A GIFT FOR:

....

FROM:

....

Leadership

PROMISES FOR EVERY DAY

A Daily Devotional

JOHN C. MAXWELL

THOMAS NELSON
Since 1798

NASHVILLE   DALLAS   MEXICO CITY   RIO DE JANEIRO

© 2003 by Maxwell Motivation, Inc.

All rights reserved. No portion of this book may be reproduced, stored in a retrieval system, or transmitted in any form by any means—electronic, mechanical, photocopy, recording, scanning, or any other—except for brief quotation in printed reviews, without the prior written permission of the publisher.

Published in Nashville, Tennessee, by Thomas Nelson. Thomas Nelson is a registered trademark of Thomas Nelson, Inc.

Published in association with Yates & Yates, www.yates2.com.

Thomas Nelson, Inc., titles may be purchased in bulk for educational, business, fund-raising, or sales promotional use. For information, please e-mail SpecialMarkets@ThomasNelson.com.

Unless otherwise indicated, all Scripture quotations in this book are from the New King James Version (NKJV) of the Bible © 1979, 1980, 1982, 1992, Thomas Nelson, Inc., Publisher.

The New International Version of the Bible (NIV) © 1984 by the International Bible Society. Used by permission of Zondervan Bible Publishers.

The Message (MSG) © 1993. Used by permission of NavPress Publishing Group.

Designed by The DesignWorks Group, www.thedesignworksgroup.com

Project editor, Kathy Baker

ISBN 978-0-8499-9594-1 (HC)
ISBN 978-1-4041-1324-4 (SC)

Printed and bound in China

12 13 14 15 16 RRD 9 8 7 6 5 4

GOD HAS PROMISED HIS GUIDANCE:

"I will lead them in paths

they have not known.

I will make darkness light before them,

and crooked places straight.

These things I will do for them,

and not forsake them."

ISAIAH 42:16

May you follow Him as you lead.

For the LORD gives wisdom;

from His mouth come

knowledge and understanding; . . .

He guards the paths of justice,

and preserves the way of His saints.

Then you will understand righteousness

and justice, equity and every good path.

—PROVERBS 2:6, 8–9

INTRODUCTION

Anyone can follow a path, but only a leader can blaze one.

That's often not easy. If you're a leader, a lot of people depend on you:

Family and friends need leaders
who model purpose-driven lives.

Children need leaders who help
them reach their potential.

Churches need leaders who chart
the course and equip the saints.

Businesses need leaders who build great
places to work while making a profit.

Communities need leaders who
create a better place to live.

As others depend on you, upon whom can *you* depend? The answer is God, the Ultimate Leader!

Leadership is not for the faint of heart, but it's encouraging to know that you're not in it alone. This daily devotional is designed to connect you to God, provide you with daily leadership thoughts to help you grow, and help you stay focused on leadership issues as you approach the challenges of the day.

If you take a few minutes every day to make sure you are following the Ultimate Leader and learning His leadership lessons, then you will undoubtedly blaze a path that takes you—and your people—where only God can lead.

May God bless you on the journey. May you live in His wisdom. May He preserve your way.

Leadership

PROMISES FOR EVERY DAY

JANUARY

The call to leadership is a
consistent pattern in the Bible.

INVITATION TO LEAD

Then God said, "Let us make man
in our image, in our likeness, and let them
rule over the fish of the sea and the birds of the air,
over the livestock, over all the earth . . ."

GENESIS 1:26 (NIV)

God is the Ultimate Leader, and He calls every believer to lead others. God could have arranged His creation in any number of ways, but He chose to create human beings who possess spirits and the capacity to relate to Him and follow Him, yet who are not forced to do so.

When mankind fell into sin, God could have executed a plan of redemption that did not include sinful people, but He has called us to participate and to lead others as we follow Him. God made that clear from the beginning when He stated, "have dominion" (Genesis 1:28).

The call to leadership is a consistent pattern in the Bible. When God decided to raise up a nation of His own, He didn't call upon the masses. He called out one leader—Abraham. When He wanted to deliver His people out of Egypt, He didn't guide them as a group. He raised up a leader to do it—Moses. When it came time for the people to cross into the Promised Land, they followed one man—Joshua.

Every time God desired to do something great, He called a leader to step forward. Today He still calls leaders to step forward for every work—both large and small.

The Maxwell Leadership Bible

GROW A LEADER—
GROW THE ORGANIZATION

So when Peter saw it, he responded to the people . . .
Many of those who heard the word believed; and
the number of the men came to be about five thousand.

ACTS 3:12, 4:4

A company cannot grow without, until its leaders grow within. I often am amazed at the money, energy, and marketing that organizations focus on areas that will not produce growth. Slick brochures and catchy slogans will never overcome incompetent leadership.

In 1981 I became senior pastor of Skyline Wesleyan Church in San Diego, California, which had averaged 1,000 in attendance from 1969–1981. It was obviously on a plateau. When I called my first staff meeting, I gave a lecture with the thesis, "Leaders determine the level of an organization." I drew a line across a marker board and wrote the number "1,000." I shared that although I knew the staff could lead 1,000 people effectively, I did not know whether they could lead 2,000 people. When the leaders changed positively, I knew the growth would become automatic. Now, I had to help them change themselves.

The strength of any organization is a direct result of the strength of its leaders.

Weak leaders = weak organizations.

Strong leaders = strong organizations.

Everything rises and falls on leadership.

Developing the Leaders Around You

IN YOUR FOOTSTEPS

*And everyone who was in distress, everyone
who was in debt, and everyone who was discontented
gathered to [David]. So he became captain
over them. And there were about four
hundred men with him.*

1 SAMUEL 22:2

The men who David attracted while he fled from Saul eventually became like him. Some even killed giants, as he did—showing that what you are is what you reproduce. Observe what David teaches us about his leadership:

1. David attracted men even without pursuing them.
2. David drew deep loyalty from them without ever trying to get it.
3. David transformed these men without disenchanting them over their initial state.
4. David fought alongside these men and turned them into winners.

Consider the astounding exploits of some of these men. Second Samuel 23 tells us that Adino slew 800 men with a spear in one battle (v. 8); Eleazar struck down the enemy until his hand clung to his sword (vv. 9,10); Shammah defended a plot of ground against an enemy army (vv. 11, 12). David attracted men like him—souls in distress. He also reproduced men like him—warriors and conquerors.

The Maxwell Leadership Bible

DON'T TAKE YOURSELF
TOO SERIOUSLY

A merry heart does good, like medicine.

PROVERBS 17:22

I work with a lot of leaders. And one thing I've found is that many times they take themselves much too seriously. Of course, they're not alone. I meet people in every walk of life who have too much doom and gloom in their attitudes. They simply need to lighten up. No matter how serious your work is, that's no reason to take yourself seriously.

If any person had a reason to take his job and himself seriously, it would be a president of the United States. Yet it's possible for even people holding that position to maintain their sense of humor and keep their egos in check. For example, when Calvin Coolidge was asked if he was attending the Sesquicentennial Exposition in Philadelphia, the President answered, "Yes."

"Why are you going, Mr. President?" a reporter asked.

"As an exhibit," answered the rotund Coolidge.

If you tend to take yourself too seriously, give yourself and everyone else around you a break. Recognize that laughter breeds resilience. Laughing is the quickest way to get up and get going again when you've been knocked down.

Failing Forward

FIRE OF GOD

"Who among us shall dwell with the devouring fire?
Who among us shall dwell with everlasting burnings?"
He who walks righteously and speaks uprightly,
He who despises the gain of oppressions,
Who gestures with his hands, refusing bribes,
Who stops his ears from hearing of bloodshed,
And shuts his eyes from seeing evil: He will dwell on high;
His place of defense will be the fortress of rocks;
Bread will be given him, His water will be sure.

ISAIAH 33:14–16

Who can stand up under the purification process of God? Who can remain unchanged through the fire of God? That's the question Isaiah asks and answers. He lays out a list of traits for the kind of people who can stand up in a crisis. Ponder his description:

Integrity: The leader's life and words match.

Justice: The leader rejects dishonest gain.

Convictions: The leader's values won't allow him or her to accept bribes.

Positive focus: The leader refuses to dwell on destructive issues.

Pure: The leader disciplines his or her mind to remain clean and pure.

Secure: The leader is firm, stable in his identity and source of strength.

The Maxwell Leadership Bible

THE HEART OF LEADERSHIP

So he got up from the meal, took off his outer clothing,
and wrapped a towel around His waist.
After that, He poured water into a basin and
began to wash His disciples' feet.

JOHN 13:4–5 (NIV)

When you think of servanthood, what do you envision? Servanthood is not about position or skill. It's about attitude. You undoubtedly have met people in service positions who have poor attitudes toward servanthood, and just as you can sense when a worker doesn't want to help people, you can just as easily detect whether a leader has a servant's heart. The truth is that the best leaders desire to serve others, not themselves.

True servant leaders . . .

- Put others ahead of their own agenda.
- Possess the confidence to serve.
- Initiate service to others.
- Are not position–conscious.
- Serve out of love.

Servant leadership is never motivated by manipulation or self–promotion. In the end, the extent of your influence depends on the depth of your concern for others. That's why it's so important for leaders to be willing to serve.

The 21 Indispensable Qualities of a Leader

BE CAREFUL WHERE YOU GET YOUR COUNSEL

Blessed is the man who walks not in the counsel of the ungodly, nor stands in the path of sinners, nor sits in the seat of the scornful; But his delight is in the law of the LORD, and in His law he meditates day and night. He shall be like a tree planted by the rivers of water, that brings forth its fruit in its season, whose leaf also shall not wither; And whatever he does shall prosper.

PSALM 1:1–3

The brilliant first psalm contrasts the righteous and the wicked. Leaders, take note because the difference between the two seems to be where they get their counsel! Observe how a foolish leader can be led astray by a corrupt inner circle:

1. The leader begins to browse for the wrong counsel.
2. The leader begins to listen to the wrong voices.
3. The leader joins the wrong inner circle.

A wise leader meditates on God's Word day and night. Note the results of receiving counsel from the right inner circle:

1. Stability
2. Inward nourishment and refreshment
3. Fruitfulness and productivity
4. Strength and durability
5. Success

The Maxwell Leadership Bible

THE BLAME GAME

The man said, "The woman whom You gave to be
with me, she gave me of the tree, and I ate."

GENESIS 3:12

When things go wrong, the natural tendency is to look for someone to blame. You can go all the way back to the Garden of Eden on this one. When God asked Adam what he'd done, he said it was Eve's fault. Then when God questioned Eve, she blamed it on the snake. The same thing happens today.

The next time you experience a failure, think about why you failed instead of who was at fault. Try to look at it objectively so that you can do better next time. Ask yourself:

What lessons have I learned?

How can I turn the failure into success?

Where did I succeed as well as fail?

People who blame others for their failures never overcome them. They simply move from problem to problem. To reach your potential, you must continually improve yourself, and you can't do that if you don't take responsibility for your actions and learn from your mistakes.

Your Road Map for Success

THE POWER OF PURPOSE

But I want you to know, brethren, that the things which happened to me have actually turned out for the furtherance of the gospel, so that it has become evident to the whole palace guard, and to all the rest, that my chains are in Christ; and most of the brethren in the Lord, having become confident by my chains, are much more bold to speak the word without fear.

PHILIPPIANS 1:12–14

Paul might have been forgiven had he chosen to take a little sabbatical as he sat in prison, awaiting his trial. Yet he used even this opportunity to advance the gospel. Paul was a leader who never drifted from his mission. He determined to leave his mark wherever he went.

How did Paul's sense of purpose keep him in the battle as he sat in prison? What did he learn behind bars? Consider the following:

A purpose will motivate you.

A purpose will keep your priorities straight.

A purpose will develop your potential.

A purpose will give you power to live in the present.

A purpose will help you evaluate your progress.

The Maxwell Leadership Bible

CHECKLIST BEFORE
TAKING NEW TERRITORY

*Arise, go over this Jordan, you and all this people,
to the land which I am giving to them—the children
of Israel. Every place that the sole of your foot will tread
upon I have given you, as I said to Moses.*

JOSHUA 1:2–3

People need to be shown the team's vision clearly, creatively, and continually. Whenever I endeavor to cast vision with the members of my team, I use the following checklist. I try to make sure that every vision message possesses . . .

Clarity: brings understanding to the vision (answers what the people must know and what you want them to do)

Connectedness: brings the past, present, and future together

Purpose: bring direction to the vision

Goals: bring targets to the vision

Honesty: brings integrity to the vision and credibility to the vision–caster

Stories: bring relationships to the vision

Challenge: brings stretching to the vision

Passion: brings fuel to the vision

Modeling: brings accountability to the vision

Strategy: brings process to the vision

The 17 Indisputable Laws of Teamwork

VISION BRINGS VICTORY

Therefore, King Agrippa, I was not disobedient
to the heavenly vision, but declared first to those
in Damascus and in Jerusalem, and throughout all
the region of Judea, and then to the Gentiles,
that they should repent, turn to God, and
do works befitting repentance.

ACTS 26:19–20

Paul's vision on the road to Damascus became the captivating force behind his success. The apostle teaches us the power of a vision. God's vision for Paul accomplished a number of things:

It stopped him. Vision allows us to see ourselves. We see things not as they are, but as we are.

It sent him. Vision allows us to see others. We feel compelled to act.

It strengthened him. Vision enables us to continue despite struggles and lack of resources.

It stretched him. Vision gives us conviction to stand, confidence to speak, and compassion to share.

It satisfied him. Obedience to this vision motivates us to act. It fulfills us.

The Maxwell Leadership Bible

LEADING THE LEADER

Lift your eyes now and look from the place
where you are—northward, southward, eastward,
and westward; for all the land which you see
I give to you and your descendants forever.

GENESIS 13:14–15

Vision is everything for a leader. It is utterly indispensable. Why? Because vision leads the leaders. It paints the targets, sparks and fuels the fire within, and draws them forward. And it is also the fire–lighter for others who follow those leaders. Show me a leader without vision, and I'll show you someone who isn't going anywhere. At best, they're traveling in circles.

To get a handle on vision and how it comes to be a part of a good leader, understand these things:
1. Vision starts within.
2. Vision draws on your history.
3. Vision meets others' needs.
4. Vision helps you gather resources.

One of the most valuable benefits of vision is that it acts like a magnet—attracting, challenging, and uniting people. The greater the vision, the more winners it has the potential to attract. The more challenging the vision, the harder the participants fight to achieve it.

The 21 Indispensable Qualities of a Leader

WHAT MAKES FOLLOWERS LOVE TO SERVE?

*And David said with longing, "Oh, that someone
would give me a drink of the water from the well
of Bethlehem, which is by the gate!" So the three mighty
men broke through the camp of the Philistines,
drew water from the well of Bethlehem that was
by the gate, and took it and brought it to
David. Nevertheless he would not drink it,
but poured it out to the LORD.*

2 SAMUEL 23:15–16

It was just a casual remark. Yet the moment David's men heard their leader mutter the words, they immediately broke through enemy lines and braved Philistine swords and spears to retrieve a cup of the precious liquid.

Such astonishing loyalty doesn't come from a mere job description. Loyalty like this comes only through modeling. David got this kind of "second–mile" effort because he had long modeled such loyalty for his men.

And it is that loyalty that drove him to do what he did next. David honored their sacrifice by presenting it to the Lord rather than drinking it. Who wouldn't go the extra mile for a leader like that?

The Maxwell Leadership Bible

LOVE PEOPLE,
REWARD PERFORMANCE

"Well done good and faithful servant; you have been faithful over a few things, I will make you ruler over many things. Enter into the joy of your lord."

MATTHEW 25:23

Educators in the United States have been seeking ways to increase students' test scores. One popular theory states that the best way to improve children's ability is to puff up their self–esteem because high–achievers tend to have high self–esteem. However, researchers have found that simply building children's egos breeds many negative traits: indifference to excellence, inability to overcome adversity, and aggressiveness toward people who criticize them.

Now, I place high value on praising people, especially children. But I also believe that you have to base your praise on truth. Here's the approach I use to encourage and lead others:

Value people

Praise effort

Reward performance

I use that method with everyone, including myself. And no matter where I fail or how many mistakes I make, I don't let it devalue my worth as a person. As the saying goes, "God uses people who fail—'cause there aren't any other kinds around."

Failing Forward

PORTRAIT OF
A GODLY LEADER

LORD, who may abide in Your tabernacle?
Who may dwell in Your holy hill? He who walks
uprightly, and works righteousness, and speaks the truth
in his heart; He who does not backbite with his tongue,
nor does evil to his neighbor, nor does he take up a
reproach against his friend; in whose eyes a vile person
is despised, but he honors those who fear the LORD;
he who swears to his own hurt and does not change;
he who does not put out his money at usury,
nor does he take a bribe against the innocent.
he who does these things shall never be moved.

PSALM 15:1-5

What qualities should every leader possess? Psalm 15 furnishes us with a list of many of the necessary traits. David pictures a godly leader as one who:

Possesses integrity

Does not participate in gossip

Does not harm others

Speaks out against wrong

Honors others who walk in truth

Keeps their word even at personal cost

Isn't greedy to gain at the expense of others

Is strong and stable

The Maxwell Leadership Bible

TALENT IS NOT ENOUGH

When a leader listens to malicious gossip,
all the workers get infected with evil.

PROVERBS 29:12 (THE MESSAGE)

Author Denis Waitley says, "The winner's edge is not in a gifted birth, in a high IQ, or in talent. The winner's edge is in the attitude, not aptitude." Unfortunately, many people resist that notion. They want to believe that talent alone (or talent with experience) is enough. But plenty of talented teams never amount to anything because of the attitudes of their players.

Take a look at how various attitudes impact a team made up of highly talented players:

ABILITIES + ATTITUDES	= RESULT
Great Talent + Rotten Attitudes	= Bad Team
Great Talent + Bad Attitudes	= Average Team
Great Talent + Average Attitudes	= Good Team
Great Talent + Good Attitudes	= Great Team

If you want great results, you need good people with great talent and awesome attitudes.

The 17 Indisputable Laws of Teamwork

CREATING A CLIMATE
FOR DEVELOPING LEADERS

All these men of war, who could keep ranks,
came to Hebron with a loyal heart, to make David
king over all Israel; and the rest of Israel were
of one mind to make David king.

1 CHRONICLES 12:38

We can conclude from the list of warriors who joined David in Ziklag that his ragtag team was diverse, loyal, and hungry for victory. So what did David do to reproduce his leadership in them?

1. *He was relational:* David's personable and approachable manner enticed hundreds of misfit volunteers to serve him. David accepted anyone.

2. *He was resourceful:* David made use of every situation and got the best out of it—even in the wilderness. He resourced his team to become all it could be and enabled it to succeed.

3. *He was rewarding:* David quickly shared both rewards and recognition for victory. He affirmed his men and motivated them with words of encouragement and spoils from battle.

4. *He was respectable:* David modeled a leadership style that others wanted to imitate. Friends and foes alike respected him; people saw in David an example of good leadership.

The Maxwell Leadership Bible

BE CAREFUL
WHAT YOU PROMISE

Do not be rash with your mouth,
And let not your heart utter anything hastily before God.
For God is in heaven, and you on earth;
Therefore let your words be few.
When you make a vow to God, do not delay to pay it;
For He has no pleasure in fools.
Do not let your mouth cause your flesh to sin,
nor say before the messenger of God that it was an error.
Why should God be angry at your excuse and destroy
the work of your hands? For in the multitude of dreams
and many words there is also vanity. But fear God.

ECCLESIASTES 5:2, 4, 6–7

Do you make promises to God? Scripture advises caution before we commit something to God— good advice for any decision a leader must make. Solomon describes three major pitfalls lying in wait for careless leaders:

Hasty speech: Leaders must listen as much as they speak.

Empty promises: Leaders tend to say what others want to hear. Don't promise what you can't deliver.

Lame excuses: Leaders diminish their influence when they try to reverse a mistake with a lame excuse.

The Maxwell Leadership Bible

NOT WITHOUT MY FAMILY!

*But if anyone does not provide for his own,
and especially for those of is household, he has denied
the faith and is worse than an unbeliever.*

1 TIMOTHY 5:8

Every day parents and spouses leave their families in the pursuit of success. It's almost as though they're driving down the road, and they get pretty far along before they realize they've left members of their family behind. The tragedy is that many value their careers, success, or personal happiness more than they do their families. They decide that it's too much work to go back, so they just keep driving.

But what many are now realizing is that the hope of happiness at the expense of breaking up a family is an illusion. You can't give up your marriage or neglect your children and gain true success. As Nick Stinnet asserted more than a decade ago, "When you have a strong family life, you receive the message that you are loved, cared for and important. The positive intake of love, affection, and respect . . . gives you inner resources to deal with life more successfully."

Your Road Map for Success

THE 101% PRINCIPLE

Now I plead with you, brethren, by the name
of our Lord Jesus Christ, that you all speak the same
thing, and that there be no divisions among you,
but that you be perfectly joined together in the
same mind and in the same judgment.

1 CORINTHIANS 1:10

The church at Corinth provided Paul with one of his greatest challenges. In this letter, he was forced to confront several problems. And his letter could have become one long, verbal spanking.

Instead, Paul saw this church's potential, despite its problems. He practiced "The 101% Principle"—finding the 1 percent you can affirm, and giving it 100 percent of your attention.

While Paul knew he must confront the issues, he began his letter with words of appreciation. Leadership rule #1 is this: Affirmation comes before confrontation. Although Corinth had some problem people, Paul still saw the good in them:

They were enriched by God.

They had fellowship with God.

They could make positive, right decisions.

Good leaders look for the good in people and affirm it. Only then do they address the problems.

The Maxwell Leadership Bible

GIVING IS THE
HIGHEST LEVEL OF LIVING

Then Abram gave a tenth of everything.
GENESIS 14:20 (NIV)

Nothing speaks to others more loudly than generosity from a leader. True generosity isn't an occasional event. It comes from the heart and permeates every aspect of a leader's life, touching their time, money, talents, and possessions. Effective leaders, the kind people want to follow, don't gather things just for themselves; they do it in order to give to others.

To cultivate the quality of generosity in your life, do the following:

1. Be grateful for whatever you have.

2. Put people first.

3. Don't allow the desire for possessions to control you.

4. See money as a resource.

5. Develop the habit of giving.

The only way to maintain an attitude of generosity is to make it your habit to give—your time, attention, money, and resources. As Richard Foster says, "Just the very act of letting go of money, or some other treasure, does something within us. It destroys the demon 'greed'."

The 21 Indispensable Qualities of a Leader

SEEK GOD, THEN ASK THESE QUESTIONS

So I say to you, ask, and it will be given to you;
seek, and you will find; knock, and it will be opened
to you. For everyone who asks receives, and
he who seeks finds, and to him
who knocks it will be opened.

LUKE 11:9–10

Most people can prioritize when faced with right or wrong issues. The challenge arises when we are faced with two good choices. Now what should we do? If you're having trouble deciding between two good things, then look at these suggestions:

Ask your overseer or coworkers their preference.

Can one of the options be handled by someone else? If so, pass it on and work on the one only you can do.

Which option would be of greater benefit to the customer? Too many times we are like the merchant who was so intent on trying to keep the store clean that he would never unlock the front door. The real reason for the store is to have customers, not to clean it!

Make your decision based on the purpose of the organization.

Developing the Leader Within You

EQUIPPING:
THE LEADER'S RESPONSIBILITY

And He Himself gave some to be apostles, some prophets, some evangelists, and some pastors and teachers, for the equipping of the saints for the work of ministry, for the edifying of the body of Christ, till we all come to the unity of the faith and of the knowledge of the Son of God, to a perfect man, to the measure of the stature of the fullness of Christ.

EPHESIANS 4:11–13

Equipping is a tough job, much harder than shepherding. The leader is to equip others for ministry. Paul explains the goal for the shepherd. If leaders wish to equip their people, they must give them certain gifts:

I must CARE for the (Communication, Affirmation, Recognition, and Example).

I must work on their weaknesses, but work out their strengths.

I must give them myself (time, energy, and focus).

I must give them ownership of the ministry.

I must become a resource person (atmosphere, training, support, tools).

I must make expectations clear.

I must eliminate unnecessary burdens.

I must catch them doing something good, then reward them for it.

The Maxwell Leadership Bible

LEADERSHIP BEGINS IN THE HEART

*No longer do I call you servants . . .
but I have called you friends.*

JOHN 15:15

What can a person do to manage and cultivate good relationships as a leader? It requires three things:

1. *Understand people:* Marketing expert Rod Nichols says, "If you deal with every customer in the same way, you will only close twenty–five percent to thirty percent of your contacts, because you will only close one personality type. But if you learn how to effectively work with all four personality types, you can conceivably close one hundred percent of your contacts."

2. *Love people:* Businessman Henry Gruland says, "Being a leader is more than just wanting to lead. Leaders have empathy for others and a keen ability to find the best in people . . . not the worst . . . by truly caring for others." You cannot be a truly effective leader unless you love people.

3. *Help people:* If your focus is on what you can put into people rather than what you can get out of them, they'll love and respect you—and those attributes are great foundations for building relationships.

The 21 Indispensable Qualities of a Leader

SECURE LEADERSHIP

Why have you despised the commandment of the LORD,
to do evil in His sight? You have killed Uriah the
Hittite with the sword; you have taken his wife
to be your wife, and have killed him with
the sword of the people of Ammon.

2 SAMUEL 12:9

Security provides the foundation for strong leadership. When we feel insecure, we drift from our mission whenever trouble arises. We must feel secure when people stop liking us, when funding drops, when morale dips, or when others reject us. If we don't feel secure, fear will eventually cause us to sabotage our leadership.

Imagine what might have happened had Nathan lacked security. David had covered up everything so well; no one else knew what happened. Further, the popular David had led Israel to prominence among the nations, and most Israelites would side with David if he put up a fight. Finally from a technical viewpoint, David had set up the man to be killed in battle by the Ammonites, but it wasn't his spear or sword that took Uriah's life. Nathan had to feel utterly secure in his plan of confrontation, or it would backfire.

The Maxwell Leadership Bible

DIAMONDS IN THE ROUGH

*On the contrary, those parts of the body that
seem to be weaker are indispensable.*

1 CORINTHIANS 12:22 (NIV)

Scripture says that every person in the body of
Christ has both value and a purpose. So how do
the people who are often undervalued by society find the
hope, direction and encouragement they need to fulfill
their God–given destinies?

The answer often comes from leadership. One of the
reasons God has put leaders in the Church is to help every
person find his or her place. I sometimes think of it as
finding and polishing hidden gems. Leaders are meant to
help others become the people God created them to be.
They are called to discover the hidden, encourage the
uncertain, develop the untrained, and empower the
powerless. They are gifted to mine the gems. Never forget
that Jesus looked at an impulsive, uneducated fisherman
named Simon and saw a diamond in the rough. Jesus even
called him Peter the rock.

Just as Jesus sees potential in you, if you are a leader,
He wants you to find and develop that potential in others.

A FRIEND INDEED

So Jonathan told David, saying, "My father Saul seeks to kill you. Therefore please be on your guard until morning, and stay in a secret place and hide. And I will go out and stand beside my father in the field where you are, and I will speak with my father about you. Then what I observe, I will tell you."

1 SAMUEL 19:2–3

 No leader succeeds on his own. Even David needed his Jonathan.

In the dark days when he fled to escape the threats of King Saul, David turned to his friend for strength and encouragement. At great risk to himself, Jonathan, hoping to pacify his father and reconcile the king to his friend, spoke well of David. And for a short while Saul relented, promising that David would not die by his hand.

Soon Saul's old animosities reasserted themselves, and Jonathan once again risked his life to help his dear friend. Jonathan remained faithful to his comrade until the very end of his life.

Do you have someone who "strengthens your hand in God?" All leaders need loyal friends who can help them to persevere through the tough times.

The Maxwell Leadership Bible

What A Leader Must See

*And I said to the king, "If it pleases the king, and
if your servant has found favor in your sight, I ask
that you send me to Judah, to the city
of my fathers' tombs, that I may rebuild it."*

NEHEMIAH 2:5

Leaders who navigate do more than control the
direction in which they and their people travel.
They see the whole trip in their minds before they leave
the dock. It seems remarkable, but Nehemiah could see
both the problem and the solution even though he had
never visited Jerusalem.

All great leaders have uncommon vision. A leader
sees . . .

Farther than others see. Nehemiah was able to see the
problem, and he could picture the solution in his
head.

More than others see. Nehemiah knew that the wall
could and should be rebuilt, and he knew what it
would take to do it.

Before others see. None of Jerusalem's neighbors wanted
to see the Jews rebuild their wall, and several enemy
leaders conspired against Nehemiah and the
people. But Nehemiah saw the danger and planned
accordingly; he refused to give in to enemy plots.

The Maxwell Leadership Bible

BLESSED FOR SUCCESS

And he blessed Joseph and said, " . . . The Angel
who has redeemed me from all evil, bless the lads;
Let my name be named upon them, and
the name of my fathers Abraham and Isaac;
and let them grow into a multitude
in the midst of the earth."

GENESIS 48: 15–16

Not everyone you influence will think the same way you do. You have to help them not only believe that they can succeed, but also show them that you want them to succeed. How do you do that?

Expect it: People can sense your underlying attitude no matter what you say or do. If you have an expectation for your people to be successful, they will know it.

Verbalize it: People need to hear you tell them that you believe in them and want them to succeed. Become a positive prophet of their success.

Reinforce it: You can never do too much when it comes to believing in people.

Once people recognize and understand that you genuinely want to see them succeed and are committed to helping them, they will begin to believe they can accomplish what you give them to do.

Becoming a Person of Influence

Buying Into the Leader

So he said to Him, "O my Lord, how can I save Israel?
Indeed my clan is the weakest in Manaseh, and I am
the least in my father's house." And the LORD said to
him, "Surely I will be with you, and you shall
defeat the Midianites as one man."

JUDGES 6:15–16

Who would have picked Gideon as a leader? Certainly not Gideon. But despite Gideon's doubts, God used him. And he grew as a leader through several stages:

He started at home with his servants by destroying an altar to Baal and building a new altar to God.

He won over his father, who was a key influencer, and Gideon's life was spared when the men of Ophrah came after him.

He broadened his circle by winning the influence of Joash, the Abiezrites, and tribes beyond his borders.

He moved at the right time, with the right number of people, and won a great victory.

People don't automatically buy into a good cause, as we see with Gideon. People buy into the leaders first, then the leader's vision.

The Maxwell Leadership Bible

GOOD LEADERS
ARE GOOD LISTENERS

Listen now to my voice; I will give you counsel,
and God will be with you.

EXODUS 18:19

As the leader of a team or an organization, you set the tone for communication. A leader's communication must be consistent, clear, and courteous. But leaders must also be good listeners. When leaders don't listen . . .

They stop gaining wisdom.

They stop "hearing" what isn't being said.

Team members stop communicating.

Their indifference begins to spread to other areas.

Ultimately, poor listening leads to hostility, miscommunication, and a breakdown of team cohesion.

How are your listening skills? Give yourself a 360–degree review. Ask for feedback concerning your ability and willingness to listen from your boss or mentor, your colleagues, and your subordinates. If you don't get good grades from all of them, then quiet down, listen up, and work to become a better communicator.

The 17 Indisputable Laws of Leadership

FEBRUARY

Effective, godly leadership
means giving what you have
so that God my be glorified
in all you do.

Choosing
the Right Circle

*But he rejected the advice which the elders had
given him, and consulted the young men who had
grown up with him, who stood before him.*

2 Chronicles 10:8

Be careful what kind of inner circle you choose!
King Rehoboam had the benefit of his father's
inner circle, men who gave him wise counsel. But the
foolish young king rejected their advice and instead looked
for advice that agreed with his own opinion. Horrible
move! He should have gone with a core team who
possessed the qualities of a solid inner circle:

1. *Experience:* People who have been down the road of life
   and understand it.

2. *Heart for God:* People who place God first and uphold
   His values.

3. *Objectivity:* People who see the pros and cons of the
   issues.

4. *Love for people:* People who love others and value them
   more than things.

5. *Complementary gifts:* People who bring diverse gifts to
   the relationship.

6. *Loyalty to the leader:* People who truly love and are
   concerned for the leader.

The Maxwell Leadership Bible

EXTENDING YOUR INFLUENCE

*And He went up on the mountain and called
to Him those He Himself wanted. And they came
to Him. Then he appointed twelve, that they might
be with Him and that He might send them out
to preach, and to have power to heal
sicknesses and to cast out demons.*

MARK 3:13–15

One of the greatest lessons I've ever learned is that the people closest to me determine my level of success or failure. On my 40th birthday discovered that the only places where my influence and productivity were growing was where I had identified potential leaders and developed them. My intention in developing leaders had been to help them improve themselves, but I found that I was also benefiting greatly. Spending time with them had been like investing. They had grown, and at the same time I had reaped incredible dividends. That's when I realized that if I was to make it to the next level, I was going to have to extend myself through others. I would find leaders and pour my life into them, and as they improved, so would I.

Your Road Map for Success

GIVE UP

*My brethren, count it all joy when
you fall into various trials.*

JAMES 1:2

What price are you willing to pay to be a more effective leader?

One of finest examples of sacrifice by a leader in the Bible can be seen in the life of Moses. He could easily be the "poster child" for leadership sacrifice. He grew up like a son of Pharaoh, a prince. As a boy, he enjoyed every privilege and pleasure of the palace.

Yet Moses risked all of that to try to help his people. And in fact, he lost everything. After murdering an Egyptian, he faced exile in the desert of Midian, and for forty years he lived with the sacrifice he had made before learning that God intended to use him as a leader. By then, Moses had undergone the breaking and remaking process required for him to be used by God.

As a leader you may not be asked to leave your country or give up all your possessions as Moses was. But you can be sure that leading others will have a price.

The 21 Most Powerful Minutes in a Leader's Day

A LEADER SPEAKS UP

*But when I saw that they were not straightforward
about the truth of the gospel, I said to Peter
before them all, "If you, being a Jew, live in the
manner of Gentiles and not as the Jews, why do
you compel Gentiles to live as Jews?"*

GALATIANS 2:14

Paul's integrity drove him to stand up to Peter, his fellow leader, in front of several Jewish and Gentile believers. He criticized Peter's hypocrisy and demanded that all Christian leaders remain consistent, regardless of the company they keep. Paul teaches us how to critique someone. Consider his checklist:

- Check your motive. Your goal should be to help, not humiliate.
- Make sure the issue is worthy of criticism. Does it really matter?
- Be specific. Don't drop hints, but clearly name the problem.
- Don't undermine the person's self–confidence or identity. Make it obvious that you value the person.
- Do not postpone needed criticism. If the issue is big, act now.
- Look at yourself looking at others. Take the log out of your own eye.
- End criticism with encouragement. Finish on a positive note.

The Maxwell Leadership Bible

THE TEAM HOLDS THE DREAM

Good–tempered leaders invigorate lives;
they're like spring rain and sunshine.

PROVERBS 16:15 (THE MESSAGE)

One of the mistakes people make is that they focus too much attention on their dream and too little on their team. But the truth is that if you build the right team, the dream will almost take care of itself.

If you want to achieve your dream—I mean really do it, not just imagine what it would be like—then grow your team. But as you do so, make sure your motives are right. Some people gather a team just to benefit themselves. Others do it because they enjoy the team experience and want to create a sense of community. Still others do it because they want to build an organization. The funny thing about those reasons is that if you're motivated by all of them, then your desire to build a team probably comes from wanting to add value to everyone on the team. But if your desire to build the team comes as the result of only one of those reasons, you probably need to examine your motives.

The 17 Indisputable Laws of Teamwork

EARN TRUST BY
DOING THE RIGHT THING

*For Ezra had prepared his heart to seek the Law
of the Lord, and to do it, and to teach
statutes and ordinances in Israel.*

EZRA 7:10

Even at a young age, Ezra diligently studied and learned to become a scholar. He won the respect of many, including the political leader of the land of his exile, King Artaxerxes. He established his connections and influence over time—a necessary step if the dream of restoring Jerusalem were to be fulfilled.

As a result of many years of consistently doing the right thing, the king finally trusted Ezra with great power and resources, acknowledging his character qualities in writing. He provided all that Ezra needed to get the job done.

Ezra led many Israelites back to Jerusalem during this time of restoration. As a spiritual leader, Ezra had prepared, studied, and connected with many ordinary Jews, and his pronounced influence prompted many to follow him to Jerusalem. Ezra did not utilize his power, intellect, and influence for personal gain, but rather to restore Jerusalem.

Throughout his life, Ezra exercised the best leader's qualities with both passion and zeal.

The Maxwell Leadership Bible

TRADING FOR
SOMETHING GREATER

And He saw also a certain poor widow putting
in two mites. So He said, "Truly I say to you that
this poor widow has put in more than all."

LUKE 21:2–3

Poet Rudyard Kipling said, "If you don't get what you want, it is a sign either that you did not seriously want it, or that you tried to bargain over the price." How badly do you want to reach your potential and fulfill your purpose in life? It will take passion on your part to keep growing, learning, and trading up.

Over the years I've found that you have to make tradeoffs throughout life in order to succeed, and only through wise exchanges can you reach your potential.

The problem many unsuccessful people is that they haven't worked to develop much in their lives that are worth trading. You can only make a trade when you've got something worth giving up. And when you do trade, you don't trade from the lowest level to the highest, skipping over all the levels in between. Usually you're only able to move one level at a time—either up or down.

Your Road Map for Success

GIVE ALL YOU CAN

*Now King Solomon gave to the queen of Sheba all she
desired, whatever she asked, much more than she had
brought to the king. So she turned and went
to her own country, she and her servants.*

2 CHRONICLES 9:12

Before he careened off course, Solomon began to
fulfill God's dream of blessing the nations
through the nation of Israel. The Queen of Sheba spoke
for those visitors from other nations when she said,
"Blessed be the LORD your God, who delighted in you,
setting you on His throne to be king for the LORD your
God!" (2 Chronicles 9:8)

Centuries later, the Lord Jesus Christ would tell His
followers that what they had received freely, they should
freely give (Matthew 10:8). Solomon had asked for
godly wisdom that he might rule in a way pleasing to
God. The Lord freely gave him that wisdom, so he freely
shared it with others—in his words, in his music, and in
his writings.

Effective, godly leadership means giving what you
have so that God may be glorified in all you do. What you
have freely received, freely give—and so bless others.

The Maxwell Leadership Bible

THE LONGEST WAY IS A SHORT CUT

*Then [Saul] waited seven days, according
to the time set by Samuel. But Samuel did not come....
So Saul ...offered the burnt offering. Now it happened,
as soon as he had finished presenting the burnt
offering, that Samuel came.... And Samuel
said, "What have you done?"*

1 SAMUEL 13:8–11

One of the most common obstacles to success is the desire to cut corners. But short cuts never pay off in the long run.

If you find that you continually give in to your moods or impulses, then you need to change your approach to doing things. Cutting corners is really a sign of impatience and poor self–discipline. But if you are willing to follow through, you can achieve a breakthrough. The best method is to set up standards for yourself that require accountability. Any time you suffer a consequence for not following through, it helps you stay on track. Once you have your standards in place, work according to them, not your moods. That will get you going in the right direction. Self–discipline is a quality that is won through practice

Failing Forward

AS YOU ARE
TRAINING OTHERS...

*And he went into the synagogue and spoke boldly
for three months, reasoning and persuading concerning
the thing of the kingdom of God. But when some were
hardened and did not believe, but spoke evil of the
Way before the multitude, he departed from them and
withdrew the disciples, reasoning daily in the school
of Tyrannus. And this continued for two years,
so that all who dwelt in Asia heard the word
of the Lord Jesus, both Jews and Greeks.*

ACTS 19:8–10

Paul began a miniature seminary in Ephesus to teach students the ins and outs of the Gospel. For two years he rounded up men and trained them in the lecture hall of Tyrannus. As he mentored students, Paul remained committed to the people, to the process, and to the purpose. Consider how we can do the same as we develop others:

Be familiar with your strengths and weaknesses.

Know the people you wish to develop.

Clearly define the goals and assignments.

Allow them to watch you serve and lead

Hold them accountable for their work.

Give them the freedom to fail.

The Maxwell Leadership Bible

GIVE UP YOUR RIGHTS

Your attitude should be the same as that of Christ Jesus:
Who, being in very nature God,
did not consider equality with God something to be grasped,
but made Himself nothing,
taking the very nature of a servant.

PHILIPPIANS 2:5–7 (NIV)

Have you been wronged? If so, you're faced with a decision. Are you going to spend your time and energy on what should have been, or are you going to focus on what can be?

Even when truth and justice are on your side, you may never be able to right your wrongs. Continually fighting for your rights will just make you resentful and angry. Those are all destructive emotions that tap our energy and make us negative. And besides, when people focus on their rights, they're often looking backward rather than forward.

When we stop worrying about our rights, it focuses us in the right direction and releases us to move forward on the journey. We recognize the wrongs, but we forgive them, and focus on what we can control—our responsibilities. When we do that, it increases our energy, builds our potential, and improves our prospects.

Your Road Map for Success

IT'S NOT JUST WHAT YOU DO,
IT'S WHEN YOU DO IT

Then the king said to me, "What do you request?"
So I prayed to the God of heaven.

NEHEMIAH 2:4

Good leaders understand that timing is everything. Nehemiah spoke to the king about Jerusalem, but not until four months after he first heard about its broken wall. He began praying about the ruined wall in December, but not until April did he approach the king about rebuilding them. What was he waiting on?

No one knows for sure, but Nehemiah might well have been waiting on . . .

1. His ownership of the burden and vision.
2. A foundation of prayer to be laid.
3. His own readiness with a plan.
4. The king's mental and emotional mood.
5. The season when he could move quickly.
6. A trust to deepen between him and the king.

How do you know when to move in leadership? How does asking at the right time increase your chance for success?

The Maxwell Leadership Bible

WORK OF REAL VALUE

*So I will consecrate the tabernacle of meeting
and the altar. I will also consecrate both Aaron
and his sons to minister to Me as priests. I will
dwell among the children of Israel and will be
their God . . . And Moses and Aaron went
into the tabernacle of meeting, and
came out and blessed the people.*

EXODUS 29:44–45, LEVITICUS 9:23

Too many people simply fall into a comfortable
niche in life and stay there rather than pursue goals
of significance. Leaders can't afford to do that. Leaders
must ask themselves whether they want survival, success,
or significance. The best leaders desire significance and
expend their time and energy in pursuit of their dreams.

Moishe Rosen teaches a mental exercise that's an
effective tool in helping a person identify his dream. He
asks a person to fill in the blanks:

If I had

_____ ,

I would

_____ .

The idea is that if you had anything you wanted—
unlimited time, unlimited money, unlimited information,
unlimited staff (all the resources you could ask for), what
would you do? Your answer to that question is your dream.
Acting on your dream adds significance to your life.

Developing the Leaders Around You

Take the High Road

And the LORD restored Job's losses when he prayed
for his friends. Indeed the LORD gave Job
twice as much as he had before.

JOB 42:10

After enduring nearly forty chapters of criticism and condemnation from Eliphaz, Bildad, and Zophar, Job has the opportunity to get even. God announces His displeasure with them, apparently giving Job a wonderful chance to say, "I told you so." Instead, Job prays for his foolish friends.

Like all great leaders, Job refused to take vengeance or hold grudges. Instead, he took the high road. He forgave his friends, interceded for them, and sent them on their way. Remind yourself of the differences between the low road and the high road:

LOW ROAD	HIGH ROAD
1. Revenge and retaliation when wronged	1. Unconditional love and forgiveness
2. Plays the same game as others	2. Refuses to play games; lives by principles
3. Guided by emotions; up and down	3. Guided by character and values
4. Reactive: lives no better than anyone else	4. Pro–active: lives above merely human standards

The Maxwell Leadership Bible

Against the Odds

You will chase your enemies, and they shall
fall by the sword before you. Five of you shall chase
a hundred, and a hundred of you shall put ten
thousand to flight; your enemies shall fall
by the sword before you.
LEVITICUS 26:7–8

Without a challenge, many people tend to fall or fade away. Charles Noble observed, "You must have a long–range vision to keep you from being frustrated by short–range failures." Vision helps people with motivation. That can be especially important for highly talented people. They sometimes fight lack of desire. That's why a great artist like Michelangelo prayed, "Lord, grant that I may always desire more than I can accomplish." A visionary compass answers that prayer.

Someone said that only people who can see the invisible can do the impossible. That shows the value of vision. But it also indicates that vision can be an elusive quality. If you can see vision for your team, then your team has a reasonably good chance at success. Vision gives team members direction and confidence, two things they cannot do without.

The 17 Indisputable Laws of Teamwork

GIVE PEOPLE PERMISSION
TO TAKE A RISK

They also gave money to the masons and the carpenters,
and food, drink, and oil to the people of Sidon
and Tyre to bring cedar logs from Lebanon to the sea,
to Joppa, according to the permission which
they had from Cyrus king of Persia.

EZRA 3:7

Most people need permission to take a risk. By issuing his proclamation, King Cyrus modeled another leadership principle.

Cyrus issued a decree to all the Jews that they could return to their homeland and begin life again there. You might think that every Jew would jump at this opportunity to leave a land of captivity and go home, but out of a population of hundreds of thousands of Jews (in 538 B.C.), only 49,897 responded to the offer. The ones who did return gave up a life of comfort and familiarity to pursue a life of rebuilding.

A risk like this is tough for most people. Most people generally take the path of least resistance and migrate toward comfort zones. This is why leaders must both model courage and call forth courage from others.

The Maxwell Leadership Bible

Begin Leading By Loving

A good leader motivates, doesn't mislead,
doesn't exploit.

Proverbs 16:10 (The Message)

If you desire to influence another person, the way to start is by nurturing them. What clergyman John Knox said over four hundred years ago is still true: "You cannot antagonize and influence at the same time."

At the heart of the nurturing process is genuine concern for others. And as we try to help and influence the people around us, we must have positive feelings and concern for them. If you want to help people and make a positive impact on them, you cannot dislike or disparage them. You must give love to them and give them respect.

You may be wondering why you should take on a nurturing role with the people you want to influence, especially if they are employees, colleagues, or friends. You may be saying to yourself, "Isn't that something they can get somewhere else, like at home?" The unfortunate truth is that most people are desperate for encouragement. If you become a major nurturer in the life of another person, then you have an opportunity to make a major impact on them.

Becoming a Person of Influence

CHOOSE YOUR MENTOR WELL

And so it was, when they had crossed over, that Elijah said to Elisha, "Ask! What may I do for you, before I am taken away from you?" Elisha said, "Please let a double portion of your spirit be upon me." So he said, "You have asked a hard thing. Nevertheless, if you see me when I am taken from you it shall be so for you; but if not, it shall not be so."

2 KINGS 2:9–10

Every leader needs mentors, especially emerging leaders. God took Elisha through the preparation necessary under Elijah. Note several principles outlined in 1 Kings 19 and 2 Kings 2 underlying his preparation:

ELISHA'S PREPARATION	LEADERSHIP PRINCIPLE
1. He was anointed to replace Elijah.	1. Leaders must understand their call and roll.
2. Elisha touched Elijah's mantle long before he entered his ministry.	2. Leaders must wait patiently on God's perfect timing for their authority.
3. He burned his farming tools.	3. Leaders must surrender former ambitions.
4. He stuck with Elijah wherever he went.	4. Leaders must pursue good mentors.
5. He absorbed all he could from Elijah.	5. Leaders must hunger to grow and develop.

The Maxwell Leadership Bible

ALL IN THE SAME BOAT

Some sailors tried to jump ship . . . .
Paul saw through their guise and told the centurion
and his soldiers, "If these sailors don't stay with
the ship, we're all going down."
ACTS 27:30–31 (THE MESSAGE)

The quality most needed among teammates amidst the pressure of a difficult challenge is collaboration. Becoming a collaborative team player requires a change in four areas:

1. *Perception:* See teammates as collaborators, not competitors—completing one another is more important than competing with one another.

2. *Attitude:* Be supportive, not suspicious, of teammates—if you trust people, you will treat them better. And both you and they will be more likely to create collaborative relationships.

3. *Focus:* Concentrate on the team, not yourself—author Cavett Roberts points out, "True progress in any field is a relay race and not a single event." If you focus on the team and not just yourself, you will be able to pass the baton when necessary.

4. *Results:* Create great victories though multiplication—collaboration has a multiplying effect on everything you do, because it releases and harnesses not only your skills but those of everyone on the team.

The 17 Essential Qualities of a Team Player

DIFFERENCES THAT
MAKE A DIFFERENCE

*Moreover David said, "The LORD, who delivered
me from the paw of the lion and from the paw
of the bear, He will deliver me from
the hand of this Philistine."*

1 SAMUEL 17:37

Consider David in his battle with Goliath. Why
was he able to stand against the giant when the
army of Israel pulled back in fear? Here's how David did it:

1. His *perspective* differed from others. He saw an
   opportunity.

2. His *methods* differed from others. He decided to use
   proven weapons that he knew would work.

3. His *conviction* differed from others. He heard
   Goliath's threats against the God of Israel and knew
   God could beat him.

4. His *vision* differed from others. He wanted to make
   Yahweh known to the world as the most powerful
   God on earth.

5. His *experience* differed from others. He brought to the
   battlefield past victories over a lion and bear, not
   months of paralyzing fear.

6. His *attitude* differed from others. He saw Goliath not
   as a threat too big to hit, but a target too big to miss.

The Maxwell Leadership Bible

GROWTH = CHANGE

Be transformed by the renewing of your mind.
ROMANS 12:2

Just about anyone would agree that growing is a good thing, but relatively few people actually dedicate themselves to the process. Why? Because growth requires change, and change is hard for most people. But the truth is that without change, growth is impossible.

Most people fight against change, especially when it affects them personally. As novelist Leo Tolstoy said, "Everyone thinks of changing the world, but no one thinks of changing himself." The ironic thing is that change is inevitable. Everybody has to deal with it in their lives. On the other hand, growth is optional. You can choose to grow or to fight it. But know this: people unwilling to grow will never reach their potential.

Making the change from being an occasional learner to someone dedicated to personal growth is tough. It goes against the grain of the way most people live. Most people celebrate when they receive their diploma or degree and say to themselves, "Thank goodness that's over. I'm done with studying." But that kind of thinking doesn't take you any higher than average.

Your Road Map for Success

MASTER COMMUNICATION
TO MANAGE CONFLICT

*A soft answer turns away wrath,
But a harsh word stirs up anger. The tongue of the wise
uses knowledge rightly, But the mouth of fools pours
forth foolishness . . . . A wholesome tongue is
a tree of life, But perverseness in it breaks
the spirit. A fool despises his father's instruction,
But he who receives correction is prudent.
In the house of the righteous there is much treasure, But
in the revenue of the wicked is trouble.
The lips of the wise disperse knowledge, But the
heart of the fool does not do so.*

PROVERBS 15:1–7

God rightly expects leaders to manage conflict within their organizations. But how can you best accomplish this? A good place to start is Proverbs 15:1. While this verse is often quoted, some leaders seldom heed its advice. Sometimes the leaders are the ones given liberty to express anger, and sooner or later this kind of unhealthy environment comes back to haunt them.

Leaders must create safe places for communication, like the environment described in the first seven verses of Proverbs 15. Master communication and you manage conflict.

The Maxwell Leadership Bible

HOW WILL THEY
MEET CHANGE?

Then Caleb . . . said, "Let us go up at once and take possession, for we are well able to overcome it." But the men who had gone up with him said, "We are not able to go up against the people."

NUMBERS 13:30–31

It is usually easier to present change as a simple refinement of "the way we've been doing it" rather than something new and different. When a proposal for change is introduced in an organization, people fall into five categories in terms of their response:

Innovators—They are the originators of new ideas and generally are not acknowledged as leaders or policy makers.

Early Adopters—They are those who know a good idea when they see it.

Middle Adopters—They are the majority. They will respond to the opinions of others.

Late Adopters—They are the last group to endorse an idea. They often speak against proposed changes and may never verbally acknowledge acceptance.

Laggards—They are always against change. Their commitment is to the status quo and the past. Often they try to create division within the organization.

Developing the Leader Within You

The Benefits of Humility, the Liability of Pride

"Woe to those who decree unrighteous decrees,
Who write misfortune,
Which they have prescribed
To rob the needy of justice,
And to take what is right from the poor of My people,
That widows may be their prey,
And that they may rob the fatherless."

ISAIAH 10:1–2

Beware of treating followers unjustly! God reserves a stern condemnation for oppressive leaders. In Isaiah 10, God speaks to both Assyria and Israel to declare the benefits of humility and the liabilities of pride. Later, God even models the leadership style He wants every leader to embrace by sending the Suffering Servant. The Messiah will come to serve, not to be served. God perfectly illustrates servant leadership. Followers come when leaders serve. Look how often God calls His leaders "servants":

1. Abraham (Genesis 26:24)
2. Moses (Exodus 14:31)
3. Caleb (Numbers 14:24)
4. Samuel (1 Samuel 3:9)
5. Elijah (2 Kings 9:36)
6. Isaiah (Isaiah 20:3)

The Maxwell Leadership Bible

THE POWER TO
CHANGE THE WORLD

Therefore go and make disciples of all nations . . .
MATTHEW 28:19 (NIV)

All the training in the world will provide only limited success if you don't turn your people loose to do the job. The way to do that is to give them responsibility, authority, and accountability.

For some people, responsibility is the easiest to give. But what is difficult for some leaders is allowing their people to keep the responsibility after it's been given. Poor managers want to control every detail of their people's work. When that happens, the potential leaders who work for them become frustrated and don't develop. Rather than desiring more responsibility, they become indifferent or avoid responsibility altogether.

With responsibility must go authority. Winston Churchill said in an address, "I am your servant. You have the right to dismiss me when you please. What you have no right to do is ask me to bear responsibility without the power of action."

Once responsibility and authority have been given to people, they become empowered to make things happen. But we also have to be sure that they are making the right things happen. That's where accountability comes into the picture

Developing the Leaders Around You

THE INTUITION OF ISSACHAR

> *Of the sons of Issachar who had understanding*
> *of the times, to know what Israel ought to do, their*
> *chiefs were two hundred; and all their*
> *brethren were at their command;*
>
> 1 CHRONICLES 12:32

One of the more popular passages in 1 Chronicles is found in chapter 12. The sons of Issachar are there described as men who "had understanding of the times, to know what Israel ought to do." What a description of the Law of Intuition! Before Israel made a decision, they got discernment. The sons of Issachar understood three key factors:

1. *The culture:* They understood the population and the place where they lived.

2. *The timing:* They understood the times and discerned when to move.

3. *The strategy:* They knew what Israel ought to do, the steps that should be taken.

How about you? Are you a "son of Issachar"? Do you understand your culture—its trends, its myths, its strengths, its dangers? Do you understand the age in which you're living—its tenor and general movement? And do you have a strategy to grapple with both the culture and the times?

The Maxwell Leadership Bible

A Leader's Courage

"Be strong and of good courage . . ."

Deuteronomy 31:7

Whenever you see significant progress in an organization, it's because the leader made courageous decisions. However, a leadership position doesn't give a person courage, but courage can give them a leadership position. As you approach the tough decisions that will challenge you, recognize these truths about courage:

1. *Courage begins with an inward battle.* Courage isn't an absence of fear. It's doing what you are afraid to do.

2. *Courage is making things right, not just smoothing them over.* Martin Luther King, Jr. said, "The ultimate measure of a man is not where he stands in moments of comfort and convenience, but where he stands at times of challenge and controversy."

3. *Courage in a leader inspires commitment from followers.* "Courage is contagious," says evangelist Billy Graham. "When a brave man takes a stand, the spines of others are stiffened." Courage by a leader inspires.

4. *Your life expands in proportion to your courage.* Roman historian Tacitus said, "The desire for safety stands against every great and noble enterprise." But courage opens doors, and that's one of its most wonderful benefits.

The 21 Indispensable Qualities of a Leader

A LEADER'S HEART

*But the LORD said to Samuel, "Do not look at his
appearance or at his physical stature, because I have
refused him. For the LORD does not see as man sees;
for man looks at the outward appearance,
but the LORD looks at the heart."*

1 SAMUEL 16:7

The selection of David to be Israel's king illustrates
how God often disregards human customs and
traditions to accomplish His purposes. By human
standards, David, as the youngest son of Jesse, appeared
least likely to be considered for a leadership position. But
God saw the heart of this young man and knew that His
people needed a leader with a tenderness of spirit. David
might have become a warrior, but gentleness was his
defining trait.

David began his leadership journey as low man on the
totem pole. He did what was asked of him with a great
attitude. While his own brothers looked down on him,
God lifted him up.

David's life illustrates that faithfulness in small things
often results in much larger assignments and greater
responsibility down the road. David loved the Lord and
lived his life as a man after God's own heart.

The Maxwell Leadership Bible

MARCH

Who you are precedes what you do...
Leadership begins with the heart.

Stay the Course

Do not turn from it to the right hand or to the left,
that you may prosper wherever you go.

Joshua 1:7

To be intentional means working with purpose making every action count. Successful leaders are intentional. They know what they're doing and why they're doing it. To become more intentional, do the following:

1. *Have a purpose worth living for:* Willis R. Whitney, the first director of General Electric's research laboratory, observed, "Some men have thousands of reasons why they cannot do what they want to, when all they need is one reason why they can."

2. *Know your strengths and weaknesses:* Playing to your strengths rekindles your passions and renews your energy.

3. *Prioritize your responsibilities:* Once you know the "why" of your life, it becomes much easier to figure out the "what" and "when."

4. *Learn to say no:* You can't accomplish much without focus. If you try to do every good thing that comes your way, you won't excel at what you were made to do.

5. *Commit yourself to long–term achievement:* Most victories in life are achieved through small incremental wins sustained over time.

The 17 Essential Qualities of a Team Player

You Gotta Have Heart

*And see, now I go bound in the spirit to Jerusalem,
not knowing the things that will happen to me there,
except that the Holy Spirit testifies in every city, saying
that chains and tribulations await me. But none
of these things move me; nor do I count my life dear
to myself, so that I may finish my race with joy, and the
ministry which I received from the Lord Jesus,
to testify to the gospel of the grace of God.*

Acts 20:22–24

Who you are precedes what you do. As Paul spoke
to the Ephesians, he described the ingredients of an
effective leader. Paul made tough calls, yet shed tears in
front of his people. One thing is sure: Leadership begins
with the heart. Paul had a heart that was . . .

Consistent—he lived steadily while moving among
them.

Contrite—he acted humbly and willingly showed his
weakness.

Courageous—he didn't shrink from doing the right
thing.

Convictional—he communicated his convictions
boldly.

Committed—he left for Jerusalem, willing to die for
Jesus.

Captivated—he showed that a surrendered man
doesn't have to survive.

The Maxwell Leadership Bible

IF YOU FALL, GET BACK UP

So the children of Israel did evil in the
sight of the LORD. They forgot the LORD their God ....
Therefore the anger of the LORD was hot against Israel
and He sold them into the hand of Cushan–Rishathaim
king of Mesopotamia, and the children of Israel
served Cushan–Rishathaim eight years.
When the children of Israel cried out to the LORD,
the LORD raised up a deliverer for the children
of Israel, who delivered them.

JUDGES 3:7–9

Austin O'Malley said, "The fact that you have been knocked down is interesting, but the length of time you remain down is important." In life, you will have problems. Are you going to give up and stay down, wallowing in your defeat, or are you going to get back on your feet as quickly as you can?

When you fall, make the best of it and get back on your feet. Learn what you can from your mistake, and then get back in the game. View your errors the way Henry Ford did his. He said, "Failure is the opportunity to begin again more intelligently."

Your Road Map for Success

THE RIGHT ATTITUDE COMES FIRST

*Then Caleb quieted the people before Moses, and said,
"Let us go up at once and take possession, for we are
well able to overcome it." But the men who had gone
up with him said, "We are not able to go up against
the people, for they are stronger than we."*

NUMBERS 13:30–31

How could there be such differing opinions on the same topic? Because there was a difference in attitude. And attitude makes all the difference. The development of a positive attitude is the first conscious step toward becoming an effective leader. Successful leadership cannot be constructed without this crucial building block. Check out the following attitude axioms suggested by the words and actions of Joshua and Caleb:

1. Our attitude determines our approach to life.
2. Our attitude determines our relationships with people.
3. Our attitude is often the only difference between success and failure.
4. Our attitude at the beginning of a task will affect its outcome more than anything else.
5. Our attitude can turn problems into blessings.
6. Our attitude is not automatically good just because we belong to God.

The Maxwell Leadership Bible

ROOM TO GROW

But Samuel was ministering before the LORD—
a boy wearing a linen ephod…And the boy Samuel
continued to grow in stature and in favor
with the LORD and with men ….The boy Samuel
ministered before the LORD under Eli ….
The LORD was with Samuel.

1 SAMUEL 2:18,26, 3:1, 19 (NIV)

Leaders in some organizations don't recognize the importance of creating a climate conducive to building potential leaders. To see the relationship between environment and growth, look at nature. One popular aquarium fish is the shark. The reason is that sharks adapt to their environment. If you catch a small shark and confine it, it will stay a size proportionate to the aquarium in which it lives. Sharks can be six inches long yet fully mature. But if you turn them loose in the ocean, they grow to their normal size.

The same is true of potential leaders. Some are put into an organization when they are still small, and the confining environment ensures that they stay small and under–developed. Only leaders can control the environment of their organization. They can be the change agents who create a climate conducive to growth.

Developing the Leaders Around You

PERSISTENCE: THE ULTIMATE GAUGE OF LEADERSHIP

And it happened, when our enemies heard that it was known to us, and that God had brought their plot to nothing, that all of us returned to the wall, everyone to his work.

NEHEMIAH 4:15

One of the great tests of leadership is how you handle opposition. Nehemiah faced the usual tactics of the opposition: ridicule, resistance, and rumor. Nehemiah modeled the right response to all three of these challenges by . . .

Relying on God.

Respecting the opposition.

Reinforcing his weak points.

Reassuring the people.

Refusing to quit.

Renewing the people's strength continually.

Nehemiah had to deal with problems from without—ridicule, resistance, and rumor—and within—disputes about food, property, and taxes.

Persistence is the ultimate gauge of our leadership; the secret is to outlast our critics. Nehemiah taught us this lesson by staying committed to his ultimate calling.

The Maxwell Leadership Bible

PREPARATION TO LEAD

But as for you, you meant evil against me; but God
meant it for good, in order to bring it about as
it is this day, to save many people alive.

GENESIS 50:20

Like most great leaders, Joseph of the Old Testament labored in obscurity before he became qualified to lead others. Nearly twenty–three years passed from the pit to the palace before Joseph was reunited with his brothers and his vision was fulfilled.

But by then, he had come to learn that true progress occurs only when God orchestrates it. He understood that self–promotion can never replace divine promotion. His self–promotion with his brothers failed miserably. Only when he finally became submissive—as a slave—and chose to work faithfully for Potiphar, did it become evident that "the Lord was with him" (Genesis 39:3 NKJV). In prison, he served the jail's keeper, and again God showed him favor and mercy. But when Joseph tried to take self–promotion back into his own hands—by recommending himself to Pharaoh's chief butler—God again made him wait. Two years passed before Joseph got an audience with the monarch. By then, Joseph had learned his lesson. He was content to recognize that God was in charge . . . and that he was being grown as a leader for a much greater purpose than he could have imagined.

The 21 Most Powerful Minutes in a Leader's Day

HAVE CHILDREN?
THEN LEAD THEM!

Train up a child in the way he should go,
And when he is old he will not depart from it.

PROVERBS 22:6

God calls parents to lead their children. And just how does a parent become a good leader for a child? Partly by focusing on three key words:

Modeling: Abraham Lincoln said, "There is but one way to train up a child in the way he should go, and that is to travel it yourself." A good example is worth a thousand sermons. What you do has more impact on your child than all the lectures you could ever give.

Management: Good management is the ability to discern the uniqueness of a child and teach him or her accordingly. We are to train up a child in the way he should go. This may mean we will have to adapt our style, depending on the child's temperament and wiring.

Memories: Memories are more important than things. Note that the verse says, "When he is old, he will not depart . . . " This implies that the child has memories of his early experiences and embraces them later in life.

The Maxwell Leadership Bible

COMMUNICATE
THE GAME PLAN

And He said to them, "Go into all the world
and preach the gospel to every creature."
MARK 16:15

Every good coach I've watched has worked from a game plan. He's got one not only for each individual game, but a plan for the development of the whole team over the course of the current and upcoming seasons. Once the game plan has been drawn up, he then communicates it to his team on an almost continual basis.

Paul "Bear" Bryant, the late Alabama football coach, had five points that explained what he believed a coach should do:

1. Tell players what you expect of them.
2. Give players an opportunity to perform.
3. Let players know how they're getting along.
4. Instruct and empower players when they need it.
5. Reward players according to their contribution.

The process must begin with communicating the game plan. That is the key to productivity. But it must continue with the exchange of information. As Sydney J. Harris said, information is "giving out" while communication is "getting through." When there is interactive communication between the team leader and his people, it empowers them to succeed.

Developing the Leaders Around You

LEADERS ORGANIZE SO THEY DON'T HAVE TO AGONIZE

*Pursue love, and desire spiritual gifts, but especially
that you may prophesy. He who speaks in a tongue
edifies himself, but he who prophesies edifies
the church. For if the trumpet makes an uncertain
sound, who will prepare for battle? But if all prophesy,
and an unbeliever or an uninformed person comes in,
he is convinced by all, he is convicted by all.
For God is not the author of confusion but of peace,
as in all the churches of the saints.
Let all things be done decently and in order.*

1 CORINTHIANS 14:1, 4, 8, 24, 33, 40

Paul wrote to bring order to a church in chaos. The Corinthians were abusing their gifts and calling attention to themselves rather than to Christ. As a leader, Paul had to change this. What can we learn about organization from this?

Identify and pursue your top priorities.

Seek to practice what will benefit the most people.

Communicate clearly.

See things through the eyes of the outsider.

Order activities simply for the purpose of adding value to others.

Make sure everything is done in a appropriate manner.

The Maxwell Leadership Bible

THOSE CLOSEST TO YOU . . .

When his brothers and all his father's house heard it,
they went down there to him. And everyone
who was in distress, everyone who was in debt,
and everyone who was discontented gathered to him.
So he became captain over them.

1 SAMUEL 22:1–2

David's heart for God made him a great man. But what made him a great leader? I assert that his leadership success had a lot to do with his inner circle.

David didn't wait until he held a leadership position to begin building his inner circle. And some of David's first followers were misfits. Yet David transformed the people who came to him into a winning team. As David gained experience and grew in his leadership, he continued to attract stronger and stronger people. And he also molded those who came to him into great warriors and leaders.

David was an incredible leader and team builder, but in many ways an ordinary person—with flaws and failures. Thanks to his inner circle, he became a great ruler. He made his inner circle great, and his inner circle made him great.

The 21 Most Powerful Minutes in a Leader's Day

LEADERSHIP INSIDE—
THEN OUT

*So the LORD's anger was aroused against Israel,
and He made them wander in the wilderness forty
years, until all the generation that had done evil
in the sight of the LORD was gone.*

NUMBERS 32:13

The first person you lead is you—and you can't
lead effectively without self–discipline. If only the
Israelites had remembered this lesson! For forty years the
Israelites wondered around in the desert. Why didn't they
get to the Promised Land more quickly? Not because it lay
so far away—they could have made the trip in two weeks.
The real reason boils down to preparation. The people
simply weren't ready for God's blessing until forty years
after they began their trip.

How about you? How is your self–discipline? Plato
said, "The first and best victory is to conquer self." If you
want to be a leader with self–discipline, follow these action
points:

1. Develop and follow your priorities.
2. Make a disciplined lifestyle your goal.
3. Challenge your excuses.
4. Remove rewards until you finish the job.
5. Stay focused on results.

Never trade what you want at the moment for what
you want most.

The Maxwell Leadership Bible

BRINGING OUT THEIR BEST

And he was called the friend of God.

JAMES 2:23

Many organizations today fail to tap into their potential. Why? Because the only reward they give their employees is a paycheck. The relationship between employer and employee never develops beyond that point. Successful organizations take a different approach. In exchange for the work a person gives, he receives not only his paycheck, but he is also nurtured by the people he works for. And nurturing has the ability to transform people's lives.

I use the BEST™ acronym as a reminder of what people need when they get started with my organization. They need me to . . .

Believe in them

Encourage them

Share with them

Trust them

Nurturing benefits everyone. What people wouldn't be more secure and motivated when their leader believes in them, encourages them, shares with them, and trusts them (BEST)? People are more productive when they are nurtured. Even more important, nurturing creates a strong emotional and professional foundation within workers who have leadership potential. Later, using training and development, a leader can be built on that foundation.

Developing the Leaders Around You

A BIGGER VISION
DRIVES GOD'S LEADERS

*God be merciful to us and bless us, And cause His face
to shine upon us, That Your way may be known on
earth, Your salvation among all nations.*

PSALM 67:1-2

God's blessings follow leaders who adopt His vision for the nations for the world. Psalm 67 contains both the "top line" and the "bottom line" of the covenant God invites us to enter. The top line represents God's blessings for His people; the bottom line represents the natural response to that blessing. When God blesses us, we are to turn around and bless all the unblessed nations of the earth. The "top line" is that God would bless us, and the "bottom line" is that we would make His name known to all of the earth.

God blesses His people so that they can bless those who have yet to be blessed. Godly leaders feel driven by this vision. Maintenance is not the goal. Getting blessed is not the goal. World conquest motivates God's heart, and He accomplishes this mission through leaders who cast vision for participating in bottom–line living.

The Maxwell Leadership Bible

EXPLANATION
AND MOTIVATION

*Now David said on that day, "Whoever climbs up by
way of the water shaft and defeats the Jebusites ... he
shall be chief and captain . . . " Then David dwelt in
the stronghold, and called it the City of David.*

2 SAMUEL 5:8–9

In this world of rapid change and discontinuities,
the leader must be out in front to encourage
change and growth and to show the way to bring it about.

Managers usually are more skilled in the technical
requirements of change, whereas leaders have a better
understanding of the attitudinal and motivational
demands that the followers need. Note the difference: In
the beginning the skills of a leader are essential. No change
will ever occur if the psychological needs are unmet. Once
change has begun, the skills of a manager are needed to
maintain needed change.

A good exercise when you face change is to make a list
of the logical advantages and disadvantages that should
result from the change, and then make another list
indicating the psychological impact. Just seeing this on a
sheet of paper can be clarifying.

Developing the Leader Within You

IT TAKES A TEAM

I am not able to bear all these people alone,
because the burden is too heavy for me.

NUMBERS 11:14

God's answer to Moses' cry for help was for Moses to share the responsibilities of leadership with a select group. We don't know a lot about the seventy elders Moses called to aid him. The Old Testament mentions them only twice, both times to witness God's presence, power, and glory (Exodus 24). But the second time the elders are called, God expanded their role. This time they were called to participate—thus revealing something remarkable about how God works with leaders. "I will take the Spirit that is upon you," God told Moses, "and will put the same upon them; and they shall bear the burden of the people with you, that you may not bear it yourself alone" (Numbers 11:17).

When a leader called by God has a burden that becomes too great, God provides help . . . if the leader will ask for it. Not only will the Lord provide helpers to share the load, He will anoint them with His power, just as He did the seventy elders of Israel.

The Maxwell Leadership Bible

Guarding Against the Sluggard

The lazy man will not plow because of winter;
He will beg during harvest and have nothing.

Proverbs 20:4

King Solomon had plenty to say about the "sluggard," or the habitually lazy person. The sluggard makes only one commitment: to his leisure. He'll try any excuse to shy away from honest labor.

The sluggard in the physical sense does nothing for the world around him; he leaves it unchanged, except for pillaging some of its resources. The sluggard in the spiritual sense is little different; he leaves the world no better than he found it, and perhaps a little poorer. When leaders become lazy and lose their diligence in doing good for God, they become spiritual sluggards and worthless to the kingdom.

Wise leaders know their time is limited. They know they have no way to retrieve misused or wasted time. Jesus stressed this when He said, "I must work the works of Him who sent Me while it is day; the night is coming when no one can work" (John 9:4). Leaders in the body of Christ must remain diligent in doing good and in encouraging others to do likewise.

The Maxwell Leadership Bible

THE WILL TO
DO WHAT'S RIGHT

*And being in agony, [Jesus] prayed more earnestly. Then
His sweat became like drops of blood.*

LUKE 22:44

Discipline is doing what you really don't want to
do, so that you can do what you really want to do.
It's paying the price in the little things so that you can buy
the bigger thing. Disciplined leaders must possess . . .

1. *Disciplined Thinking:* You can't get far in life if you
   don't use your head. If you keep your mind active
   and regularly take on mental challenges, you will
   develop the kind of disciplined thinking that will
   help you with whatever you endeavor to do.

2. *Disciplined Emotions:* People have just two choices
   when it comes to their emotions: they can master
   their emotions or be mastered by them. You
   shouldn't let your feelings prevent you from doing
   what you should or drive you to do things you
   shouldn't.

3. *Disciplined Actions:* Sharpening your mind and
   controlling your emotions are important, but they
   can take you only so far. Action is what separates
   the winners from the losers. Your actions always
   reflect your degree of discipline.

The 17 Essential Qualities of a Team Player

COMMITMENT PRECEDES RESOURCES

But Ruth said: "Entreat me not to leave you,
Or to turn back from following after you;
For wherever you go, I will go; And wherever you lodge,
I will lodge; Your people shall be my people,
And your God, my God."

RUTH 1:16

While every leader needs financial and human resources to reach his or her goals, commitment should always precede those resources. When a leader demonstrates a commitment to the mission and goals of the organization, then God moves and a whole stream of events begin to flow.

In the very first chapter of the book that bears her name, Ruth chooses to stay with Naomi, her mother–in–law, even after she loses her husband. She didn't know it, but her commitment would lead to all kinds of open doors. Ruth finds work during a difficult time, makes friends in a foreign land, and eventually gains a new husband, Boaz. Most impressively, God includes her—a Moabite adopted into the family of Israel—in the line of Christ. The child she bore became part of the lineage of the Messiah.

The key? Commitment. Once a leader definitely commits, God moves and all manner of unforeseen incidents, meetings, persons, and material assistance begin to stream forth.

The Maxwell Leadership Bible

LEADERS WHO
ATTRACT LEADERS

*And men of all nations, from all the kings of the earth
who had heard of his wisdom, came
to hear the wisdom of Solomon.*

1 KINGS 4:34

As you look for potential leaders, you need to realize that there are really two kinds of leaders: those who attract followers and those who attract other leaders. People who attract and team up only with followers will never be able to do anything beyond what they can personally touch or supervise. Look for leaders who attract other leaders. They will be able to multiply your success.

LEADERS WHO ATTRACT FOLLOWERS . . .	LEADERS WHO ATTRACT LEADERS . . .
Need to be needed.	Want to be succeeded.
Want recognition.	Want to reproduce themselves.
Focus on others' weaknesses.	Focus on others' strengths.
Spend their time with others.	Invest their time in others.
Experience some success.	Experience incredible success.

But also know this: In the long run, you can only lead people whose leadership ability is less than or equal to your own. To keep attracting better and better leaders, you will have to keep developing your own leadership ability.

Your Road Map for Success

MODELING: LEADERSHIP IS CAUGHT MORE THAN TAUGHT

For I think God has displayed us, the apostles, last, as men condemned to death; for we have been made a spectacle to the world, both to angels and to men.

1 CORINTHIANS 4:9

The greatest missing ingredient in Christian leaders today is credibility. Paul tests his level of credibility with his Corinthian followers by reminding them of how he had modeled what was right. He pleads with them to imitate him.

Leaders add infinite weight to their words by incarnating the principles they teach. Paul was able to scold the erring people and sternly correct them because he never asked them to do something he hadn't already done. Observe his life:

His leadership was on display and open for ridicule.

He was willing to play the fool in order to model a surrendered life.

He endured mocking from others, but didn't waver.

He sacrificed luxuries that others enjoyed.

He urged his followers to imitate his life.

He sent Timothy to help them live up to godly standards.

He reminded them that God's kingdom was not about talk, but power.

The Maxwell Leadership Bible

SPEND TIME WITH YOUR BEST

*Now after six days Jesus took Peter, James,
and John, and led them up on a high
mountain apart by themselves.*

MARK 9:2

Years ago I learned the Pareto Principle and began applying it to my life. It's a useful tool for determining priorities for any person's life or for any organization.

THE PARETO PRINCIPLE

20 percent of your priorities will give you 80 percent of your production

IF you spend your time, energy, money, and personnel on the top 20 percent of your priorities.

Every leader needs to understand the Pareto Principle in the area of people oversight and leadership. For example, 20 percent of the people in an organization will be responsible for 80 percent of the company's success. The following strategy will enable a leader to increase the productivity of an organization.

Determine which people are the top 20 percent producers.

Spend 80 percent of your "people time" with the top 20 percent.

Spend 80 percent of your personal development dollars on the top 20 percent.

Ask the top 20 percent to do on–the–job training for the next 20 percent.

Developing the Leader Within You

The Leader and Stress

The LORD is my shepherd; I shall not want.

PSALM 23:1

Have you discovered the differences between problems and facts? Problems are things we can do something about; we can solve problems. Facts are things we can do nothing about; therefore we do well not to worry about them. We should apply energy only to those things we can change. When we do, we can feel peace and act with poise, because we no longer beat our heads against an unbreakable wall.

Psalm 23 reminds us of what God alone can control and what we can control. It distinguishes between problems and facts. It defines God as . . .

Our possession
Our provision
Our peace
Our pardon
Our partner
Our preparation
Our praise
Our paradise

The Maxwell Leadership Bible

QUALITIES OF INITIATORS

So I prayed to the God of heaven. And I said to the king, "If it pleases the king, and if your servant has found favor in your sight, I ask that you send me to Judah, to the city of my fathers' tombs, that I may rebuild [the wall]."

NEHEMIAH 2:4–5

 Nehemiah displayed the qualities that make for initiative in leaders:

They know what they want: Desire is the starting point of all achievement. Nehemiah knew that he wanted that wall up.

They push themselves to act: At first, Nehemiah acted alone. He pushed to get the facts that would move others.

They take more risks: Nehemiah took some major risks as he got permission to go, to get wood, and to survey the job.

They make more mistakes: Nehemiah wasn't afraid to mobilize men who weren't professional contractors to build or soldiers to fight.

They go with their gut: What Nehemiah lacked in experience, he made up for with the passion of his heart.

The Maxwell Leadership Bible

USE EVERY TOOL YOU HAVE

Abraham said to the oldest servant of his house . . . "Go to my country and to my family, and take a wife for my son Isaac."
GENESIS 24:2, 4

Delegation is the most powerful tool leaders have. Delegation increases individual productivity according to the number of people to whom leaders can delegate. It increases the productivity of their department or organization. Leaders who can't or won't delegate create a bottleneck to productivity. So why do some leaders fail to delegate effectively?

1. Insecurity
2. Lack of confidence in others
3. Lack of ability to train others
4. Personal enjoyment of the task
5. Habit
6. Inability to find someone else to do it
7. Lack of time
8. An "I do it best" mind–set

If you recognize yourself in any of the issues above, you probably aren't doing enough delegating. Here are some other indicators that you need to delegate: When deadlines are missed often; crises become frequent; someone else could do the job; or those under your leadership need another world to conquer.

Developing the Leaders Around You

TRUST BUSTER

Then three thousand men of Judah went down
to the cleft of the rock of Etam, and said to Samson,
"Do you not know that the Philistines rule over us?
What is this you have done to us?"
And he said to them, "As they did to me, so I have
done to them." But they said to him, "We have come
down to arrest you, that we may deliver
you into the hand of the Philistines."

JUDGES 15:11–12

Samson learned the hard way that trust provides the foundation for all genuine leadership. This impetuous, volatile, lustful, moody, emotional, and unpredictable man provides a very good example of a very bad leader. Since no one could trust him, none followed his leadership.

Leaders who erode the solid ground of trustworthy leadership usually exhibit one or more of the following signs—Samson displayed them all. Leaders in trouble . . .

1. Fail to address glaring character weaknesses.
2. Count on deception to safeguard themselves.
3. Act impulsively.
4. Are overcome by an area of weakness.
5. Misuse their God–given gifts.

Samson's self–centered, undisciplined, and arrogant nature made him an ineffective leader.

The Maxwell Leadership Bible

BE A WORTHY FOLLOWER

*Then the woman said to Elijah, "Now by this I know
that you are a man of God, and that the word of the
LORD in your mouth is truth . . . . So Elisha . . . arose
and followed Elijah, and became his servant.*

1 KINGS 17:24, 19:21

When you find someone who can personally
mentor you, use these guidelines to help develop a
positive mentoring relationship with that person:

Ask the right questions. Give thought to the questions
you will ask before your time with your mentor. Make the
questions strategic for your growth.

Don't let ego get in the way of learning.

Respect the mentor but don't idolize them. Making the
mentor an idol removes our critical faculty for adapting a
mentor's knowledge and experience to ourselves.

Put into effect immediately what you are learning.

Be disciplined in relating to the mentor. Arrange for
ample time, select the subject matter in advance, and do
your homework to make sessions profitable.

Don't threaten to give up. Let your mentor know that
you have made a decision for progress, so they will know
they are not wasting their time.

Developing the Leaders Around You

THE MARK OF A BELIEVER

A new command I give you:
Love one another. As I have loved you, so you
must love one another. By this all men will know that
you are my disciples, if you love one another.

JOHN 13:34–35 (NIV)

Bud Wilkinson states, "If a team is to reach its potential, each player must be willing to subordinate his personal goals to the good of the team."

Some sports teams seem to embrace an everyone–for–themselves mind set. Others weave the attitude of subordination and teamwork into the fabric of everything they do. Notre Dame and Penn State don't put the names of the players on their jerseys. Lou Holtz once said, "At Notre Dame, we believed the interlocking ND was all the identification you needed . . . If your priority is the team rather than yourself, what else do you need?"

Winning teams have players who put the good of the team ahead of themselves. They want to play in their area of strength, but they're willing to do what it takes to take care of the team. They are willing to sacrifice their role for the greater goal.

The 17 Indisputable Laws of Teamwork

YOUR ADVISORS
WILL MAKE OR BREAK YOU

Where there is no counsel, the people fall;
But in the multitude of counselors there is safety.
PROVERBS 11:14

Every leader ought to build an inner circle that adds value to him or her and to the leadership of the organization. But choose well, for the members of this inner circle will become your closest confidantes; your inner circle will make you or break you.

So who belongs in the "council" in this inner circle? Strive for the following:

Creative people
Loyal people
People who share your vision
Wise and intelligent people
People with complementary gifts
People with influence
People of faith
People of integrity

So how about it? Do those closest to you exemplify these qualities?

The Maxwell Leadership Bible

TOOL TIME

If it pleases the king, let letters be given to me for the governors of the region beyond the River, that they must permit me to pass through till I come to Judah, and a letter to Asaph the keeper of the king's forest, that he must give me timber to make beams for the gates of the citadel which pertains to the temple, for the city wall, and for the house that I will occupy." And the king granted them to me according to the good hand of my God upon me.

NEHEMIAH 2:7–8

When we give our people authority and responsibility, we must also give them the tools they need. Giving responsibility without resources is ridiculous. It is incredibly limiting. If we want our people to be creative and resourceful, we need to provide resources.

Tools, however, include much more than just equipment. Be willing to spend money, on things like books, tapes, professional conferences, etc. Fresh ideas from outside an organization can stimulate growth. Be creative in providing tools. It will keep your people growing and equip them to do the job well.

Developing the Leaders Around You

A BROTHER IN MORE THAN ONLY BLOOD

Is not Aaron the Levite your brother?
I know that he can speak well. And look, he is also
coming out to meet you. When he sees you, he will be
glad in his heart. Now you shall speak to him
and put the words in his mouth . . . .
So he shall be your spokesman to the people.
And he himself shall be as a mouth for you,
and you shall be to him as God.

EXODUS 4:14–16

Who wouldn't tremble at receiving a call like the one given to Moses? From the very beginning, Moses' feelings of inadequacy prompted him to build an "inner circle" of close supporters. His brother, Aaron, quickly became a critical member of his team, and through the years Moses added to his inner circle, each time including individuals who possessed different gifts but the same vision as he.

Who sits in your inner circle? Do they share your vision? Do they have complementary gifts, useful where you need them most? Find yourself some Aarons, Jethros, and Joshuas, or you won't be able to accomplish all that God has for you.

The Maxwell Leadership Bible

APRIL

You can tell a lot about which direction
your life is heading by looking
at the people with whom you've chosen
to spend your time and share your ideas.

SWALLOW YOUR PRIDE
OR BE SWALLOWED UP

And Moses said: "By this you shall know
that the LORD has sent me to do all these works,
for I have not done them of my own will. If these men
die naturally like all men, or if they are visited
by the common fate of all men, then the LORD has
not sent me. But if the LORD creates a new thing,
and the earth opens its mouth and swallows
them up with all that belongs to them,
and they go down alive into the pit,
then you will understand that
these men have rejected the LORD."

NUMBERS 16:28–30

The Scripture makes clear that God places people in authority, and it is dangerous to oppose God's anointed. Korah had rebelled against both Moses and the Lord, thus illustrating the tragic flaw of many leaders—a desire for power and authority beyond what God has ordained.

Godly leaders must be willing to submit themselves to those in leadership above them. Many who hold leadership positions based on their strength and personality find this difficult to accept, yet willing subordination may qualify a person for greater leadership responsibilities later.

The Maxwell Leadership Bible

HOPE FLOATS

Therefore my heart is glad, and my glory rejoices;
My flesh also will rest in hope.

PSALM 16:9

Writer Mark Twain said: "Keep away from people who try to belittle your ambitions. Small people always do that, but the really great make you feel that you, too, can become great." How do most people feel when they're around you? Do they feel small and insignificant, or do they believe in themselves and have great hope about what they can become?

The key to how you *treat* people lies in how you *think* about them. It's a matter of attitude. What you believe is revealed by how you act. Johann Wolfgang von Goethe said: "Treat a man as he appears to be and you make him worse. But treat a man as if he already were what he potentially could be, and you make him what he should be."

Hope is perhaps the greatest gift you can give another person as the result of nurturing, because even if people fail to see their own significance, they still have a reason to keep trying and striving to reach their potential in the future.

Becoming a Person of Influence

FAMILY FIRST

Now the sons of Eli were corrupt;
they did not know the LORD.

1 SAMUEL 2:12

As a priest, Eli mentored Samuel; however, Eli's failure to lead his family eventually led to his downfall as a religious leader. This revered judge in Israel failed to discipline his two sons and ended up rearing spiritual rebels. Eli lost his credibility, his job, and eventually his life.

The Scripture teaches that if we do not faithfully lead our own household, we lack the qualifications to lead beyond the home—in other words, if it doesn't work at home, don't export it. How could a priest like Eli miss the mark? By making some crucial errors.

1. *Emphasis:* Eli emphasized teaching his colleagues and clients, not his family.

2. *Expectations:* Eli thought his sons would "get it" just because they lived in the house of the Lord.

3. *Example:* Eli failed to live out in his home what he taught in his work.

4. *Entanglements:* Eli got so caught up with his profession, he blinded himself to his failure.

The Maxwell Leadership Bible

THE COMMITMENT CRUCIBLE

*Then Jesus said to the twelve, "Do you also want
to go away?" But Simon Peter answered Him,
"Lord, to whom shall we go? You have the
words of eternal life."*

JOHN 6:67–68

People often associate commitment with their
emotions. If they feel the right way, then they can
follow through on their commitments. But true
commitment doesn't work that way. It's not an emotion;
it's a character quality that enables us to reach our goals.
Human emotions go up and down all the time, but
commitment has to be rock solid.

There are some things every leader needs to know
about being committed:

1. It usually is discovered amid adversity
2. It does not depend on gifts or abilities
3. It comes as the result of choice, not conditions
4. It lasts when it's based on values

The 17 Essential Qualities of a Team Player

AN UNEXPECTED LEADER

Now the city shall be doomed by the LORD
to destruction, it and all who are in it.
Only Rahab the harlot shall live,
she and all who are with her in the house,
because she hid the messengers that we sent.

JOSHUA 6:17

The story of Rahab proves that God will use anybody. This woman worked as a prostitute in Jericho. Although the Hebrew spies needed someone to help them scope out the best approach to conquering the city, there seemed little logical reason why Rahab should have been considered for the role.

But because leadership depends less on titles than it does on influence, God chose Rahab. She helped the spies by her quick wisdom, gutsy style, and clever plan. She saved not only her own life, but aided in accomplishing the purposes of God in Jericho.

Wise leaders remember that God sees the human heart; while many would never trust a woman with a personal history like that of Rehab, God selected her. Because Rahab faithfully served God, her family lived and was adopted into Hebrew society—and she became an ancestor of the Lord Jesus Himself (Matthew 1:5).

The Maxwell Leadership Bible

LEADERS ARE LEARNERS

A wise man will hear and increase learning.

PROVERBS 1:5

If you continually invest in your leadership development, the inevitable result is growth over time. Although it's true that some people are born with greater natural gifts than others, the ability to lead is really a collection of skills, nearly all of which can be learned and improved. But that process doesn't happen overnight. Leadership is complicated. It has many facets: respect, experience, emotional strength, people skills, discipline, vision, momentum, timing—the list goes on. As you can see, many factors that come into play in leadership are intangible. That's why leaders require so much seasoning to be effective.

In a study of ninety top leaders from a variety of fields, leadership experts Warren Bennis and Burt Nanus made a discovery about the relationship between growth and leadership: "It is the capacity to develop and improve their skills that distinguishes leaders from their followers." Successful leaders are learners. And the learning process is ongoing, a result of self–discipline and perseverance. The goal each day must be to get a little better, to build on the previous day's progress.

The 21 Irrefutable Laws of Leadership

WHEN THE REAL
LEADER SPEAKS

Then Elijah said to all the people, "Come near to me."
So all the people came near to him. And he repaired the
altar of the LORD that was broken down.

1 KINGS 18:30

When Elijah spoke, people jumped. But most amazing of all, by the end of the day after all the theatrics, Elijah turned his face toward heaven and cried, "Hear me, O LORD, hear me, that this people may know that You are the LORD God, and that You have turned their hearts back to You again" (1 Kings 18:37)—and God did.

How did the prophet gain the ear of everyone who heard his voice? We can discern a number of reasons:

His courage: He was willing to stand alone for God.

His conviction: He has a passion for what he believed.

His character: He was honest and forthright with everyone.

His connection: He magnetically drew the people to himself and to God.

His credibility: He eventually gained the people's ear because he got the results he wanted.

The Maxwell Leadership Bible

EXPANDING THE CIRCLE BEYOND TWELVE

Then the seventy returned with joy, saying, "Lord, even the demons are subject to us in Your name." And He said to them, "I saw Satan fall like lightening from heaven. Behold, I give you the authority to trample on serpents and scorpions, and over all the power of the enemy, and nothing shall by any means hurt you."

LUKE 10:17–19

If you look at the roster of any successful team, you will see that the starters are always outnumbered by the other players on the team. In pro football, twenty–two people start on offense and defense, but teams are allowed to have fifty–three players on a team. (College teams often have more than 100!)

You find similar situations in every field. In the entertainment industry, the actors are often known, but the hundreds of crew members it takes to make a movie aren't. For any politician or corporate executive or big–name fashion designer that you know about, hundreds of people are working quietly in the background to make their work possible. Nobody can neglect the majority of the team and hope to be successful.

The 17 Indisputable Laws of Teamwork

THE HEART OF A LEADER

Have mercy upon me, O God,
According to Your lovingkindness;
According to the multitude of Your tender mercies,
Blot out my transgressions.
Wash me thoroughly from my iniquity,
And cleanse me from my sin.
For I acknowledge my transgressions,
And my sin is always before me . . .
Create in me a clean heart, O God,
And renew a steadfast spirit in me.

PSALM 51:1–3, 10

All leaders make mistakes. They are a part of life. Successful leaders recognize their errors, learn from them, and then work to correct their faults. A study of 105 executives determined many of the characteristics of successful executives, but one particular trait they shared was identified as the most valuable. It was that they admitted their mistakes and accepted the consequences, rather than trying to blame others.

Most people don't want to reap the consequences of their actions. You can see this type of attitude everywhere. A leader who is willing to take responsibility for their actions and be honest or "transparent" with their people is someone they will admire, respect, and trust. That leader is also someone they can learn from.

Developing the Leaders Around You

INVEST TO EMPOWER

Barnabas took [Paul] and brought him to the apostles,
And he declared to them how he had seen the
Lord on the road, and that He had spoken
to him, and how he had preached boldly
at Damascus in the name of Jesus.

ACTS 9:27

Barnabas let no opportunity escape to add value to others, and his greatest single contribution in terms of empowerment can be seen in his interaction with Paul.

He believed in Paul before anyone else did.

He endorsed Paul's leadership to other leaders.

He empowered Paul to reach his potential.

To be an empowering leader, you must do more than believe in emerging leaders. You need to take steps to help them become the leaders they have the potential to be. You must invest in them if you want to empower them to become their best.

Empowering people takes a personal investment. It requires energy and time. But it's worth the price. If you do it right, you will have the privilege of seeing someone move up to a higher level. And when you empower others, you create power in your organization.

The Maxwell Leadership Bible

BIRDS OF A FEATHER

Take firm hold of instruction, do not let go;
Keep her, for she is your life.
Do not enter the path of the wicked,
And do not walk in the way of evil.
Avoid it, do not travel on it;
Turn away from it and pass on.

PROVERBS 4:13–15

A factor in your personal development comes in the area of your relationships with others. You can tell a lot about which direction your life is heading by looking at the people with whom you've chosen to spend your time and share your ideas. Their values and priorities impact you the way you think and act. If they're positive people dedicated to growth, then their values and priorities will encourage you and reinforce your desire to grow.

It's not always comfortable to associate with people who are ahead of you in their growth, but it's always profitable. Try to cultivate relationships with those people who can help you grow, but don't think only in terms of what you can gain. Always bring something to the table yourself. You've got to make the relationship win–win or it won't last.

Your Road Map for Success

THE CALL OF A LEADER

In the year that King Uzziah died, I saw the Lord sitting on a throne, high and lifted up, and the train of His robe filled the temple. Also I heard the voice of the Lord, saying: "Whom shall I send, And who will go for Us?" Then I said, "Here am I! Send me."

ISAIAH 6:1, 8

The first eight verses of Isaiah 6 illustrate how God calls many leaders. When Isaiah receives a vision from God, the Lord lays out a need for someone to speak for Him. God has a message and is looking for a messenger. God issued a general call, for anyone, and Isaiah took it personally. He did so because of three factors that make up a divine call to lead:

Opportunity: We see a specific place where we can make a difference. This has to do with timing.

Ability: We recognize that we have the God–given gifts to do something about the need. This has to do with competence.

Desire: We want to step out and address the need; our hunger pushes us. This has to do with our passion.

The Maxwell Leadership Bible

FALLING SHORT

Then Saul said to Samuel,
"I have sinned, for I have transgressed the
commandment of the LORD and your words,
because I feared the people and obeyed their voice."

1 SAMUEL 15:24

Saul never won the inward battles. On the outside he was tall, good–looking, and well built; however, on the inside he was a small man. When faced with a challenge he panicked. He lacked the courage necessary to lead the people of Israel.

Some lessons about courage we learn from Saul are that:

Courage and cowardice are both contagious: When Saul fled so did his men.

Without courage, it doesn't matter how good your intentions are: Saul had good intentions when he presented burnt offerings to the Lord. But he let his fear that people would desert him control his actions.

Without courage, we're slaves of our own insecurity and possessiveness: Saul was captive to his fears of being replaced by David.

A leader without courage will never let go of the familiar: Saul employed a medium to ask counsel of Samuel's spirit.

Lack of courage will eventually sabotage a leader. Saul's lack of courage cost him everything.

The Maxwell Leadership Bible

TEAM SUCCESS BRINGS
INDIVIDUAL SUCCESS

But God composed the body, having given greater honor
to that part which lacks it, that there should be no
schism in the body, but that the members should have
the same care for one another.
And if one member suffers, all the members
suffer with it; or if one member is honored,
all the members rejoice with it.

1 CORINTHIANS 12:24–26

If your team members believe in the goals of the team and begin to develop genuine trust in one another, they will be in a position to demonstrate true teamwork. Notice that I mention the team members will be in a position to demonstrate true teamwork. That does not necessarily mean that they will do it.

For there to be teamwork, several things must happen. First, team members must genuinely believe that the value of the team's success is greater than the value of their own individual interests. Second, personal sacrifice must be encouraged and then rewarded—by the team leader and the other members of the team. As this happens, the people will identify themselves more and more with the team, and they will recognize that individualism wins trophies, but teamwork wins pennants.

Developing the Leaders Around You

EVERYONE'S A CRITIC

Then Miriam and Aaron spoke against Moses
because of the Ethiopian woman whom he had
married; for he had married an Ethiopian woman.

NUMBERS 12:1

Leaders can bank on two truths. First, they will be criticized. Second, criticism always changes the leader. Unhappy people tend to attack the point person. Moses' only family criticized him. Notice what God and Moses teach us on how to handle criticism (Numbers 12):

1. Maintain your humility. (v. 3)
2. Face the criticism squarely. (v. 4)
3. Be specific about the issue. (vv. 5–8)
4. Lay out consequences. (vv 9, 10)
5. Pray for the criticizers. (vv. 12, 13)
6. Restore them when appropriate. (v. 14)

Beyond that, consider the ways leaders should handle criticism:

1. Understand the difference between constructive and destructive criticism.
2. Look beyond the criticism to see the critic.
3. Guard your own attitude toward the critic.
4. Keep yourself spiritually in shape. Associate with people of faith.
5. Wait for time to prove the critic wrong.
6. Concentrate on your mission; change your mistakes.

The Maxwell Leadership Bible

A LIFE OF PRIORITIES

I have finished the work which
You have given Me to do.

JOHN 17:4

When Peter was a young fisherman in Galilee, no one would have thought he was destined to become the passionate leader of a world movement. After all, he had almost no education and probably would have been happy to live the remainder of his life in obscurity. But God had something else in mind, and when Peter met Jesus, his priorities began to change.

Like many leaders, Peter had to learn how to put first things first. In fact, Scripture reveals a lot about the inconsistencies of his behavior and his many irrational decisions. But the more time Peter spent with Jesus, the more he learned the difference between mere activity and accomplishment.

Like Peter, great leaders sift through the many things that demand their time, and they discern not only what needs to be done first, but also what doesn't need to be done at all. That starts with a passion to excel. When you focus your passion on what's most important, your leadership climbs to new heights.

The 21 Most Powerful Minutes in a Leader's Day

COUNT ON CHARACTER

A thick bankroll is no help when life falls apart,
but a principled life can stand up to the worst.
PROVERBS 11:4 (THE MESSAGE)

How a leader deals with the circumstances of life tells you a lot about their character. Crisis doesn't necessarily make character, but it certainly does reveal it. Adversity is a crossroads which makes a person choose one of two paths: character or compromise. Every time leaders choose character, they become stronger, even if that choice brings negative consequences. As Nobel Prize winning author Alexander Solzhenitsyn said, "The meaning of earthly existing lies, not as we have grown used to thinking, in prospering, but in the development of the soul." The development of character is at the heart of our development, not just as leaders, but as human beings.

What must every person know about character?

• Character is more than talk.

• Talent is a gift, but character is a choice.

• Character brings lasting success with people.

Leaders cannot rise above the limitations of their character.

The 21 Indispensable Qualities of a Leader

WARNING SIGNS OF A LEADER OUT OF CONTROL

Then Haman told them of his great riches, the multitude of his children, everything in which the king had prompted him, and how he had advanced him above the officials and servants of the king . . . "Yet all this avails me nothing, so long as I see Mordecai the Jew sitting at the king's gate." Then his wife Zeresh and all his friends said to him, ". . . in the morning suggest to the king that Mordecai be hanged on it. . . ." And the thing pleased Haman; so he had the gallows made . . . And Esther said, "The adversary and enemy is this wicked Haman!" So Haman was terrified before the king and queen . . . So they hanged Haman on the gallows that he had prepared for Mordecai.

ESTHER 5:11,13–14; 7:6 & 10

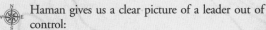 Haman gives us a clear picture of a leader out of control:

1. He lost joy over little problems.
2. He needed friends to build his self–image.
3. His greed made him unhappy.
4. He listened to the wrong people.
5. He thought too highly of himself.
6. He set himself up for a fall.
7. He reaped what he sowed.

The Maxwell Leadership Bible

CONSIDER THEIR DREAM

Then He bought [Abram] outside and said,
"Look now toward heaven, and count the stars if you
are able to number them." And He said to him,
"So shall your descendants be."

GENESIS 15:5

Most people who are dissatisfied and discouraged feel that way because they haven't grasped a vision for themselves. As a leader you can help others discover their dreams and then get moving.

You may already recognize much of the potential of the people you're leading, but you need to know more about them. To help them recognize the destination they will be striving for, you need to know what really matters to them. To do that, find out these things:

What do they cry about? To know where people truly want to go, you've got to know what touches their hearts.

What do they sing about? In the long run, people need to focus a lot of energy on what gives them joy.

What do they dream about? If you can help people discover their dreams and truly believe in them, you can help them become who they were designed to be.

Becoming a Person of Influence

LEARNING FROM
YOUR PREDECESSOR

So the king commanded Benaiah the son of Jehoiada;
and he went out and struck him down, and he
died. Thus the kingdom was established
in the hand of Solomon.

1 KINGS 2:46 (NKJV)

Solomon had to make some tough but crucial leadership decisions at the beginning of his reign. First, he had to deal with men scheming for power—even his own brother, Adonijah, tried to set up his own kingdom. One by one, King Solomon discerned the loyalties of his associates, then removed all who refused to cooperate with him.

Solomon knew he could never work with renegades, no matter how influential or strategic they might seem. The young king ensured that his inner circle would include only loyal men who wanted to work with him.

David had seen these troubles brewing on the horizon. He knew he was placing his successor in a precarious leadership situation, but twice he confidently declared that Solomon would know what to do. David understood that those closest to Solomon would greatly hinder or improve his level of success. Solomon understood the same thing—and wisely acted on it.

The Maxwell Leadership Bible

SPEAK UP TO YOUR LEADER

Good leaders cultivate honest speech;
they love advisors who tell them the truth.
PROVERBS 16:13 (THE MESSAGE)

Good team leaders never want yes–men. They need direct and honest communication from their people. I have always encouraged people on my team to speak openly and directly with me. Our meetings are often brainstorming sessions where the best idea wins. Often, a team member's remarks or observations really help the team. Sometimes we disagree. That's okay, because we've developed strong enough relationships that we can survive conflict. Getting everything out on the table always improves the team. The one thing I never want to hear from a teammate is, "I could have told you that wouldn't work." If you know it beforehand, that's the time to say it.

Besides directness, the other quality team members need to display when communicating with their leaders is respect. Leading a team isn't easy. It takes hard work. It demands personal sacrifice. It requires making tough and sometimes unpopular decisions. We should respect the people who take on leadership roles and show them loyalty.

The 17 Indisputable Laws of Teamwork

FOLLOWING
IN YOUR FOOTSTEPS

*So Aaron and his sons did all the things that
the LORD had commanded by the hand of Moses.*

LEVITICUS 8:36

Aaron, like many leaders through history, received a divine calling. God chose Aaron and his sons to serve as Israel's priests and charged them with carrying out rituals and sacrifices on behalf of all Israelites. Scripture gives meticulous detail to their ordination and calling. Their conduct was to be beyond reproach—God made it crystal clear that failure to uphold His established guidelines would result in death.

Despite his high calling, Aaron at times struggled with his authority. He once caved into the depraved wishes of the people and led Israel in a pagan worship service, an abomination that led to the deaths of many Israelites. Aaron had been set apart for God's service, but on that occasion, he chose to live and lead otherwise.

The failure of a leader usually results in consequences far more grave that the fall of a non–leader; On the day Aaron failed, "about three thousand men of the people fell [died]" (Exodus 32:28). When leaders fall, followers also pay the price.

The Maxwell Leadership Bible

REPAIR CHARACTER FAULTS

Now about that time Herod the king stretched
out his hand to harass some from the church. Then he
killed James the brother of John with the sword.
And because he saw that it pleased the Jews,
he proceeded further to seize Peter also.

ACTS 12:1–3

Ego drove King Herod of Paul's day, just as it had driven his father and grandfather. They all desperately lacked character. Herod's lack of character provides many examples of what not to do as a leader:

1. He mistreated his own citizens.

2. He made decisions based on popularity.

3. He acted irrationally in difficult times.

4. He harbored anger toward others.

5. He sought power out of insecurity.

6. He projected an infallible image.

7. He was blinded by his ego.

To improve your character and build a solid foundation of your own leadership, you must:

Identify where you're weak or have taken shortcuts.

Look for patterns.

Apologize to those you've wronged.

Stay teachable and rebuild.

The Maxwell Leadership Bible

LISTENING LIKE SAMUEL

*. . . and after the earthquake a fire, but the LORD was
not in the fire; and after the fire a still small voice.
So it was, when Elijah heard it."*

1 KINGS 19:12&13

Someone once asked Joan of Arc why God spoke
only to her. She responded, "Sir, you are wrong.
God speaks to everyone. I just listen."

When God spoke to Samuel, it was as the boy lay
down quietly in the middle of the night. Even then,
Samuel did not at first recognize that the voice belonged
to God. He needed the wisdom of his experienced
mentor, Eli, to understand who was communicating with
him. But based on how often Samuel heard God's voice
as an adult, it's clear that he did learn to identify, listen to,
and obey God's voice.

Leaders are often very busy people. And they can
easily get caught up in the activity of their obligations. If
you're a leader, that's why it's important to set aside times
to quiet yourself and listen for God's direction. As Bill
Hybels says, "Leaders need to ask God to give them
Samuel's ear."

The 21 Most Powerful Minutes in a Leader's Day

As Responsibilities Increase, Rights Decrease

For everyone to whom much is given, from him much will be required; and to whom much has been committed, of him they will ask the more.

LUKE 12:48

Leaders must live by higher standards than their followers. This insight is exactly opposite of most people's thoughts concerning leadership. In a world of perks and privileges that accompany the climb to success, little thought is given to the responsibilities of the upward journey. Leaders can give up anything except responsibility, either for themselves or their organizations. John D. Rockefeller, Jr., said, "I believe that every right implies a responsibility; every opportunity, an obligation; every possession, a duty."

Too many people are ready to assert their rights, but not to assume their responsibilities. Richard L. Evans, in his book *An Open Road,* said: "It is priceless to find a person who will take responsibility . . . to know when someone has accepted an assignment that it will be effectively, conscientiously completed. But when half-finished assignments keep coming back—to check on, to verify, to edit, to interrupt thought, and to take repeated attention—obviously someone has failed to follow the doctrine of completed work."

Developing the Leader Within You

RECOGNIZE THE
NEED TO TRANSITION

*Then it was, when the wall was built and I had hung
the doors, when the gatekeepers, the singers, and the
Levites had been appointed, that I gave the charge
of Jerusalem to my brother Hanani, and Hananiah the
leader of the citadel, for he was a faithful man
and feared God more than many.*

NEHEMIAH 7:1-2

Two emotions usually follow a great achievement: a sign of relief and celebration and a sense of . . . now what? The period after a success can become a dangerous time. Sometimes we feel tempted toward complacency, especially if we lack another goal. We can become satisfied and let down our guard. Momentum leaks.

The moment of victory is a crucial time for any organization. A transitional problem occurs when the leader does not know how to grow with the organization. Nehemiah's life illustrates the difference between a catalyst and a consolidator:

TWO TYPES OF LEADERSHIP SEASONS

1. Catalyst: Gets it going	1. Consolidator: Keeps it going
2. Designer: Thinks it up	2. Developer: Follows it up
3. Motivator: Encourages	3. Manager: Organizes
4. Entrepreneur: Relies on self	4. Executive: Relies on others

The Maxwell Leadership Bible

UNCHECKED EMOTION— UNSUCCESSFUL LEADERSHIP

Then Jonadab the son of Shimeah, David's brother,
answered and said, "Let not my lord suppose they have
killed all the young men, the king's sons, for only
Amnon is dead. For by the command of Absalom
this has been determined from the day that
he forced his sister Tamar."

2 SAMUEL 13:32

After David sinned with Bathsheba, the prophet Nathan warned the king that the sword would never depart from his house. And David endured domestic problems from that day on. No one saw this more clearly than his son, Absalom. When Amnon raped Absolom's sister Tamar and David did nothing about it, Absalom became irate. After his attempts to get an audience with his father failed, Absalom decided to get everyone's attention. He avenging his sister Tamar by murdering Amnon, his half–brother; for this crime his father banished him. After he was permitted to return, Absalom got angry with general Joab and set his field on fire.

Despite his actions, Absalom couldn't get the fatherly attention he wanted so desperately. So he used his passion to sabotage his father's leadership. In the end, Absalom died a maverick leader whose passion went awry.

The Maxwell Leadership Bible

SHARP FOCUS
SHARPENS LEADERSHIP

Then the twelve summoned the multitude
of the disciples and said, "It is not desirable that we
should leave the word of God and serve tables…
but we will give ourselves continually to prayer
and to the ministry of the word."

ACTS 6:2,4

What does it take to have the focus required to be a truly effective leader? The keys are priorities and concentration. To focus your time and energy use these guidelines to help you:

Focus 70 percent on developing strengths: Effective leaders who reach their potential spend more time focusing on what they do well than on what they do wrong.

Focus 25 percent on new things: If you want to get better, you have to keep changing and improving. That means stepping out into new areas. If you dedicate time to new things related to your strength areas, then you'll grow as a leader.

Focus 5 percent on areas of weakness: Nobody can entirely avoid working in areas of weakness. They key is to minimize it as much as possible, and leaders can do it by delegating.

The 21 Indispensable Qualities of a Leader

MOTIVE MATTERS

Mean–tempered leaders are like mad dogs;
the good–natured are like fresh morning dew.
PROVERBS 19:12 (THE MESSAGE)

In a culture that sings the praises of individual gold medals and where a person fights for rights instead of focusing on responsibility, people tend to lose sight of the big picture. In fact, some people seem to believe that they are the entire picture: Everything revolves around their own needs, goals, and desires. I once saw this message on a T–shirt that expresses the attitude well: "My idea of a team is a whole lot of people doing what I tell them to do."

A team isn't supposed to be a bunch of people being used as a tool by one individual for their own selfish gain. Members of a team must have mutually beneficial shared goals. They must be motivated to work together, not manipulated by someone for individual glory. Anyone who is accustomed to pulling together people and using them to benefit only himself isn't a team builder; he's a dictator.

The 17 Indisputable Laws of Teamwork

GOD GRANTS REST

And the LORD spoke to Moses on Mount Sinai,
saying, "Speak to the children of Israel, and say to
them: 'When you come into the land which I give you,
then the land shall keep a sabbath to the LORD.'"

LEVITICUS 25:1–2

Ever hear of the Sabbath Year or the Year of Jubilee? Those are the topics of Leviticus 25. The first occurred every seven years, while the second was to take place every fifty years.

These special years called for special behavior. God's people were to stop their usual labor, alter their daily routines, and change their normal existence. Consider a few lessons leaders can learn from these special Sabbaths:

They gave the people a time of rest.
They gave the people an opportunity for redemption.
They gave the people time for reflection.
They gave the people time for reward and repair.
They gave the people time for relationships.
They gave the people a time to refocus.

The Maxwell Leadership Bible

MAY

*Your leadership ability
always determines your effectiveness
and the potential impact
of your organization.*

ARE PEOPLE DRAWN TO YOU?

And a great multitude from Galilee followed Him,
and from Judea and Jerusalem and Idumea and beyond
the Jordan; and those from Tyre and
Sidon, a great multitude ...
MARK 3 : 7 – 8

Most people think of charisma as something mystical, almost undefinable. They think it's a quality that comes at birth or not at all. But charisma is the ability to draw people to you. And like other character traits, it can be developed.

How do you rate when it comes to charisma? Are other people naturally attracted to you? If not, it could be because possess one these roadblocks to charisma:

Pride—nobody wants to follow a leader who thinks he is better than everyone else.

Insecurity—if you are uncomfortable with who you are, others will be too.

Moodiness—if people never know what to expect from you, they stop expecting anything.

Perfectionism—people respect the desire for excellence, but dread unrealistic expectations.

Cynicism—people don't want to be rained on by someone who sees a cloud around every silver lining.

If you can stay away from those qualities, you can cultivate charisma.

The 21 Indispensable Qualities of a Leader

To Communicate, Listen

Now when Job's three friends heard
of all this adversity that had come upon him,
each one came from his own place . . . For they had
made an appointment together to come and mourn
with him, and to comfort him. And when
they raised their eyes from afar, and did not
recognize him, they lifted their voices and wept;
and each one tore his rove and sprinkled dust on his
head toward heaven. So they sat down with him
on the ground seven days and seven nights,
and no one spoke a word to him, for they saw
that his grief was very great.

JOB 2: 11–13

Job's friends wanted to help. They felt his pain and were horrified to see a friend in such need. Mercifully, they kept their mouths shut for one whole week. They sat with their friend and listened.

These friends realized an important truth: People don't lose intimacy when they stop talking, but when they stop listening. Leaders seldom realize how much their listening empowers the other person. Because they are leaders, the sheer act of listening speaks volumes that even a great speech can't communicate.

The Maxwell Leadership Bible

TRADE YOUR FEARS
FOR FAITH IN GOD

*When the LORD saw that he turned aside to look,
God called to him from the midst of the bush.*

EXODUS 3:4

Brokenness involves removing inappropriate pride and self–reliance and building healthy God–reliance. God tamed Moses' self–reliance and pride in the desert, but to create trust He had to break the man's fears. Moses dealt with different kinds of fear in his encounter with God:

Fears concerning himself. God responded by assuring Moses of his purpose.

Fears concerning God. God responded by overwhelming Moses with His presence.

Fears concerning others. God responded by demonstrating His power and commitment.

Fears concerning his ability. God responded by proving him with a partner, his brother, Aaron.

With his willfulness broken, his fears overcome, and his purpose affirmed, Moses finally placed himself in the hands of God.

Life is filled with trade–offs. Moses sacrificed his status and material possessions to prepare for his life purpose. And then to fulfill it, he had to sacrifice again, relinquishing the security and safely of obscurity in the desert. If you desire to lead, then you must be ready to make sacrifices.

The Maxwell Leadership Bible

LET GOD WORRY
ABOUT YOUR PROMOTION

Don't work yourself into the spotlight;
Don't push your way into the place of prominence.
It's better to be promoted to a place of honor
Than face humiliation by being demoted.

PROVERBS 25:6–7 (THE MESSAGE)

In his first letter to Timothy, the Apostle Paul tells us that aspiring to a position of leadership is a good thing (3:1). However, there's a difference between stepping forward to accept the responsibility of leadership and stepping forward to put yourself into the spotlight for the benefit of self-promotion.

The road to biblical leadership comes through service. Leaders may find themselves in the spotlight, but they also take the heat that often comes with that place of prominence. They speak up for the sake of the mission, but they are also willing to remain silent when it serves the organization. And at any moment, they must be willing to make all kinds of sacrifices for the sake or their people.

When you have the opportunity to lead, serve well. You cannot force yourself into a position God does not want you to have, nor will you miss the opportunity to serve where God desires you to be.

DREAM ON

Go, for he is a chosen vessel of Mine to bear My name before Gentiles, kings, and the children of Israel.
ACTS 9:15

Many people discover their dream in a flash of insight after working in an area for years. Some receive it in a time of prayer. Others are motivated by an event from their past. If you haven't already discovered your dream, read the following five steps that will help you clear away the clutter and discover your dream:

1. *Believe in your ability to succeed.* You must believe that you can succeed if you are to succeed.

2. *Get rid of your pride.* People full of themselves usually don't have much room left over for a life–changing dream.

3. *Cultivate constructive discontent.* Discontent is the driving force that makes people search for their dreams. Complacency never brings success.

4. *Escape from habit.* Don't accept what is without considering what could be.

5. *Balance creativity with character.* When it comes to their dreams, truly successful people have enough creativity to think it out, and enough character to try it out.

Your Road Map for Success

THE TOUGH
AND TENDER LEADER

*For godly sorrow produces repentance leading
to salvation, not to be regretted; but the
sorrow of the world produces death.*

2 CORINTHIANS 7:10

In his previous letter to the church, Paul played the role of the tough leader. He instigated conflict. In this letter, he speaks more from a personal viewpoint, more from his heart. He exudes tenderness.

In 2 Corinthians 7, the apostle discusses how he caused the Corinthians sorrow, but distinguished between good sorrow and bad sorrow. Every leader will find this distinction profitable to understand. Consider the differences:

BAD SORROW

1. Pain goes on indefinitely
2. Example: Judas (Matthew 27:3–5)
3. Leads to regret and death
4. Suffering based on selfishness

GOOD SORROW

1. Pain is temporary
2. Example: Peter (Luke 22:54–62)
3. Leads to repentance and life
4. Suffering based on God's will

Leaders should never seek revenge or desire to hurt someone just to vindicate their action. The pain they bring should have the constructive purpose of repentance and recovery.

The Maxwell Leadership Bible

IT TAKES A MENTOR

Then Moses spoke to the LORD, saying,
"Let the LORD . . . set a man over the congregation . . .
that the congregation of the LORD may not be like sheep
which have no shepherd." And the LORD said to Moses:
"Take Joshua the son of Nun with you,
a man in whom is the Spirit."

NUMBERS 27:15–18

Joshua was an impressive leader. One of the major factors in Joshua's increase in influence was the impact of Moses on his life. Wherever Moses went, Joshua went with him, whether it was up Mount Sinai or to meet with God in the tabernacle.

After the Hebrews refused to enter the Promised Land, the mentoring relationship between the two men continued. In fact, the process continued for forty years and culminated with Moses imparting his authority to the younger man. And after Moses died, no one questioned Joshua's leadership.

Pastor A. W. Tozer said, "God is looking for people through whom He can do the impossible—what a pity that we plan only the things we can do by ourselves." Moses' investment in Joshua released God's power in him.

The 21 Most Powerful Minutes in a Leader's Day

PETTY DIFFERENCES
PREVENT VICTORY

*I implore Euodia and I implore Syntyche
to be of the same mind in the Lord. And I urge you
also, true companion, help these women who labored
with me in the gospel, with Clement also,
and the rest of my fellow workers, whose names are
in the Book of Life. Rejoice in the Lord always. Again I
will say, rejoice! Let your gentleness be known
to all men. The Lord is at hand.*

PHILIPPIANS 4:2–5

Paul knew the importance of teamwork, so he encouraged two women who had been quarreling to make peace. Euodia and Syntyche, members of the Philippian church, had by their disharmony created some division. Paul uses them as examples to launch into an entire chapter on peace. He doesn't ask these women to act uniformly, but rather to be of the same mind.

The term he uses connotes harmony. Singing in harmony doesn't mean singing in unison. Players should play different positions on a team. Harmony means their efforts complement the efforts of others, rather than conflict with them.

The Maxwell Leadership Bible

CHARTING THE COURSE
FOR OTHERS

Lead good people down a wrong path
and you'll come to a bad end;
do good and you'll be rewarded for it.
PROVERBS 28:10 (THE MESSAGE)

Leaders who navigate do even more than control the direction in which they and their people travel. They see the whole trip in their minds before they leave the dock. They have a vision for their destination, they understand what it will take to get there, they know who they'll need on the team to be successful, and they recognize the obstacles long before they appear on the horizon.

First–rate navigators always have in mind that other people are depending on them and their ability to chart a good course, and the secret to successful navigation is preparation When you prepare well, you convey confidence and trust to the people. You see, it's not the size of the project that determines its acceptance, support, and success—it's the size of the leader. Leaders who are good navigators are capable of taking their people just about anywhere.

The 21 Irrefutable Laws of Leadership

CREATE AN INNER CIRCLE

Now these were the heads of the mighty men
whom David had, who strengthened themselves
with him in his kingdom, with all Israel,
to make him the king, according to the word
of the LORD concerning Israel.

1 CHRONICLES 11:10

There are no Lone Ranger leaders. If you're alone, you're not leading anybody. Examine the way David pulled together the core people who made him great:

1. *He started building a strong inner circle before he needed it:* David began building his team long before he was crowned king.

2. *He attracted people with varied gifts:* David attracted men of diverse abilities. We read of experienced warriors with a variety of skills, many men of valor, and hundreds of captains. With the help of these men, David felt ready for anything.

3. *He engendered loyalty:* David's followers displayed incredible loyalty to him throughout his life. Those closest to him seemed willing to put their lives on the line for him.

4. *He delegated responsibility based on ability:* David continually gave authority to others. He designated Joab as commander of the army, and he felt equally secure in giving others civil authority.

The Maxwell Leadership Bible

GIVE THEM THEMSELVES

And [the Angel] said, "Your name shall no longer be called Jacob, but Israel; for you have struggled with God and with men, and have prevailed."

GENESIS 32:28

Team members always love and admire a person who is able to help them go to another level, someone who enlarges them and empowers them to be successful. Players who enlarge their teammates have several things in common.

1. Enlargers value their teammates: People's performances usually reflect the expectations of those they respect.

2. Enlargers know and relate to what their teammates value: Players who enlarge others understand what their teammates value. That kind of knowledge, along with a desire to relate to their fellow players, creates a strong connection between teammates.

3. Enlargers add value to their teammates: An enlarger looks for the gifts, talents, and uniqueness in other people, and then helps them to increase those abilities for their benefit and for that of the entire team.

4. Enlargers make themselves more valuable: You cannot give what you do not have. If you want to increase the ability of a teammate, make yourself better.

The 17 Essential Qualities of a Team Player

Balancing Your Gifts
with Character

For people who hate discipline and
only get more stubborn, there'll come a day
when life tumbles in and they break, but by then
it'll be too late to help them.

Proverbs 29:1 (The Message)

How many leaders have ruined their lives and damaged the lives of others through immorality? Character has become a crucial issue today precisely because of the myriad leaders in the political, business, and religious worlds who have fallen morally. Leaders need to remember that they influence many others beyond themselves; they never fall in a vacuum. They also need to realize that replacing fallen leaders is a slow and difficult process.

So how can we guard against falling? First, we must take care not to emphasize the gifts of a leader over his or her character. We have an unhealthy tendency to see and reward the gift more than the character; but both are to be developed. We must strike the following balance if we are to finish well:

What I Am	What I Do	What I Gain
Humble	Rely on God	Power from God
Visionary	Set Goals	High Morale
Convicted	Do the Right Thing	Credibility

The Maxwell Leadership Bible

NOT A 'NATURAL'

Now the man Moses was very humble, more than all men who were on the face of the earth.

NUMBERS 12:3

What words come to mind when you think of great leaders? It's doubtful that "meek" appears at the top of your list—yet that is the precise word God used to describe Moses.

Moses had reasons to be humble. He certainly wasn't a natural leader. Nothing in Scripture indicates he attracted or led anyone during the first eighty years of his life. So far as we know, his first attempt at exerting his influence to help the people resulted in the murder of an Egyptian and his flight from the country. The next forty years Moses spent in exile in the desert of Midian, a time so uneventful that Scripture sums it up in three verses (Exodus 2:21–23).

You don't have to be a "natural" to become a great leader; you simply need a heart for God and a teachable spirit. Most of the great leaders in Scripture were made, not born. Happily for us, God is still making them today. Could you be one?

The Maxwell Leadership Bible

HONOR EVERYONE
ON THE TEAM

And those members of the body with we think to be less
honorable, on these we bestow greater honor …

1 CORINTHIANS 12:23

People who build successful teams never forget that every person's role is contributing to the bigger picture. One of the best examples of this involves Winston Churchill. During World War II when Britain was experiencing its darkest days, the country had a difficult time keeping men working in the coal mines. Many wanted to give up their dirty, thankless jobs in the dangerous mines to join the military service, which got much public praise and support. Yet without coal, the military and the people at home would be in trouble.

So Churchill faced thousands of coal miners one day and passionately told them of their importance to the war effort, how their role could make or break the goal of maintaining England's freedom. It's said that tears appeared in the eyes of those hardened men. And they returned to their inglorious work with steely resolve. That's the kind of mindset it takes to build a team.

The 17 Indisputable Laws of Teamwork

Me First

Whoever desires to become great among you
shall be your servant. And whoever of you desires
to be first shall be slave of all.

MARK 10:43–44

People always project on the outside how they feel on the inside. Have you ever interacted with someone for the first time and suspected that their attitude was poor, yet you were unable to put your finger on exactly what was wrong? Here are six common attitudes that ruin a team so that you can recognize them for what they are when you see them.

An inability to admit wrongdoing

Failing to forgive

Petty jealousy

The disease of me

A critical spirit

A desire to hog all the credit

Certainly this isn't every bad attitude—just the most common ones. Simply put, most bad attitudes are the result of selfishness. If one of your teammates puts others down, sabotages teamwork, or makes themselves out to be more important than the team, then you can be sure that you've encountered someone with a bad attitude.

The 17 Indisputable Laws of Teamwork

THE DOCTOR IS IN

Trust in the LORD, and do good;
Dwell in the land, and feed on His faithfulness.
Delight yourself also in the LORD, And He shall give you
the desires of your heart. Commit your way
to the LORD, Trust also in Him, And He shall
bring it to pass. He shall bring forth your righteousness
as the light, and your justice as the noonday.
Rest in the LORD, and wait patiently for Him;
Do not fret because of him who prospers in his way,
Because of the man who brings wicked schemes to pass.
Cease from anger, and forsake wrath; Do not fret—
it only causes harm. For evildoers shall be cut off;
But those who wait on the LORD,
They shall inherit the earth.

PSALM 37:3–9

Do you ever feel like you need a therapist? If so, then Psalm 37 is for you. David writes as a counselor, providing wise steps to take as you face crises and decisions. Whenever you feel the pressure of competition or the compulsion to perform, pause and remember the assurances in this passage. David brings eternal perspective and long-term vision that prevents mistakes in short-term decisions.

The Maxwell Leadership Bible

LEADING FROM THE SHADOWS

Yet I consider it necessary to send to you Epaphroditus,
my brother, fellow worker, and fellow soldier,
but your messenger and the one who ministered
to my need; since he was longing for you all,
and was distressed because you had heard that he was
sick. For indeed he was sick almost unto death;
but God had mercy on him, and not only on him but
on me also, . . . I sent him the more eagerly, that
when you see him again you may rejoice, and I may
be less sorrowful. Receive him therefore in the Lord
with all gladness, and hold such men in esteem;
because for the work of Christ he came close
to death, not regarding his life, to supply what
was lacking in your service toward me.

PHILIPPIANS 2:25–30

Epaphroditus never became famous like David or Paul, but remained obscure, even though he played a vital role in the kingdom. He was a "nobody" who became a "somebody" to Paul. Note how Paul describes him as:

People lover—minister.
Risk taker—fellow soldier.
Tireless worker—fellow worker.
Servant leader—messenger.

The Maxwell Leadership Bible

UNEQUAL IN INFLUENCE

Then all who heard were amazed . . . But Saul
increased all the more in strength, and confounded the
Jews who dwelt in Damascus, proving that this Jesus
is the Christ. Now after many days were past,
the Jews plotted to kill him.

ACTS 9:21–23

Influence is a curious thing. Even though we make some kind of impact on nearly everyone around us, we need to recognize that our level of influence is not the same with everyone. To see this principle in action, try ordering around your best friend's dog the next time you visit.

You may not have thought much about it, but you probably know instinctively which people you have great influence with and which ones you don't. One person may think all your ideas are great. Another may view everything you say with a great deal of skepticism. Yet that same skeptical person may love every single idea presented by your boss or one of your colleagues. That just shows your influence with him may not be as strong as that of someone else.

Becoming a Person of Influence

KEEP THE MAIN THING
THE MAIN THING

You shall love the LORD your God with all your heart,
with all your soul, and with all your strength.
And these words which I command you today
shall be in your heart. You shall teach them diligently
to your children, and shall talk of them when you
sit in your house, when you walk by the way,
when you lie down, and when you rise up.

DEUTERONOMY 6:5–7

An old phrase says, "The leader's job is to keep the main thing, the main thing." Moses attempts this in Deuteronomy 6 by reminding the Israelites that their existence revolves around loving God. He also tells family leaders how to transfer truth to their children. Reggie Joiner notes the principles Moses develops:

1. Relationship comes before rules.
2. Truth must be in you before it can be in them.
3. Each day offers natural opportunities for teaching.
4. Repetition is the teacher's best friend.

Make use of all of these opportunities. Decide on issues you can discuss and ask questions of each other. Pray about your priorities together.

The Maxwell Leadership Bible

LIFT YOUR LID

When good people run things, everyone is glad,
but when the ruler is bad, everyone groans.

PROVERBS 29:2 (THE MESSAGE)

Success is within the reach of just about everyone. But personal success without leadership ability brings only limited effectiveness. A person's impact is only a fraction of what it could be with good leadership. The higher you want to climb, the more you need leadership. The greater the impact you want to make, the greater your influence needs to be. Whatever you will accomplish is restricted by your ability to lead others.

Leadership ability is the lid that determines a person's level of effectiveness. The lower a person's ability to lead, the lower the lid on his potential. The higher the leadership, the greater the effectiveness. Your leadership ability—for better or for worse—always determines your effectiveness and the potential impact of your organization. To reach the highest level of effectiveness, you have to raise the lid on your leadership ability. The good news is that you can—if you're willing to pay the price to change.

The 21 Irrefutable Laws of Leadership

THE VALUE OF VISION

Where there is no vision, the people perish.

PROVERBS 29:18 (KJV)

Have you ever been part of a team that didn't seem to make any progress? Maybe the group had plenty of talent, resources, and opportunities, and team members got along, but the group just never went anywhere. There's a strong possibility that the situation was caused by lack of vision.

Great vision precedes great achievement. Every team needs a compelling vision to give it direction. A team without vision is at worst, purposeless. At best, it is subject to the personal—and sometimes selfish—agendas of various teammates.

Author Ezra Earl Jones points out: "Leaders do not have to be the greatest visionaries themselves. The vision may come from anyone. The leaders do have to state the vision, however. Leaders also have to keep the vision before the people and remind them of the progress that is being made to achieve the vision. Otherwise, the people might assume that they are failing and give up."

If you lead your team, then you are responsible for identifying a worthy and compelling vision and articulating it to your team members.

The 17 Indisputable Laws of Teamwork

Exam Time

*And Abraham stretched out his hand and
took the knife to slay his son. But the Angel
of the LORD called to him from heaven.*

Genesis 22:10–11

Did you know that God provides tests as measures
of progress and proving grounds for every person
He calls to lead? Genesis 22 begins with a divine test. God
calls Abraham to climb Mount Moriah and sacrifice his
beloved son. If Abraham would resolve to give up Isaac,
God knew he would be willing to do anything asked of
him——and would be a perfect candidate to become the
father of the Hebrew people.

Leadership tests differ from one another, but all have
a few things in common:

1. Leaders get tested at each stage of growth.
2. The leader's goal is to pass the test.
3. Testing always precedes promotion.
4. Self–promotion can never replace divine promotion.
5. Promotion requires sacrifice.

While Abraham's trial foreshadowed what God
intended to do with His only begotten Son thousands of
years later, it also provided Abraham with a leadership test.

When is the last time God tested you? If you aren't
being tested, then you're not really moving forward!

The Maxwell Leadership Bible

VALUE VALUES

... fear the LORD your God,
to keep all His statutes and His commandments ...
DEUTERONOMY 6:2

Even if some members of a team don't share common experiences or have a personal relationship with each other, they can still possess a cohesiveness that defies the size of the team. What it takes is a common vision and shared values. If everyone embraces the same values, team members can still have a connection to each other and to the larger team.

If you've never really thought about how your team's values impact its identity and increase its potential, go through the following process with your team:

- Articulate the values.
- Compare values with practices.
- Teach the values.
- Practice the values.
- Institutionalize the values into the fabric of the team.
- Publicly praise the values.

If you are the leader of your team, if you don't work to help the team embrace the values you know to be important, team members will create an identity of their choosing.

The 17 Indisputable Laws of Teamwork

PREPARE YOUR PEOPLE
FOR THE FUTURE

*Finally, my brethren, be strong in the Lord and
in the power of His might. Put on the whole
armor of God, that you may be able to stand
against the wiles of the devil.*

EPHESIANS 6:10–11

Like any good leader, Paul issues a warning at the
end of his letter about the tough times his people
will face. They are up against Satan himself, an enemy
who will do everything to stop their progress.

Instead of moping about the situation, however, Paul
lays out a specific plan for his Ephesian friends. They are
not to approach this fight in their own strength, but
remember that only God can defeat the enemy. Paul then
instructs his readers to put on the whole armor of God, in
order to stand and prevail. Serving as an officer under God,
Paul issues the orders for the troops.

When leaders practice the Law of Intuition, they
provide their people with:

- A strategy to win.
- Knowledge of the opposition.
- The resources they need.
- A plan for how to use them.
- Detailed communication.

The Maxwell Leadership Bible

SEEK GOD
WHEN SETTING GOALS

Everyone tries to get help from the leader,
but only God will give us justice.

PROVERBS 29:26 (THE MESSAGE)

The number of people today who lack a strong sense of purpose is astounding. Pulitzer–winning writer Katherine Anne Porter observed: "I am appalled at the aimlessness of most people's lives. Fifty percent don't pay any attention to where they are going; forty percent are undecided and will go in any direction. Only ten percent know what they want, and even all of them don't go toward it."

Goals give you something concrete to focus on, and that has a positive impact on your actions. Goals help us focus our attention on our purpose and make it our dominant aspiration. And as philosopher–poet Ralph Waldo Emerson said, "The world makes way for the man who knows where he is going."

Use the following guidelines to keep your goals on target. Goals must be . . .

• Written
• Personal
• Specific
• Achievable
• Measurable
• Time–sensitive

Your Road Map for Success

WHO YOU ARE
IS WHO YOU ATTRACT

Then he arose and followed Elijah,
and became his servant.

1 KINGS 19:21

Effective leaders are always on the lookout for good people. But who you get is not determined by what you want, but by who you are. In most situations, you draw people who possess the same qualities you do.

What enabled Elijah to draw like–minded people to his side? This truth: who you are is who you attract.

1. Every leader has a measure of magnetism.
2. A leader's magnetism may impact others intellectually, emotionally, or volitionally.
3. Magnetism is neither good nor bad in itself—it depends on what a leader does with it.
4. Secure leaders draw both similar and complementary followers.
5. A leader's magnetism never remains static.

It is possible for a leader to go out and recruit people unlike himself, but it's crucial to recognize that people who are different will not naturally be attracted to him. Their quality depends on you. If you think the people you attract could be better, then it's time for you to improve yourself.

The Maxwell Leadership Bible

Pay Now, Play Later

*Enter by the narrow gate; for wide is the gate
and broad is the way that leads to destruction, and
there are many who go in by it. Because narrow
is the gate and difficult is the way which leads
to life, and there are few who find it.*

MATTHEW 7:13–14

Great leaders always have self–discipline. As General Dwight D. Eisenhower said, "There are no victories at bargain prices." When it comes to self–discipline, people choose one of two things: Either they choose the pain of discipline, which comes from sacrifice and growth, or they choose the pain of regret, which comes from taking the easy road and missing opportunities. Each person in life chooses.

We must look for two areas of self–discipline in potential leaders. The first is in the area of the emotions. Effective leaders recognize that their emotional reactions are their responsibility. The second area concerns time. Every person on the planet is given the same allotment of minutes in a day. But each person's level of self–discipline dictates how effectively those minutes are used. Disciplined people maximize the use of their time.

Developing the Leaders Around You

LEADERS HAVE A
FEW THINGS TO LEARN

But Naaman became furious, and went away
and said, "Indeed, I said to myself,
He will surely come out to me, and stand
and call on the name of the LORD his God,
and wave his hand over the place,
and heal the leprosy."

2 KINGS 5:11

Naaman had earned the love and respect of his king. Yet for all his strength and might, Naaman suffered from the dreaded disease of leprosy. When his king learned of a Hebrew prophet named Elisha who might be able to help, he sent Naaman off with great expectations.

But rather than an impressive meeting with the prophet, Naaman received instructions by messenger to wash seven times in the Jordan River. This enraged Naaman and he angrily refused to follow the prescription. He struggled with pride, faulty expectations, and inflexibility—much like many leaders today.

Yet as a strong leader, Naaman had surrounded himself with individuals who could speak up and disagree with him, and his inner circle provided good counsel. Naaman changed his mind, followed the prophet's directives, and was healed. Leaders who remain teachable receive ongoing blessings.

The Maxwell Leadership Bible

GUIDE THE WAY

*I will instruct you and teach you
in the way you should go; I will guide you with My eye.*

PSALM 32:8

God does not expect leaders to be perfect, but to be whole. To have integrity means to be whole, as in a whole number (an "integer"). Despite their human frailties, leaders can effectively guide those who follow.

This scripture reminds us that leaders must closely observe the flock for its needs and problems. God expects spiritual leaders to serve as guides. A guide takes a person or group safely to a planned destination. The Hebrew words for "guide" gives us several clues as to what God expects from those He uses as leaders:

A guide is a spiritual head who unites and directs people in their walk with God.

A guide takes people on the straight path that leads to fellowship with God.

A guide gives accurate and godly counsel to those who need it.

A guide leads with gentleness and trustworthiness, making others feel safe.

A guide bases his or her direction on the Spirit and the Word of God.

The Maxwell Leadership Bible

LEADERSHIP DEVELOPMENT, NOT FULFILLMENT

*Leaders can't afford to make fools of themselves,
gulping wine and swilling beer, lest, hung over, they
don't know right from wrong, and the people
who depend on them are hurt.*

PROVERBS 31:4–5 (THE MESSAGE)

Beginning in the late 60s and early 70s, people began talking about "finding themselves," meaning that they were searching for a way to become self–fulfilled. It's like making "happiness" your goal, because self–fulfillment is about feeling good.

But self–development is different. Sure, much of the time it will make you feel good, but that's a by–product, not the goal. Self–development is a higher calling; it is the development of our potential so that we can fulfill the purpose for which we were created. There are times when that's fulfilling, but other times it's not. But no matter how it makes us feel, self–development always has one effect: It draws us toward our destiny. As Rabbi Samuel M. Silver said, "The greatest of all miracles is that we need not be tomorrow what we are today, but we can improve if we make use of the potential implanted in us by God."

Your Road Map for Success

DOUBLE VISION

Now it shall come to pass, if you
diligently obey the voice of the LORD your God,
to observe carefully all His commandments which
I command you today, that the LORD your
God will set you high above all nations of the earth....
But it shall come to pass, if you do not obey
the voice of the LORD your God, to observe carefully
all His commandments and His statutes which
I command you today, that all these curses
will come upon you and overtake you.

DEUTERONOMY 28:1,15

The vision Moses cast to the new generation of Israelites looked quite different from anything most leaders have communicated since then: He cast vision for what life would look like if the people obeyed God fully. But Moses also cast vision for how life would turn out if they failed to obey. Not many leaders do this! From then on, the people could see clearly the blessing of obedience and the curses of disobedience.

That's the power of vision, from two angles. Such a vision helps people sort out what they will do, because they can think with the end in mind.

The Maxwell Leadership Bible

JUNE

As the leader, your communication
sets the tone for interaction
among your people.

DON'T TRY TO FLY SOLO

Two are better than one ...
and a threefold cord is not quickly broken.
ECCLESIASTES 4:9,12

As much as we admire solo achievement, the truth is that no lone individual has done anything of value. Frontiersman Daniel Boone had companions from the Transylvania Company as he blazed the Wilderness Road. Sheriff Wyatt Earp had his brothers and Doc Holiday looking out for him. Aviator Charles Lindbergh had the backing of nine businessmen from St Louis and the services of the Ryan Aeronautical Company who built his plane. Even scientist Albert Einstein didn't work in a vacuum.

The history of America is marked by the accomplishments of many strong leaders and innovative individuals who took great risks—but those people always were part of teams.

A Chinese proverb states that "behind an able man there are always other able men." The truth is that teamwork is at the heart of great achievement. One is too small a number to achieve greatness. You cannot do anything of real value alone.

The 17 Indisputable Laws of Teamwork

THE GREATEST EDGE

I heard the voice of the LORD, saying:
"Whom shall I send, and who will go for Us?"
Then I said, "Here am I! Send me."

ISAIAH 6:8

Teams are always looking for an edge. I'm sure you've seen it: Businesses invest in the latest technology hoping to improve their productivity. Companies fire their ad agencies and hire others to launch new campaigns. Corporations cycle through the latest management fads like channel surfers through television reruns. Everyone is seeking the magic formula that will lead to success. The more competitive the field, the more relentless the search.

What is the key to success? To be successful, a team needs all of those things, but it still needs something more. It needs leadership. I believe . . .

Personnel determine the potential of the team.

Vision determines the direction of the team.

Work ethic determines the preparation of the team.

Leadership determines the success of the team.

Everything rises and falls on leadership. If a team has great leadership, then it can gain everything else it needs to go to the highest level.

The 17 Indisputable Laws of Teamwork

A WEAK LINK

*But the children of Israel committed
a trespass regarding the accursed things, for Achan ...
took of the accursed things; so the anger of the LORD
burned against the children of Israel.*

JOSHUA 7:1

After an incredible victory over Jericho, Achan, an Israelite soldier, chose to disobey clear directives regarding treasures captured in war. Joshua told his men that all the spoils taken from Jericho were to be considered "devoted things" belonging in God's treasure. Achan defied Joshua's orders by taking valuables and hiding them under his family's tent.

In an act of severe judgment, Achan, his entire family, their livestock and possessions were all destroyed. By this fearsome act, Joshua determined to follow God and to remove those who would stand in the way of God's work.

The story of Achan illustrates the principle that leaders may become vulnerable following major success. Although it can be very difficult, leaders must take the appropriate steps to remove those who block God's blessing and work. When a team member compromises a core value, the ripple effect of his or her action can hurt many others. Godly leaders must stop the trickle before it becomes a flood.

The Maxwell Leadership Bible

LEADERS SPEAK TO TRANSFORM, NOT MERELY INFORM

*Then Agrippa said to Paul, "You are permitted to speak
for yourself." So Paul stretched out his hand and
answered for himself: "I think myself happy, King
Agrippa, because today I shall answer for myself before
you concerning all the things of which I am accused by
the Jews, especially because you are expert in all customs
and questions which have to do with the Jews.
Therefore I beg you to hear me patiently."*

ACTS 26:1–3

In a compelling court speech, Paul addressed King
Agrippa. Try to sense Paul's strategy. Paul believed
the best defense is a good offense and nearly converted
King Agrippa. Observe how this leader attempted to
persuade his audience:

He appeared relaxed, yet used animated gestures.

He humbly thanked the king for allowing him to
speak.

He affirmed the king's knowledge and expertise.

He identified with their opposition to the life he now
embraced.

He described his motives as pure and constructive.

He explained that his obedience to God caused his
trouble.

He challenged them with reasonable and verifiable facts.

He pled with them to obey God.

The Maxwell Leadership Bible

SPARE CHANGE

Love and truth form a good leader;
sound leadership is founded on loving integrity.
PROVERBS 20:28 (THE MESSAGE)

A leader's history of successes and failures makes a big difference in their credibility. It's a little like earning and spending pocket change. Each time you make a good leadership decision, it puts change into your pocket. Each time you make a poor one, you have to given some of your change to the people.

All leaders have a certain amount of change in their pockets when they start in new positions. From then on, they either build up their change or pay it out. Bad decisions cost them until they run out of change. It doesn't matter whether the blunders were big or small, when you're out of change, you're out as a leader.

Leaders who keep making good decisions and recording wins build up change. If they make huge blunders, they still have plenty of change left over, because they still have the trust of their people.

The 21 Irrefutable Laws of Leadership

CHOOSE ACHIEVEMENT
OVER AFFIRMATION

Instead, to suit their own desires,
they will gather around them a great number
of teachers to say what their itching ears want to hear.

2 TIMOTHY 4:3 (NIV)

If you want to make an impact during your lifetime, you have to trade the praise you could receive from others for the things of value that you can accomplish.

A friend once explained something to me that illustrates this concept very well. He told me that as people catch crabs, they'll toss the crustaceans into a basket. If you have only one crab in the basket you need a lid to keep it from crawling out, but if you've got two or more, you don't. When there are several crabs, they will drag one another down so that none of them can get away.

A lot of unsuccessful people act the same way. They'll do things to keep others from getting ahead. But the good news is that if you observe someone trying to do that, you don't have to buy into their belief system. You can get out and stay out of the basket by refusing to be a crab.

Your Road Map for Success

LEADERS ARE BROKERS OF GIFTS

Having gifts differing according to the grace
that is given to us, let us use them.

ROMANS 12:6

Paul describes seven spiritual gifts, distributed to different members in the body of Christ. And every believer is a steward of the abilities he or she has been given. Every leader is a manager whose goal should be to maximize everyone's gift.

The gifts in Romans 12 are commonly called "motivational gifts," which means they are central to our lives. Paul's gift list includes:

Prophecy: to challenge others by declaring God's truth and calling for action.

Service or ministry: to serve others and meet their needs.

Teaching: to explain truth so that others can understand and apply it.

Exhortation: to encourage, strengthen, and inspire others to be their best.

Giving: to generously share what God has given.

Leadership: to govern and oversee others so that the group moves forward.

Mercy: to empathize with, cheer, and show compassion to those who hurt.

The Maxwell Leadership Bible

IN THE HANDS OF THE ARTIST

But now, O LORD,
You are our Father;
We are the clay, and You our potter;
And all we are the work of Your hand.

ISAIAH 64:8

There is an interesting story about an English artist named William Wolcott who went to New York in 1924 to record his impressions of that great city. One morning he was visiting in the office of a former colleague when the urge to sketch came over him. Seeing some paper on his friend's desk, he asked, "May I have that?"

His friend answered, "That's not sketching paper. That's ordinary wrapping paper."

Not wanting to lose that spark of inspiration, Wolcott took the wrapping paper and said, "Nothing is ordinary if you know how to use it." On that ordinary paper Wolcott made two sketches. Later that same year, one of those sketches sold for $500 and the other for $1,000, quite a sum for 1924.

People under the influence of an empowering person are like paper in the hands of a great artist. No matter what they're made of, they can become treasures.

Becoming a Person of Influence

WHERE IS YOUR CONFIDENCE?

"When you go out to battle against your enemies,
and see horses and chariots and people
more numerous than you, do not be afraid of them;
for the LORD your God is with you, who
brought you up from the land of Egypt."

DEUTERONOMY 20:1

It's always a good idea to have a battle plan if you intend to lead an army into war. Moses possessed a plan for the army of Israel, a set of instructions that came straight from the top—the very top. Imagine the confidence a field commander could instill in his troops knowing that he could not lose. Yet that was just the kind of guarantee God gave Moses and the people of Israel. God assured them they had nothing to fear—as long as they remembered that He would remain with them always.

Christian leaders today can bank on the same promise that gave Moses such courage: "For the LORD your God is He who goes with you, to fight for you against your enemies, to save you" (Deuteronomy 20:4). And so God gives us the same word He gave to Moses: "Do not be afraid."

The Maxwell Leadership Bible

SOW A SEED, CHANGE A LIFE

*So he went to him and bandaged his wounds, pouring
on oil and wine; and he set him on his own animal,
brought him to an inn, and took care of him.
On the next day, when he departed, he took out two
denarii, gave them to the innkeeper, and said to him,
"Take care of him; and whatever more you spend, when
I come again, I will repay you."*

LUKE 10:34–35

It's been said that we make a living by what we get,
but we make a life by what we give. Helping others
is something you can start doing today, whether it's
spending more time with your family, developing an
employee who shows potential, helping people in the
community, or putting your own desires on hold to
benefit your team. The key is to find your purpose and
help others while you're pursuing it. As entertainer Danny
Thomas said: "All of us are born for a reason, but all of us
don't discover why. Success in life has nothing to do with
what you gain in life or accomplish for yourself. It's what
you do for others."

Your Road Map for Success

HELP THOSE WHO
HAVE HELPED YOU

*On that day King Ahasuerus gave Queen Esther
the house of Haman, the enemy of the Jews.
And Mordecai came before the king, for Esther had told
how he was related to her. So the king took
off his signet ring, which he had taken from Haman,
and gave it to Mordecai; and Esther appointed
Mordecai over the house of Haman.*

ESTHER 8:1–2

Twice Mordecai protected the king from destructive leaders—first from the men who intended to kill the king, and then from the man who intended to kill the queen and her people—and twice he was rewarded. He reaped the benefits of a track record that showed him to be a leader who could be trusted. He demonstrated that a leader cannot be successful unless other people want him to be.

Who has helped you to become more successful as a leader? How have you helped and rewarded them?

The Maxwell Leadership Bible

HOW TO ADD
VALUE TO OTHERS

*And Jesus went about all Galilee, teaching in their
synagogues, preaching the gospel of the kingdom,
and healing all kinds of sickness and all kinds
of disease among the people.*

MATTHEW 4:23

When people think about you, do they say to
themselves, "My life is better because of that
person"? Their response probably answers the question of
whether you are adding value to them. To succeed
personally, you must try to help others. That's why Zig
Ziglar says, "You can get everything in life you want if you
help enough other people get what they want." How do
you do that? How can you turn your focus from yourself
and start adding value to others? You can do it by:

1. Putting others first in your thinking.
2. Finding out what others need.
3. Meeting that need with excellence and generosity.

Failing Forward

VESSELS FOR VICTORY

When the children of Israel cried out to the LORD,
the LORD raised up a deliverer for the children
of Israel, who delivered them . . .

JUDGES 3:9,15

True leaders always find a way to help the team win. Othniel found his people surrounded by enemies from Mesopotamia. He stepped forward, led the armies of Israel against a pagan king, and prevailed. His victory led to forty years of peace. Later, Moab formed an alliance with the Ammonites and Amalekites and attacked Israel. The Hebrews suffered defeat and served these enemies for eighteen years. When the people cried out to the Lord, Ehud stepped forward and led them to victory. This peace lasted for eighty years. A third judge, Shamgar, personally struck down 600 Philistines and rallied his people over Philistia.

What can we learn from this? True leadership starts when a person:

1. *Perceives a need*—spots a specific problem.
2. *Possesses a gift*—has the competence to address the need.
3. *Parades a passion*—casts vision for a passion to act.
4. *Persuades a people*—attracts others to join the cause.
5. *Pursues a purpose*—employs measures to accomplish the desired goal.

The Maxwell Leadership Bible

PASSING THE TRUST TEST

Among leaders who lack insight, abuse abounds,
but for one who hates corruption, the future is bright.

PROVERBS 28:16 (THE MESSAGE)

People today are desperate for leaders, but they want to be influenced by someone they can trust, a person of good character. If you want to become someone who can positively influence other people:

Model consistency of character. Solid trust can only develop when people can trust you all the time

Employ honest communication. To be trustworthy, you have to be like a good musical composition: your words and music must match.

Value transparency. If you're honest with people and admit your weaknesses, they appreciate your honesty. And they are able to relate to you better.

Exemplify humility. People won't trust you if they see that you are driven by ego, jealousy, or the belief that you are better than they are.

Demonstrate your support of others. Nothing develops or displays your character better than your desire to put others first.

Fulfill your promises. One of the fastest ways to break trust with others is in failing to fulfill your commitments.

Becoming a Person of Influence

WHO'S THE BOSS?

*Bondservants, be obedient to those who
are your masters according to the flesh, with fear
and trembling in sincerity of heart, as to Christ; not
with eyeservice, as men–pleasers, but as bondservants
of Christ, doing the will of God from the heart, with
goodwill doing service, as to the Lord, and not to men,
knowing that whatever good anyone does, he will
receive the same from the Lord, whether he is a slave
or free. And you, masters, do the same thing to them,
giving up threatening, knowing that your
own Master also is in heaven, and
there is no partiality with Him.*

EPHESIANS 6:5–9

The principles Paul taught to owners and slaves apply today to employees and employers. He twice states that we are not to be people pleasers. We aren't to work while others watch, then slack off when alone. We are to render service as though we are working for God. Not only does God always watch us, He rewards the good we do.

People may forget how fast you did your last job, but they will remember how well you did it. Ultimately, we all work for ourselves and for God.

The Maxwell Leadership Bible

RECRUIT PEOPLE
WHO SEIZE OPPORTUNITIES

*And when Saul had come to Jerusalem; he tried to join
the disciples; but they were all afraid of him, and did
not believe that he was a disciple. But Barnabas
took him and brought him to the apostles.*

ACTS 9:26–27

Many people are able to recognize an opportunity
after it's already passed them by. That's pretty easy.
But seeing opportunities coming, that's a different matter.
Opportunities are seldom labeled. That's why you have to
learn what they look like—and how to seize them.

The best people to take with you on the leadership
journey don't simply sit back and wait for opportunities to
come to them. They make it their responsibility to go out
and find them

Good potential leaders don't rely on luck. As Walter P.
Chrysler said, "The reason so many people never get
anywhere in life is because when opportunity knocks, they
are out in the backyard looking for four–leaf clovers."

Of the people around you, who always seems able to
recognize opportunities and grab hold of them? The
people with those qualities are the ones you're probably
going to want to take with you.

Your Road Map for Success

MEETING A
GOD–SIZED CHALLENGE

*And it happened, when all our enemies heard of it, and
all the nations around us saw these things, that they
were very disheartened in their own eyes; for they
perceived that this work was done by our God.*

NEHEMIAH 6:16

Commitment comes before anything else in a
leader's life. Because Nehemiah had it and drew it
out of others, the people finished the wall in 53 days,
despite much adversity. Their great accomplishment so
thrilled Nehemiah that he wrote, "When all our enemies
heard of it, and all the nations around us saw these things
. . . they were very disheartened in their own eyes; for they
perceived that this work was done by our God."

Leaders who complete a task possess these characteristics:

Compelling purpose: They make a great commitment
to a great cause.

Clear perspective: They don't let fear cloud their view
of the future.

Continual prayer: They pray about everything and
gain God's favor.

Courageous persistence: They move ahead despite the odds.

If you're facing a God–sized challenge, cultivate these
characteristics to give yourself the best opportunity for
success.

The Maxwell Leadership Bible

AN INVESTMENT
FOR THE FUTURE

So [David] became captain over them.
And there were about four hundred men with him.

1 SAMUEL 22:2

Most people recognize that investing in a team brings benefits to everyone on the team. Here are ten steps you can take to invest in your team.

1. Make the decision to build a team.

2. Gather the best team possible.

3. Pay the price to develop the team.

4. Do things together as a team.

5. Empower team members with responsibility and authority.

6. Give credit for success to the team.

7. Watch to see that the investment in the team is paying off.

8. Stop your investment in players who do not grow.

9. Create new opportunities for the team.

10. Give the team the best possible chance to succeed.

One of the great things about investing in a team is that it almost guarantees a high return for the effort, because a team can do so much more than individuals. Or as Rex Murphy, one of my conference attendees, told me: "Where there's a will there's a way; where there's a team, there's more than one way."

The 17 Indisputable Laws of Leadership

REAPING WHAT YOU SOW

Now may He who supplies seed to the sower,
and bread for food, supply and multiply the seed you
have sown and increase the fruits of your righteousness,
while you are enriched in everything for all liberality,
which causes thanksgiving through us to God.

2 CORINTHIANS 9:10–11

Paul uses dozens of metaphors throughout 2 Corinthians. In the above passage, he compares stewardship to farming. In trying to encourage the Corinthian church to give generously to their brothers and sisters in Jerusalem, he instructs the church to view its resources as a farmer views his sowing seed. A good farmer liberally sows seed, trying to ensure a good fall harvest. The more he sows, the more he reaps. You can't harvest what you haven't planted.

Some leaders, like the Corinthians, find it hard to invest resources because they seem so deficient—feeling their commodities are about to run out. Good leaders see the same resources as sufficient seed to be sown—knowing the harvest will come and more will be created. We must guard against poverty; we should give our life because it is plentiful.

The Maxwell Leadership Bible

TAKE THE LEAD

And Barak said to her,
"If you will go with me, then I will go;
but if you will not go with me, I will not go!"

People follow men and women whose leadership they respect. The less-skilled follow the more highly skilled. In general, followers seek those who are better leaders than themselves.

Deborah's leadership gifts commanded the respect of both men and women, even though few women in her day rose to leadership positions. Even Barak, the military commander of the northern tribes of Israel, sought her help.

The more leadership ability someone has, the more quickly they recognize leadership—or its lack—in others. When groups of people get together for the first time, take a look at what happens. Leaders in the group immediately take charge. They think about the direction they desire to go and whom they want to take with them. At first, individuals may make tentative moves in several directions, but after they get to know one another, it doesn't take long for them to recognize the strongest leaders and to follow them.

The Maxwell Leadership Bible

COMMUNICATE WELL TO LEAD

And so it was, when Jesus had ended these sayings, that the people were astonished at His teaching, for He taught them as one having authority, and not as the scribes.

MATTHEW 7:28–29

John W. Gardner observed, "If I had to name a single all-purpose instrument of leadership, it would be communication." If you cannot communicate, you will not lead others effectively.

If you lead your team, give yourself three standards to live by as you communicate to your people.

Be Consistent—Nothing frustrates team members more than leaders who can't make up their minds.

Be Clear—Your team cannot execute if they don't know what you want. Don't try to dazzle anyone with your intelligence; impress them with your simple straightforwardness.

Be Courteous—Everyone deserves to be shown respect, no matter what their position or what kind of history you might have with them. If you are courteous to your people, you set a tone for the entire organization.

Never forget that as the leader, your communication sets the tone for the interaction among your people.

The 17 Indisputable Laws of Teamwork

THE GENEROUS LEADER

If there is among you a poor man of your brethren, within any of the gates in your land which the LORD your God is giving you, you shall not harden your heart nor shut your hand from your poor brother, but you shall open your hand wide to him and willingly lend him sufficient for his need, whatever he needs.

DEUTERONOMY 15:7–8

If great leaders err, they do so on the side of generosity. They are givers, not takers. They feel motivated to:

1. *Serve others*—to help them grow and thrive.
2. *Solve problems*—that prevent potential from being reached.
3. *Save causes*—that benefit mankind.

God instructs His leaders and the entire nation of Israel to imitate His generosity and grace. At the end of every seventh year, every Israelite was to cancel all debts owed by fellow citizens. If they would indeed cancel debts, model graciousness and forgiveness, and care for the poor, God would favor their land with abundant crops and freedom from invasion. Imagine! They simply needed to trust that God was in control and let Him worry about rain and sun and fruitful harvest times.

The Maxwell Leadership Bible

SHARE THE BURDEN

Moreover you shall select from all the people
able men …And let them judge the people at all times.
Then it will be that every great matter they shall bring
to you, but every small matter they themselves
shall judge. So it will be easier for you,
for they will bear the burden with you.

EXODUS 18:21–22

Easing people into delegation is important. You can't simply dump tasks on people, not if you want them to succeed. Delegate according to the following steps:

Ask them to be fact finders only. It gives them a chance to become acquainted with the issues and objectives.

Ask them to make suggestions. This gets them thinking and it gives you a chance to become acquainted with their thought processes.

Ask them to implement one of their recommendations, but only after you give your approval. Set them up for success, not failure.

Ask them to take action on their own, but to report the results immediately. This will give them confidence, and you will still be able to perform damage control if necessary.

Give complete authority. This is the final step—what you've been working toward.

Developing the Leaders Around You

A PART FOR EVERYONE

But David said, "My brethren, you shall not do so with
what the LORD has given us, who has preserved us and
delivered into our hand the troop that came against us.
For who will heed you in this matter? But as his part is
who goes down to the battle, so shall his part be who
stays by the supplies; they shall share alike."

1 SAMUEL 30:23–24

When some "wicked and worthless men" suggested that those who stayed behind should receive none of the spoil. David resolved the conflict by declaring that since God had given them victory, even those who had protected the supplies had played a role and therefore should share equally in the plunder.

Clearly, David valued partnership. What did his act of partnership do for his leadership?

1. It helped others see the contribution of every man's gift.

2. It reminded everyone that God was the true source of every good gift.

3. It promoted goodwill in potential allies.

4. It enabled David to prepare for the future and make friends all over Israel.

5. It developed a nationwide value of mutual benefit and good faith.

The Maxwell Leadership Bible

GIVE YOURSELF AWAY

Speak up for the people who have no voice,
for the rights of all the down–and–outers.
Speak out for justice! Stand up for the poor and destitute!
PROVERBS 31:8–9 (THE MESSAGE)

Nothing has such a positive impact on a person as giving to others. And people who have a giving spirit are some of the most positive people I know. That's because giving is the highest level of living. They focus their time and energy on what they can give to others rather than what they can get from them. And the more a person gives, the better his attitude.

Most unsuccessful people don't understand this concept. They believe that how much people give and their attitude about it are based on how much they have. But that's not true. I know many people who have very little but are tremendous givers. And I know people who have been blessed with money, good families, and wonderful careers who are stingy and suspicious of others. In life, it's not what you have that makes a difference. It's what you do with what you have. And that is based completely on attitude.

Your Road Map for Success

FATHER KNOWS BEST

If you walk in My statutes
and keep My commandments, and perform them,
then I will give you rain in its season,
the land shall yield its produce, and the trees
of the field shall yield their fruit ... I will walk among
you and be your God, and you shall be My people.

LEVITICUS 26: 3, 4, 12

Have you noticed that rules, regulations, and laws bring out the human tendency to ask, "But why?"

Many of our problems arise from ignoring God's Word when we don't think His instructions make sense. Moses tells us the rules and regulations God gave to His people not only kept them clean—make that *holy*—before Him, but they also protected them from discomfort, sickness, and untimely death.

In some ways, the law can be seen as God solving a problem before it ever occurs. Moses reminds us that God always knows what is best—for us and for our relationship with Him.

The Maxwell Leadership Bible

NEED A LIFT?

Good leadership is a channel of water controlled by God;
He directs it to whatever ends he chooses.

PROVERBS 21:1 (THE MESSAGE)

With good leadership, everything improves. Leaders are lifters. They push the thinking of their teammates beyond old boundaries of creativity. They elevate others' performance, making them better than they've ever been before. They improve people's confidence in themselves and others. While managers are often able to maintain a team at its current level, leaders are able to lift it to a higher level than it has ever reached before. The key to that is working with people and bringing out the best in them. For example:

> Leaders transfer ownership for work to those who execute the work.
>
> Leaders create an environment where each team member wants to be responsible.
>
> Leaders coach the development of personal capabilities.
>
> Leaders learn quickly and encourage others to learn efficiently also.

If you want to give a team a lift, then provide it with better leadership.

The 17 Indisputable Laws of Teamwork

THE POWER OF EMPOWERMENT

*All authority has been give to Me
in heaven and on earth.*

MATTHEW 28:18

The ability to empower others is one of the keys to personal and professional success. John Craig said, "No matter how much work you can do, no matter how engaging your personality may be, you will not advance far in business if you cannot work through others."

When you become an empowerer, you certainly work with and through people, but you also do much more. Simply defined, empowering is giving your influence to others for the purpose of personal and organizational growth. It's seeing others' potential, then sharing yourself—your influence, position, power, and opportunities—with others with the purpose of investing in the lives of others so that they can function at their best. The act of empowering others changes lives, and one of the greatest things about it is that it's a win–win for you and the people you empower. If you empower others by giving them your authority, it has the same effect as sharing information. You haven't lost anything. You've increased the ability of others without decreasing yourself.

Becoming a Person of Influence

A Leader's Heart of Love
for the Unlovely

Therefore I will bewail the vine of Sibmah,
With the weeping of Jazer; I will drench you with my
tears, O Heshbon and Elealeh; for battle cries have
fallen over your summer fruits and your harvest.

Isaiah 16:9

Someone must have forgotten to tell Isaiah that he lived in Old Testament times. The picture of most ancient Hebrew leaders is anger and eagerness for God's righteous judgment to fall upon the wicked. And yet, here stands Isaiah, crying out for heathen Moab and weeping for wayward Heshbon.

Isaiah demonstrates the attitude of a godly leader who sees approaching judgment for unbelievers. He grieves over what is coming for lost souls. Isaiah's lament over the fate of these ancient nations reveals the attitude of a truly godly leader.

We ought to stand in awed silence when we see the judgment of God falling on those who have forsaken His way. But we should never see His judgment as an occasion to celebrate our own righteousness. We should grieve for the lost and reflect deeply on the grace and mercy God has extended to us.

The Maxwell Leadership Bible

HOW DO YOU EXPECT
PEOPLE TO RESPOND?

*Death and life are in the power of the tongue,
And those who love it will eat its fruit.*

PROVERBS 18:21

Few muscles in the body wield more power than the little one inside the mouth. Leaders who understand this can greatly increase their influence. Many have said the American culture has witnessed four styles of leadership since 1950, each having different expectations concerning how followers should respond to words:

Military Commander—Leaders came out of the army and expected unquestioning obedience from subordinates.

Chief Executive Officer—Most leaders migrated to a different style driven by vision and shared by everyone. Yet it was still top down and possibly very narrow in scope.

Coach—Leaders moved toward a coach model where they saw employees as players on a team. This produced even better results, but still limited the possibilities to the vision of the coach.

Poet—Today, leaders see the need to express the heart of the team, as a poet gives words to the heart of readers. They develop players using encouragement and direction. They recognize the power of words and use them wisely.

The Maxwell Leadership Bible

JULY

Leadership is more art than science.
The principles of leadership are constant,
but the application changes with every
leader and every situation.

LEAD AS A SHEPHERD DOES

The LORD is my shepherd; I shall not want. He makes me to lie down in green pastures; He leads me beside the still waters. He restores my soul; He leads me in the paths of righteousness for His name's sake. Yea, though I walk through the valley of the shadow of death, I will fear no evil; For You are with me; Your rod and Your staff, they comfort me. You prepare a table before me in the presence of my enemies; You anoint my head with oil; my cup runs over. Surely goodness and mercy shall follow me All the days of my life; And I will dwell in the house of the LORD forever.

PSALM 23: 1–6

In Psalm 23, we learn not only about God's nature, but also about His leadership. Both the Old and New Testaments use the term "shepherd" to illustrate leadership. The word communicates the love, nurture, and spiritual care a godly leader provides. It involves both the rod (correction) and staff (direction). Psalm 23 describes the Ultimate Shepherd performing several functions. The Shepherd . . .

Provides necessities	Gives rest
Confidently leads	Renews and restores
Guides and directs	Protects from harm
Feeds and anoints	Corrects and comforts
Loves unconditionally	Furnishes permanent shelter

The Maxwell Leadership Bible

GIVE UP TO GO UP

*This is the law of the Nazirite who vows to the LORD
the offering for his separation, and besides that,
whatever else his hand is able to provide; according
to the vow which he takes, so he must do according
to the law of his separation.*

NUMBERS 6:21

Through the vow of the Nazirite, God provided a
way for both men and women to specially
consecrate themselves to the Lord for a special time and
purpose. Leaders such as Samson (and perhaps Samuel)
made this vow, committing to abstain from wine and
strong drink, to leave their hair uncut, and to avoid
contact with corpses. They gave up certain rights or
options in order to live at a higher standard—in other
words, they practiced the Law of Sacrifice. They did so
not to stand in judgment of others, but to discipline
themselves against the temptations of the day.

How can today's leaders apply the principle behind
the Nazirite vow?

DISCIPLINE	APPLICATION
Abstinence from wine/ strong drink	Self–control: discipline to prevent addiction
Uncut hair	Image: refuse to allow fashion to lead you
Avoid defilement from corpse	Integrity: stay pure; pursue a holy standard

The Maxwell Leadership Bible

GIVE YOURSELF AWAY

*And walk in love, as Christ also has loved us
and given Himself for us, an offering and a sacrifice
to God for a sweet–smelling aroma.*

EPHESIANS 5:2

 As a team leader, how do you cultivate an attitude of selflessness? Begin by doing the following:

1. *Being generous:* If team members are willing to give of themselves generously to the team, then it is being set up to succeed.

2. *Avoiding internal politics:* Good team players worry about the benefit of their teammates more than themselves.

3. *Displaying loyalty:* If you show the people on your team loyalty, they will return loyalty in kind. Loyalty fosters unity, and unity breeds team success.

4. *Valuing interdependence more than independence:* In the United States, we value independence highly, because it is often accompanied by innovation, hard work, and a willingness to stand for what's right. But independence taken too far is a characteristic of selfishness, especially if it begins to harm or hinder others. Seneca stated, "You must live for others if you wish to live for yourself."

The 17 Essential Qualities of a Team Player

READING BETWEEN THE LINES

> *When the country is in chaos,*
> *everybody has a plan to fix it—*
> *But it takes a leader of real understanding*
> *to straighten things out.*

PROVERBS 28:2 (THE MESSAGE)

Leadership intuition is often the factor that separates the greatest leaders from the merely good ones. Some people are born with great leadership intuition. Others have to work hard to develop and hone it. But both ways it is a combination of natural ability and learned skills. The best way to describe this informed intuition is an ability to discern intangible factors, understand them, and work with them to accomplish leadership goals.

Successful leaders see every situation in terms of available resources: money, raw materials, technology, and people. They can sense people's hopes, fears, and concerns. And they can step back from the moment and see not only where they and their people have gone, but also where they are heading. It's as if they can smell change in the wind.

Leadership is more art than science. The principles of leadership are constant, but the application changes with every leader and every situation. That's why it requires intuition. Without it, you can get blindsided, and that's one of the worst things that can happen to a leader.

The 21 Irrefutable Laws of Leadership

BE A GOOD FOLLOWER FIRST

But David said to Abishai, "Do not destroy him;
for who can stretch out his hand against
the LORD's anointed, and be guiltless?"

1 SAMUEL 26:9

Leadership operates on the basis of trust. Before David became king, he showed respect for the king who preceded him. Saul failed to practice this law, and lost his kingdom. The Bible provides a vivid contrast between the leadership of Saul and David:

SAUL	DAVID
Self–conscious from the beginning	Displayed God–confidence from the beginning
Presumed the priestly office	Didn't assume any right or privilege
Disobeyed God in the little things	Obeyed God in the little things
Lost integrity by covering his sin	Maintained integrity by respecting Saul
Failed to submit to God–given authority	Consistently submitted to authority
Preoccupied with his own fame	Desired to increase God's reputation

The Maxwell Leadership Bible

CONNECT BEFORE CALLING

When He had stopped speaking, He said to Simon,
"Launch out into the deep and let down your nets
for a catch." . . . And Jesus said to Simon,
"Do not be afraid. From now on you will catch men."
So when they had brought their boats to land,
they forsook all and followed Him.

LUKE 5:4, 10–11

Connection is absolutely critical if you want to influence people in a positive way. When I think of connecting with people, I compare it to trains and what happens to them in a train yard. The cars sitting on the tracks have great value because they're loaded with cargo; they have a destination; and they even have a route to follow. But they don't have a way of getting anywhere on their own. They have to hook up with a locomotive.

Have you ever watched how a bunch of pieces form a working train? It all begins with the locomotive. It switches itself to the same track as the car it's going to pick up, then it backs up to the car, makes contact, and connects. Then it repeats the process until the cars are all hooked up, and together they start moving toward their destination.

A similar thing must happen before you are able to get people go with you on any kind of journey. You have to find out where they are, move toward them to make contact, and connect with them. If you can do that successfully, you can take them to new heights in your relationship and in their development.

Becoming a Person of Influence

A MODEL TO BE FOLLOWED

So it was, whenever Moses went out to the tabernacle,
that all the people rose, and each man stood
at his tent door and watched Moses until
he had gone into the tabernacle.

EXODUS 33:8

Modeling provides the basis of all true leadership. Leaders must set the example for their followers. The number one management principle in the world is this: *People do what people see.*

Moses demonstrated this truth. The people watched him as he spent time with God, interceding for them in intimate, personal communion—and it changed them more than any sermon could have. If you want to enjoy an intimate relationship with God, as Moses did, you must practice what he did:

1. Separate yourself regularly.
2. Seek God with all your heart.
3. Risk being watched and scrutinized.
4. Learn to listen and obey God's voice.
5. Enter covenant partnership with God.

The Maxwell Leadership Bible

WHAT'S THE SCORE?

I planted, Apollos watered, but God gave the increase.
So then neither he who plants is anything, nor he
who waters, but God who gives the increase.

1 CORINTHIANS 3:6–7

Every endeavor or "game" in life has its own rules and its own definition of what it means to win. Some teams measure their success in points scored, others in profits. Still others may look at the number of people they serve. But no matter what the game is, there is always a scoreboard. And if a team is to accomplish its goals, it has to know the score.

Why is the score so important? Because teams that succeed make adjustments to continually improve themselves and their situations. In preparation, teams come up with a detailed game plan. But as the game goes on, the game plan means less and less, while the scoreboard becomes more and more important. Why? Because the game is constantly changing. You see, the game plan tells you what you *want* to happen. But the scoreboard tells what *is* happening.

The 17 Indisputable Laws of Teamwork

WISE WORDS FROM A LEADER

Blessings are on the head of the righteous, but violence covers the mouth of the wicked. The mouth of the righteous is a well of life, but violence covers the mouth of the wicked. Wisdom is found on the lips of him who has understanding, but a rod is for the back of him who is devoid of understanding. Wise people store up knowledge, but the mouth of the foolish is near destruction. In the multitude of words sin is not lacking, but he who restrains his lips is wise. The lips of the righteous feed many, but fools die for lack of wisdom.

PROVERBS 10:6,11,13–14,19,21

Many verses in Proverbs speak of the tongue and how to use it as a positive influence. Leaders who use words skillfully increase their influence. Leaders who understand the power of their words accomplish the following:

They proclaim justice and are blessed (v.6).

They speak hope for the future, becoming a fountain of life to others (v. 11).

They speak forth wisdom and save others from ruin (vv. 13–14).

They know when silence is more powerful than words (v. 19).

Their words feed and nourish many others (v. 21).

The Maxwell Leadership Bible

KEEP IMPROVING

*Everyone who competes in the games
goes into strict training.*

1 CORINTHIANS 9:25 (NIV)

We live in a society with destination disease. Too many people want to do enough to "arrive," and then they want to retire. My friend Kevin Myers says it this way: "Everyone is looking for a quick fix, but what they really need is fitness. People who look for fixes stop doing what's right when pressure is relieved. People who pursue fitness do what they should no matter what the circumstances are." People who are constantly improving themselves make three processes an ongoing cycle in their lives:

1. *Preparation:* When individuals are intentional about learning something every day, then they become better prepared to handle whatever challenges they meet.

2. *Contemplation:* Time alone is essential to self–improvement. It allows you to gain perspective on your failures and successes so that you can learn from them. It gives you the time and space to sharpen your personal or organizational vision. And it enables you to plan how you can improve in the future.

3. *Application:* Musician Bruce Springsteen said, "A time comes when you need to stop waiting for the man you want to become and start being the man you want to be." In other words, you need to apply what you've learned.

The 17 Essential Qualities of a Team Player

THE VALUE OF VISION

*Then all the tribes of Israel came to David at Hebron
and spoke, saying, "Indeed we are your bone and your
flesh. Also, in time past, when Saul was king over us, you
were the one who led Israel out and brought them in;
and the LORD said to you, "You shall shepherd My people
Israel, and be ruler over Israel."* Therefore all the elders
of Israel came to the king at Hebron, and King David
made a covenant with them at Hebron before the LORD .
. . And the king and his men went to Jerusalem against
the Jebusites, the inhabitants of the land . . .*

2 SAMUEL 5:1–3 & 6

David's vision energized the Hebrew nation far
beyond anything Saul had ever imagined. Notice
what the vision of David did for the Israelite nation:

1. *Vision united:* For the first time in years, "all the tribes"
   and "all the elders" came together.

2. *Vision provides a center for leadership:* David began his
   reign from Hebron, but desired to unite a divided
   land and lead from Jerusalem.

3. *Vision dominates inner conversation:* All of us indulge
   in "inner conversation." David's vision focused his
   men as they neared Jerusalem.

4. *Vision inspires greatness:* David's dream for Jerusalem
   helped him and his people realize a great goal together.

5. *Vision attracts others to the leader:* Once David had
   taken Jerusalem, others began to join the cause.

The Maxwell Leadership Bible

ACKNOWLEDGING GOD'S ROLE

*When I consider Your heavens, the work of Your
fingers, The moon and the stars, which You have
ordained, What is man that You are mindful of him,
And the son of man that You visit him? For You have
made him a little lower than the angels, And you have
crowned him with glory and honor. You have made
him to have dominion over the works of Your hands;
You have put all things under his feet . . . O LORD, our
Lord, How excellent is Your name in all the earth!*

PSALM 8:3–6 & 9

Have you ever asked, "When does a leader's
confidence become arrogance? What does humility
look like in a leader's life?" Psalm 8 answers those
questions. It shows leaders how to balance their identity
with their self-esteem. Consider how David perceives his
identity and maintains both confidence and humility:

1. *David sees his own weakness and humanity.* David
   realizes that in the sweep of the galaxy, man accounts
   for only a very small part.

2. *David sees his God-given position and privileges.* David
   knows that God has made humankind a little lower
   than Himself.

3. *David sees a balance by giving all the glory to God.*
   David closes the psalm the way he began. He
   magnifies the Lord and gives Him the credit for the
   good that has come from his life and leadership.

The Maxwell Leadership Bible

FIRE UP YOUR LEADERSHIP WITH VISION

Every promise of God proves true;
he protects everyone who runs to him for help.

PROVERBS 30:5 (THE MESSAGE)

Where does a leader's vision come from? To find your vision, you must listen to . . .

The Inner Voice: Vision starts within. Do you know what your life's mission is? If what you're pursuing in life doesn't come from the depths of who you are and what you believe, you will not be able to accomplish it.

The Unhappy Voice: Where does inspiration for great ideas come from? From noticing what doesn't work. Discontent with the status quo is a great catalyst for vision. No great leader in history has fought to prevent change.

The Successful Voice: Nobody can accomplish great things alone. If you want to lead others to greatness, find a good mentor, an advisor who can help you sharpen your vision.

The Higher Voice: Don't let your vision be confined by your own limited capabilities. A truly valuable vision must have God in it. Only He knows what you're really capable of. Have you looked beyond yourself, even beyond your own lifetime as you've sought your vision? If not, you may be missing the true potential of your life.

The 21 Indispensable Qualities of a Leader

HELP YOUR PEOPLE GROW

Then He called His twelve disciples together
and gave them power and authority over all demons,
and to cure diseases. He sent them to preach
the kingdom of God and to heal the sick.

LUKE 9:1-2

In an organization, it is the team leader's responsibility to orchestrate the team's growth. He must make sure that his people grow both personally and professionally. And he must insure that their growth happens with them together—as a team.

When I work on growing my team members, I take several different approaches. First, we all learn together on a regular basis, at least once a month. In this way, I know that that everyone in the organization shares the common experience of learning things together, regardless of their position or responsibilities. Second, I regularly build small teams of learners. I periodically have groups of three or four cooperate on a project that requires them to learn. It builds strong relational bonds between those people. Third, I send people to conferences, workshops, seminars, and other development opportunities. Then when they return, I ask them to teach others in the organization what they've learned.

Shared experiences and the give–and–take of communication are the greatest ways to promote team growth.

Developing the Leaders Around You

READ, THEN LEAD

But Zerubbabel and Jeshua and the rest of the heads
of the fathers' houses of Israel said to them,
"You may do nothing with us to build a house
for our God; but we alone will build
to the LORD God of Israel, and King Cyrus
the king of Persia has commanded us."

EZRA 4:3

Leaders must practice discernment. Relationships can get messy; people often harbor personal agendas and attempt to mask their true motives or to make them sound more noble than they really are.

Such was the case when a group of outsiders approached Zerubbabel and offered to help. "Let us build with you, for we seek your God as you do; and we have sacrificed to Him since the days of Esarhaddon king of Assyria, who brought us here," (Ezra 4:2). Zerubbabel, however, quickly recognized these folks had really arrived only to discourage the builders. His relational discernment kept these negative influences from infiltrating the flock.

Leaders must read the people, then lead the people. They must understand the timing, the people, the situation, and the priorities, then act accordingly. Their action depends upon how they read these factors. Discernment always precedes decision. Analysis always precedes action.

The Maxwell Leadership Bible

NOT EVERYONE
WILL TAKE THE JOURNEY

Therefore many of His disciples, when they heard this,
said, "This is a hard saying, who can understand it?"
. . . From that time many of His disciples went back
and walked with Him no more.

JOHN 6:60, 66

Having exceptional people on the journey with you doesn't happen by accident. It's true that the greater your dream is, the greater the people who will be attracted to you. But that alone isn't enough. You need to make sure they're compatible with you.

The first question to ask is, "Does this person want to go?" That was a hard lesson for me to learn, because early on, I wanted to take everybody with me. I just assumed that everyone wanted what I did. But that's not true.

The second question you need to ask is whether that person is able to go. There has to be a match between the journey you want to take and their gifts and talents.

The third question you should ask is, "Can this person make the trip without me?" If so, make friends with them and try to keep in touch. Though you may not take the journey together, you may be able to help one another down the road as colleagues.

Your Road Map for Success

INITIATE USING INTUITION

*Then the king said to me (the queen also sitting
beside him), "How long will your journey be?
And when will you return?" So it pleased the king
to send me; and I set him a time.*

NEHEMIAH 2:6

Nehemiah couldn't imagine sitting still when he heard the walls of Jerusalem lay in shambles. He had to act. Of all the things a leader should fear, complacency ought to head the list. Leaders don't know everything, but they know enough to act. Nehemiah had insight into the following areas:

He knew how long the project would take. Nehemiah gave King Artaxerxes a definite time period for his absence.

He knew how to get there. Nehemiah asked for letters of permission to pass through the provinces beyond the river to Judah.

He knew what he would need to get the job done. Nehemiah requested timbers from Asaph to make beams and gates for the wall.

He knew that God's hand was upon him. Nehemiah got all that he requested because the hand of God rested on him.

What is your intuition telling you right now? Are you listening?

The Maxwell Leadership Bible

ENCOURAGE
OTHERS' STRENGTHS

*And Saul said to David, "You are not able to go
against this Philistine to fight with him; for you are a
youth, and he a man of war from his youth."*

1 SAMUEL 17:33

When some leaders begin to work with others on their development, they gravitate to weaknesses rather than strengths. Maybe that's because it's so easy to see other people's problems and shortcomings. But if you start by putting your energies into correcting people's weaknesses, you will demoralize them and unintentionally sabotage the enlarging process.

Instead, of focusing on weaknesses, give your attention to people's strengths. Focus on sharpening skills that already exist. Compliment positive qualities. Bring out the gifts inherent in them. Weaknesses can wait—unless they are character flaws. Only after you have developed a strong rapport with the person and they have begun to grow and gain confidence should you address areas of weakness. And then those should be handled gently and one at a time.

Becoming a Person of Influence

SIGNS OF VICTORY

"...that this may be a sign among you when your children ask in time to come, saying, 'What do these stones mean to you?' Then you shall answer them that the waters of the Jordan were cut off before the ark of the covenant of the LORD; when it crossed over the Jordan, the waters of the Jordan were cut off. And these stones shall be for a memorial to the children of Israel forever."

JOSHUA 4:6–7

Effective leaders look for ways to use the successes of today to empower their people for the challenges of tomorrow. Joshua did exactly that.

Although God worked a miracle to allow the people to cross the Jordan on dry ground, Joshua wanted to communicate God's greatness to the children of Israel yet to be born. To accomplish his goal, Joshua devised a plan called "Stones of Remembrance." He directed that twelve stones be taken from the middle of the dry riverbed— one for each of the Twelve Tribes who crossed the river— and be piled in a monument on shore. The stones served as "handles" to communicate what God had done.

Good leaders always provide "handles" to enable their people to grab hold of the vision. Effective leaders find a way to communicate future vision and past victories, because their people need to be constantly reminded of both.

The Maxwell Leadership Bible

A POSITION
DOESN'T MAKE A LEADER

*Then all Israel came together to David at Hebron,
saying, "Indeed we are your bone and your flesh. Also,
in time past, even when Saul was king, you were the
one who led Israel out and brought them in; and the
LORD your God said to you, 'You shall shepherd My
people Israel, and be ruler over My people Israel.'"*

1 CHRONICLES 11:1–2

As the most influential man in the country, David
was leading long before Saul lost his throne.

Like it or not, position doesn't make a person a leader.
Title may give someone authority, but not influence.
Influence comes from the person; it must be earned.
David had earned it and Saul had not. What was this so?

Unity: David rallied the people and created unity.

Identification: David identified with his followers as
family.

Credibility: David effectively led military campaigns.

Anointing: David enjoyed God's hand and power on
his life.

Partnership: David worked cooperatively with key
leaders.

The Maxwell Leadership Bible

BE PREPARED

And that servant who knew his master's will,
and did not prepare himself or do according to his will,
shall be beaten with many stripes.

LUKE 12:47

Spanish Novelist Miguel de Cervantes said, "The man who is prepared has his battle half-fought." If you want to prepare yourself so that you can help your team as it faces the challenges ahead, then think about the following:

1. Assessment: Where are you and your team heading? What will conditions be along the way? What price will you have to pay to get there?

2. Alignment: Golf has taught me a valuable lesson: Even if you know where you want to go, if you're not lined up right, you'll never get to your desired destination. That's true of personal preparation as well as for golf. Good alignment makes success possible.

3. Attitude: To succeed in any endeavor, you need to do your homework to take care of the mental aspects of your game. You need to have a positive attitude about yourself, your teammates, and your situation.

4. Action: Being prepared means being ready to take that first step when the time comes. Remember this: Courage has no greater ally than preparation, and fear has no greater enemy.

The 17 Essential Qualities of a Team Player

MENDING THE WALLS

*Then I said . . . "Come and let us build the wall of
Jerusalem, that we may no longer be a reproach." . . .
So they said, "Let us rise up and build." Then
they set their hands to this good work.*

NEHEMIAH 2:17–18

A city wall in ruins was a very bad thing in ancient
days. It left a city vulnerable to both physical attack
and hurtful ridicule from neighboring powers. In
Jerusalem's case, the unrepaired wall also gave foreigners a
reason to scorn God, whose holy city it was. And that is
why Nehemiah wept, mourned, fasted, and prayed for
several days when he heard the news of the condition of
the wall, which had been destroyed and neglected for
more than a century.

During the 120 years after the walls were torn down by
the Chaldeans (2 Chronicles 36:19), generations of
Jerusalem's people had looked at the ruins and done
nothing. Maybe to them, rebuilding the wall looked like
an impossible challenge, even though the city possessed
plenty of workers. What the people needed was someone
to rally them, plan their course of action, and take them
through the rebuilding process. What they needed was a
leader. They needed Nehemiah. Remarkably, it took the
people only fifty–two days to rebuild the city wall. And
they were able to do it because they had a great leader to
navigate for them.

The 21 Most Powerful Minutes in a Leader's Day

HOPE CHEST

"Teach me, and I will hold my tongue;
Cause me to understand wherein I have erred."

JOB 6:24

All of Job's friends posed a theory about his troubles, but Job simply asked them to survey his life and point out any place where he lacked integrity. He felt so certain of the blamelessness of his heart that he invited the scrutiny of his peers. Only a leader with strong character and a strong sense of security can do that!

C. S. Lewis calls this quality, "Leaders with chests." Lewis likened the properly ordered soul to the human body: the head (reason) must rule the belly (the sensual appetites) through the chest (character and spirit). The chest is the indispensable liaison between reason and the appetites. Without a strong "chest," men would succumb to excuses, relativism, and compromise. Lewis called those with no character or integrity, "men without chests."

What enabled Job to possess such integrity as a leader?

1. *Strong security.* He felt emotionally secure enough to take criticism.

2. *Clear conscience.* He kept a clear and sensitive conscience regarding sin.

3. *Pure motives.* He refused to entertain self–indulgent motives.

4. *Solid character.* He was committed to doing the right thing at any cost.

The Maxwell Leadership Bible

LIKE A ROCK

Now when Jesus looked at him, He said, "You are Simon the son of Jonah. You shall be called Cephas" (which is translated, A Stone).

JOHN 1:42

Dependability is important to every team's success. Everyone on the team knows upon whom they can and can't depend. Allow me to give you what I consider to be the essence of dependability:

1. *Pure motives:* If someone on the team continually puts themselves and their agenda ahead of what's best for the team, they have proven themselves to be undependable. When it comes to teamwork, motives matter.

2. *Responsibility:* While motivation addresses why people *are* dependable, responsibility indicates that they *want to be* dependable.

3. *Sound thinking:* Dependability means more than just wanting to take responsibility. That desire must also be coupled with good judgement to be of real value to the team.

4. *Consistent contribution:* The final quality of a dependable team player is consistency. If you can't depend on teammates all the time, then you can't really depend on them any of the time. Consistency takes a depth of character that enables people to follow through no matter how tired, distracted, or overwhelmed they are.

The 17 Essential Qualities of a Team Player

THE PLAN OF AN EFFECTIVE LEADER

Now I will come to you when I pass through
Macedonia . . . And it may be that I will remain, or
even spend the winter with you, that you may send me
on my journey, wherever I go . . . But I will tarry in
Ephesus until Pentecost. For a great and effective door
has opened to me, and there are many adversaries.

1 CORINTHIANS 16:5–9

Paul had a plan to reach the major cities of his day. In a conversational manner, he describes his plan to start in Macedonia, then move south to Corinth, and finally visit Asia Minor and the major port city of Ephesus, where "a great and effective door opened" to him.

Effective leaders don't drift from one place to another. Paul had a plan to impact major cities that would in turn influence those who visited these cities. He focused on the metropolitan areas, knowing that well-trained followers would bring God's message to the smaller towns and villages in the region.

Leaders can do anything, but they can't do everything. Paul did not spend his energies haphazardly, but charted the course to reach the Roman Empire in his lifetime.

What kind of plan do you have?

The Maxwell Leadership Bible

CHARTING THE COURSE

*Thus the children of Israel did according to all that the
LORD commanded Moses; so they camped by their
standards and so they broke camp, each one by his
family, according to their fathers' houses.*

NUMBERS 2:34

As a good leader, Moses methodically arranged the tribal camps in the wilderness. We would do well to plan and organize as Moses did:

Give time for planning and organizing. Determine your primary purpose.

Understand where you are before trying to develop a strategy.

Prioritize the needs and goals of the team by asking the right questions.

Write goals that are realistic, measurable, and convicting.

Clarify goals and communicate with your team.

Identify possible obstacles. Have an open system approach to your planning.

Budget your cost and time by scheduling everything you can and setting deadlines.

Study the results. Evaluation prevents stagnation and exaggeration.

Remember, anyone can steer the ship, but it takes a leader to chart the course.

The Maxwell Leadership Bible

IT'S NOT ABOUT POSITION, BUT CREDIBILITY

A wise servant will rule over a son who causes shame, and will share an inheritance among the brothers.

PROVERBS 17:2

Our influence has less to do with our position or title than it does with the life we live. It's not about position, but production. It is not the education we get, but the empowerment we give, that makes a difference to others.

The key word is credibility. We gain credibility when our life matches our talk and when both add value to others. How are you doing when it comes to credibility? To find out, answer the following vital questions:

Consistency: Are you the same person no matter who's with you?

Choices: Do you make decisions based on how they benefit you or others?

Credit: Are you quick to recognize others for their efforts when you succeed?

Character: Do you work harder at your image or your integrity?

Credibility: Have you recognized that credibility is a victory, not a gift?

The Maxwell Leadership Bible

CARE ENOUGH TO CONFRONT

Then Nathan said to David, "You are the man!"

2 SAMUEL 12:7

Many people avoid confrontation. Some fear being disliked and rejected. Others are afraid confrontation will make things worse by creating anger and resentment in the person they confront. But avoiding confrontation always worsens the situation. Confrontation can be a win–win situation, a chance to help and develop your people—if you do it with respect and with the other person's best interests at heart. Here are ten guidelines to help you confront positively:

1. Confront ASAP.
2. Address the wrong action, not the person.
3. Confront only what the person can change.
4. Give the person the benefit of the doubt.
5. Be specific.
6. Avoid sarcasm.
7. Avoid words like "always" and "never."
8. If appropriate, tell the person how you feel about what was done wrong.
9. Give the person a game plan to fix the problem.
10. Affirm him or her as a person and a friend.

Positive confrontation is a sure sign that you care for a person and have their best interests at heart. Each time you build up your people and identify their problems, you give them an opportunity to grow.

Developing the Leaders Around You

TAKE CARE OF THOSE
CLOSEST TO YOU

*Just before the Passover Feast, Jesus knew that the time
had come to leave this world to go to the Father.
Having loved his dear companions, he continued
to love them right to the end.*

JOHN 13:1 (THE MESSAGE)

If you lead your team, you are responsible for
making sure the revolving door (through which
current employees leave the organization and new
employees enter) swings in such a way that better players
are joining the team than are leaving. One of the ways you
can facilitate that is to place high value on the good people
you already have on the team.

Every team has three groups of players. There are the
starters, who directly add value to the organization or who
directly influence its course, and the *bench players*, who add
value to the organization indirectly or who support the
starters who do. The third group is a core group within the
starters that I call the inner circle members. These are
people without whom the team would fall apart. Your job
is to make sure each group is continually developed so that
bench players are able to step up to become starters, and
starters are able to step up to become inner circle members.

If your treatment of key people doesn't match their
value, you run the risk of losing them.

The 17 Indisputable Laws of Teamwork

CONNECTION FIRST

*And Moses went up to God, and the LORD called to
him form the mountain, saying, "Thus you shall say to
the house of Jacob, and tell the children of Israel: 'You
have seen what I did to the Egyptians, and how I bore
you on eagles' wings and brought you to Myself. Now
therefore, if you will indeed obey My voice and keep My
covenant, then you shall be a special treasure to Me
above all people; for the earth is Mine. And you shall
be to Me a kingdom of priests and a holy nation.'"*

EXODUS 19:3–6

Have you ever noticed how God introduced the
Ten Commandments? Before He spoke His laws
to the people in Exodus 20, He took time to remind them
of three vital truths:

1. The love He had for them.
2. The victories He had won for them.
3. The future He planned for them.

God spoke about how He intended to bless Israel as
His children, and He warned them of the boundaries to
keep. Only then did He give them His commandments to
obey. Do you see the genius of the sequence?

Leaders touch a heart before they ask for a hand.
Before God demanded His people keep His rules, He
reminded them of His relationship and blessings. That
gave them all the incentive they needed to follow through
on their commitment!

The Maxwell Leadership Bible

INTEGRITY IS ABOUT
THE SMALL THINGS

Good leaders abhor wrongdoing of all kinds;
sound leadership has a moral foundation.

PROVERBS 16:12 (THE MESSAGE)

As important as integrity is to your business success, it's even more critical if you want to become an influencer. It is the foundation upon which many other qualities are built, such as respect, dignity, and trust. If that foundation of integrity is weak or fundamentally flawed, then being a person of influence becomes impossible.

That's why it's crucial to maintain integrity by taking care of the little things. Ethical principles are not flexible. A little white lie is still a lie. Theft is theft—whether it's $1, $1,000, or $1 million. Integrity commits itself to character over personal gain, to people over things, to service over power, to principle over convenience, to the long view over the immediate.

Anytime you break a moral principle, you create a small crack in the foundation of your integrity. And when times get tough, it becomes harder to act with integrity, not easier. Character isn't created in a crisis; it only comes to light. Everything you have done in the past—and the things you have neglected to do—come to a head when you're under pressure.

Becoming a Person of Influence

AUGUST

One of the greatest gifts leaders can give

to those around them is hope.

Never underestimate its power.

IF IT AIN'T BROKE . . .

*Then Jacob was left alone; and a Man wrestled with
him until the breaking of day. Now when He saw that
He did not prevail against him, He touched the socket
of his hip; and the socket of Jacob's hip was out
of joint as He wrestled with him.*

GENESIS 32:24–25

Natural leaders have it easy, right? Not always.
Even leaders gifted with tremendous natural
leadership can have a very difficult time, especially with
issues of character.

That was true for Jacob. From the very beginning he
wielded great influence. No matter what he did or where
he went, he stirred things up . . . Wealthy, strong,
influential, and blessed with a large family, Jacob seemed
to have everything. But a leader who goes his own way
and seeks to benefit only himself cannot be an effective
instrument in God's hands. God had to break Jacob to
make him useful. In the breaking process, Jacob—the
deceiving "heel–catcher"—became Israel, a "prince of
God" who purposed to serve God rather than himself.

Natural leaders often need to be broken. Consider your
natural ability to lead a gift from God, but your character a
gift to present back to God. Remember: Every time you
stand up under the weight of adversity, you are being
prepared, as Jacob was, to better serve God and lead people.

The Maxwell Leadership Bible

NO GREATER LOVE

*Greater love has no one than this, than to
lay down one's life for his friends.*

JOHN 15:13

Teams that don't bond, can't build. Why? Because
they never become a cohesive unit. Why do
wounded soldiers strive to rejoin their buddies on the
battlefield? Because after you work and live with people,
you soon realize that your survival depends on one
another.

For a team to be successful, the teammates have to
know that they will look out for one another. When a
team member cares about no one but himself, the whole
team suffers. I have found that one of the best ways to get
members of a team to care about one another is to get
them together outside of a work context in order to build
relationships. Every year in our organization we plan
retreats and other events that put our people together in
social settings. And during those times, we also make sure
that they spend part of their time with staff members they
don't really know very well. That way they're not only
building relationships, but they're being prevented from
developing cliques.

Developing the Leaders Around You

TIME TO MAKE A DECISION

*Then the LORD spoke to Moses and Aaron, "Because
you did not believe Me, to hallow Me in the eyes
of the children of Israel, therefore you shall not bring
this assembly into the land which I have given them."*

NUMBERS 20:12

We learn something invaluable about leadership at the expense of Moses in Numbers 20. By this point Moses felt weary of the complaining, the stagnation, and the lack of progress among the people. He was running on empty. And in his weakened condition he made a decision that cost him his future.

Directed by God to speak to a rock in order to get water for the nation, in anger he struck it. He reacted in fury rather than obeying with poise, and for his disobedience he was barred from entering the Promised Land. This sad incident teaches us at least two lessons. First, never make a major decision during an emotionally low time. Second, choose to be proactive, not reactive, in your leadership. Don't let your mandate come from the grumbling of the crowd. Get your cues from God and the mission He has given you. Ask yourself these questions:

1. Am I a reactor or a creator when I lead?
2. Do I play defense or offense when I lead?
3. Am I a people–pleaser or a God–pleaser when I lead?
4. Do I boss my calendar, or does someone else choose where I give my time?

The Maxwell Leadership Bible

DON'T OVERSTEP
YOUR LEADERSHIP

*[Uzziah] sought God in the days of Zechariah, who
had understanding in the visions of God; and as long as
he sought the LORD, God made him prosper . . .
But when he was strong his heart was lifted up,
to his destruction, for he transgressed
against the LORD his God . . .*

2 CHRONICLES 26:5, 16

The choices we make nearly always reflect our true character. Uzziah's reign mirrored that of Asa, Josiah, and Amaziah—it began very strong and ended in disgrace. In the early years, Uzziah displayed strong, godly leadership skills. The Lord blessed him with military success. During this time, his inner circle included a godly spiritual counselor, Zechariah, who exerted significant influence for good. Uzziah sought after God, and the Lord prospered him.

As Uzziah's kingdom and wealth increased, however, his priorities shifted to personal success rather than the things that delighted God's heart. A raw desire for power consumed his soul, and the king intentionally stepped out of his God–ordained role. As a result, Uzziah left a legacy of disgrace. "He dwelt in an isolated house, because he was a leper; for he was cut off from the house of the LORD." (2 Chronicles 26:21). A sad ending to a promising start.

The Maxwell Leadership Bible

LEADERSHIP BEGINS A HOME

Choose for yourselves this day whom you will serve,
whether the gods which your fathers served that were on
the other side of the River, or the gods of the Amorites
in whose land you dwell. But as for me
and my house, we will serve the LORD.

JOSHUA 24:15

As a leader, where should your influence begin? A good answer can be drawn from the life of Joshua. For him—as for other leaders wanting to make an impact beyond their lifetimes—it began at home. Before anything else, Joshua took responsibility for the spiritual life of his family. Joshua's leadership of his family was more important than his leadership of the country. It may sound ironic, but when leaders put their families first, the community benefits. When leaders put the community first, both their familes and the community suffer. Starting at home is always the key to affecting others in a positive way. Because Joshua had his priorities right and had led his household well, he gained credibility to lead the entire house of Israel.

If you have a family, put them first in your leadership. There's no legacy like that of the positive influence leaders can exercise with their family.

The 21 Most Powerful Minutes in a Leader's Day

IT TAKES MORE
THAN POTENTIAL

*Remove impurities from the silver and the silversmith
can craft a fine chalice; Remove the wicked
from leadership and authority will be
credible and God–honoring.*

PROVERBS 25:4–5 (THE MESSAGE)

Samson had everything going for him. He was a special child, foretold by the Angel of the Lord to his parents. He had a divine destiny and purpose. Scripture reports that the Angel said, "The child shall be a Nazirite to God from the womb; and he shall begin to deliver Israel out of the hand of the Philistines" (Judges 13:5).

Why didn't Samson become the great leader he had the potential to be? His despicable character made him untrustworthy and that destroyed his leadership. He was impetuous, volatile, lustful, moody, emotional, and unpredictable. He also broke his Nazirite vows. Samson repeatedly flirted with disaster, and it finally overtook him.

I think many people believe that if they had been given a start like that Samson's, they would find it easy to lead and to finish well. But God gives every one of us a good enough start to be able to finish well. It's up to us to see to our character and build trust with others so that God can use our leadership.

The 21 Most Powerful Minutes in a Leader's Day

RAISING UP A LEADER TAKES TIME

*And the LORD said to Moses: "Take Joshua the son
of Nun with you, a man in whom is the Spirit, and lay
your hand on him; set him before Eleazar the priest
and before all the congregation, and inaugurate him
in their sight. And you shall give some of your authority
to him, that all the congregation
of the children of Israel may be obedient.*

NUMBERS 27:18–20

Of all the wonderful ways Moses expressed his leadership, the most strategic had to be his training of Joshua. Moses passed along his authority, abilities, and anointing to Joshua. He gave Joshua his time, his insight, a learning environment, an opportunity to prove himself, and a strong belief in his future.

The interaction of Moses and Joshua demonstrates that reproducing leaders is not a quick, simple process. It requires time, emotional investment, and sacrifice.

When you begin developing the next generation of leaders, recognize that your protégés will need certain things:

1. *From themselves: Conviction, courage, and obedience*

2. *From their mentor: Equipping*

3. *From God: Vision*

4. *From the people: Buy–In*

With time, investment, and sacrifice, you will build a legacy of leadership.

The Maxwell Leadership Bible

WHEN A LEADER SPEAKS

*And with many other words he testified and exhorted
them, saying, "Be saved from this perverse generation."
Then those who gladly received his word
were baptized; and that day about three
thousand souls were added to them.*

ACTS 2:40–41

When somebody asks a question in a meeting,
whom do people look to for the answer? Whom do
they wait to hear? The person they look to is the real leader.

Identifying a real leader can be easy—if you
remember what you're looking for. Don't listen to the
claims of the person professing to be the leader. Instead,
watch the reactions of the people around him. The proof
of leadership is found in the followers. People listen to
what someone has to say not necessarily because of the
message, but because of their respect for the messenger.

So I must ask you this : How do people react when
you communicate? When you speak, do people listen—I
mean *really* listen? Or do they wait to hear what someone
else has to say before they act? You can find out a lot about
your level of leadership if you have the courage to ask and
answer that question.

The 21 Irrefutable Laws of Leadership

MOSES' FIRST FORTY YEARS IN THE DESERT

But Moses fled from the face of Pharaoh and dwelt in the land of Midian . . . Then Moses was content to live with the man, and he gave Zipporah his daughter to Moses.
EXODUS 2:15, 21

How did God prepare Moses to be His man to lead the Hebrews out of Egyptian bondage? He prepared him not in a day, but over time; not through an event, but with a process. God also led others through a lengthy leadership development process:

Noah—waited 120 years before the predicted rains arrived.

Abraham—waited 25 years for a promised son.

Joseph—waited 14 years in prison for a crime he didn't commit.

Job—waited perhaps a lifetime, 60–70 years, for God's justice.

God prepares leaders in a slow–cooker, not in a microwave oven. More important than the awaited goal is the work God does in us while we wait. Waiting deepens and matures us, levels our perspective, and broadens our understanding. Tests of time determine whether we can endure seasons of seemingly unfruitful preparations, and indicate whether we can recognize and seize the opportunities that come our way.

The Maxwell Leadership Bible

OBSERVE YOUR INFLUENCE

*"But only speak a word, and my servant will be healed.
For I also am a man under authority, having soldiers
under me. And I say to this one, 'Go,' and he goes;
and to another, 'Come,' and he comes; and
to my servant, 'Do this,' and he does it."*

MATTHEW 8:8–9

Sociologists tell us that even the most introverted individual will influence ten thousand other people during his or her lifetime. This amazing statistic was shared with me by my associate Tim Elmore. Tim and I concluded that all of us are leading in some areas, while in other areas we are being led. No one is excluded from being a leader or a follower. Realizing your potential as a leader is your responsibility.

The prominent leader of any group is quite easy to discover. Just observe the people as they gather. If an issue is to be decided, who is the person whose opinion seems most valuable? Who is the one others watch the most when the issue is being discussed? Who is the one with whom people quickly agree? Most importantly, who is the one the others follow? Answers to these questions will help you discern who the real leader is in a particular group.

Developing the Leader Within You

LEADERS MUST BE
EXAMPLES, NOT EXCEPTIONS

Then Hezekiah and all the people rejoiced
that God has prepared the people, since
the events took place so suddenly.

2 CHRONICLES 29:36

Far too often, leaders drift. Once they get some experience under their belt and a track record of accomplishments, they often abandon the lifestyle that helped them reach the top. They chafe under the very rules that they once established or endorsed. Sadly, leaders like these forget the number one management principle in the world: People do what people see. If they want to succeed, leaders must incarnate the life they desire in their followers.

The kings of Judah had drifted badly when Hezekiah inherited an unholy mess from his father, King Ahaz. But Hezekiah repaired the Temple, restored legitimate worship, removed the idols, repented for the people, and required a change in the land. Once the population saw his example of worship, they followed suit. These events took place quickly not only because of a sovereign God who replaced Ahaz with the king's godly son, but because Hezekiah modeled the life he expected of others.

The Maxwell Leadership Bible

IT DOESN'T HURT TO ASK

Why did I not die at birth? Why did I not perish
when I came from the womb? . . . How long?
Will You not look away from me, And let
me alone till I swallow my saliva?

JOB 3:11 & 7:19

 God doesn't mind questions; it's doubt that He hates.

For many wearying hours, the three friends of Job—Eliphaz, Bildad, and Zophar—accused Job of all kinds of evil. They spoke the kind of foolish words that the healthy and ill–informed often speak to those in pain. But Job wanted to take his case to the Lord Himself! Only at the end of the book does God at last break His silence, and although He answers not one of Job's questions, neither does He chastise Job for asking them. God rebukes Job for only one thing: doubting His righteous character.

Leaders must never be afraid to ask hard questions of God, but neither must they demand that He answer. No matter how dark our circumstances may grow, we must resist the temptation to doubt God's holy nature. When we, like Job, through trembling lips confess the awesome majesty of God, we may at last be ready for the awesome blessing of God.

The Maxwell Leadership Bible

Playing Favorites

Peter, seeing him, said to Jesus, "But Lord, what about this man?" Jesus said to him, "If I will that he remain till I come, what is that to you? You follow Me."

JOHN 21:21–22

One of the biggest mistakes a coach can make is to believe that he must treat all of his players the same. Coaches are hired to win—not to make everyone happy or give everyone equal time, money, or resources. Every player must be given support and encouragement. But to believe that everyone must receive the same treatment is not only unrealistic but destructive. Poor or mediocre performance should not be rewarded the same as the outstanding contributions.

Great coaches give opportunities, resources, and playing time according to players' past performance. The greater the performer, the greater the opportunity. When you have a player like Michael Jordan, you want to put the ball in his hands as often as possible.

There will be times that you aren't sure about a player's performance level because you haven't had time to observe him, especially with a "rookie" player. Give that player frequent but small opportunities to determine his caliber of play, and that will show you how to respond.

Developing the Leaders Around You

Become a Momentum Maker

And all Israel heard of the judgment which the king had rendered; and they feared the king, for they saw that the wisdom of God was in him to administer justice.

1 Kings 3:28

It takes a leader to create momentum. Followers catch it. And managers are able to continue it once it has begun. But creating momentum requires someone who can motivate others, not one who needs to be motivated. Just as every sailor knows you can't steer a ship that isn't moving forward, strong leaders understand that to change direction, you first have to create forward progress. Without momentum, even the simplest tasks can seem insurmountable. But with momentum on your side, nearly any kind of change is possible.

Consider the ways young Solomon created momentum:

• He started with what David provided.

• He made wise decisions that won him credibility.

• He maintained the peace.

No leader can ignore the impact of momentum. If you've got it, you and your people will be able to accomplish things you never thought possible. The choice to build momentum is yours. *The Maxwell Leadership Bible*

A GROWING COMMUNITY

*They devoted themselves to the apostles' teaching
and to the fellowship, to the breaking of bread and
to prayer. Everyone was filled with awe, and many
wonders and miraculous signs were done by the apostles.
All the believers were together and had everything
in common…And the Lord added to their number
daily those who were being saved.*

ACTS 2:42–44, 47 (NIV)

Just as the growth of tropical fish is limited by the size of the aquarium in which they live, we also are affected by our environment. If your current circumstances do nothing to help you grow, you're going to have a hard time enlarging yourself to reach your potential. That's why it's crucial that you create an environment of growth around you. That kind of place should look like this:

1. Others are ahead of you.
2. You are still challenged.
3. Your focus is forward.
4. The atmosphere is affirming.
5. You are out of your comfort zone.
6. Others are growing.
7. There is a willingness to change.
8. Growth is modeled and expected.

A life of continual growth is never easy, but a good environment makes the swim upstream a little less difficult.

Your Road Map for Success

TROUBLE? TURN TO GOD

I waited patiently for the LORD; And He inclined to me, And heard my cry. He also brought me up out of a horrible pit, Out of the miry clay, And set my feet upon a rock, And established my steps.

PSALM 40:1–2

King David knew something about suffering, particularly suffering caused by his own actions. But he also knew to whom he could turn during those times of trouble.

What great comfort and joy come to us when we understand that God is rich in grace and mercy, that He not only forgives, but restores and redeems! The Lord lifts us up from our personal pits of despair and puts us in right standing with Him.

When times of trouble arrive—even trouble we bring on ourselves—we must turn to God and wait patiently for His help. He'll never fail us. Remember these truths about the God you serve, then proclaim them to everyone who will hear.

The Maxwell Leadership Bible

WITHOUT BUY-IN, THE VISION PERISHES

*And the Angel of the LORD appeared to [Gideon],
and said to him, "The LORD is with you,
you mighty man of valor!"*

JUDGES 6:12

All leaders have vision. But all people who possess vision are not leaders. A compelling vision alone will not make someone a leader. Nor will a great vision automatically be fulfilled simply because it is compelling or valuable. Followers need to buy in to the leader.

Once Gideon possessed the vision to deliver Israel from its enemies, he still needed to get the people to buy into his leadership. Even though the vision was ordained by God, it still required time and action from Gideon. Ultimately, so many people bought into Gideon's leadership so completely that God had to send a bunch of them home to make sure He got the glory for their victory.

Just because a person has vision and occupies a leadership position doesn't necessarily mean that the people will follow. Before they get on board, they have to buy in. And that doesn't happen in an instant. Buy-in is an ongoing process.

The 21 Most Powerful Minutes in a Leader's Day

CURSED SELF-INTEREST

Afterward, when David heard it, he said,
"My kingdom and I are guiltless before the LORD
forever of the blood of Abner the son of Ner.
Let it rest on the head of Joab and on all
his father's house; and let there never fail to be
in the house of Joab one who has a discharge
or is a leper, who learns on a staff or
falls by the sword, or who lacks bread."

2 SAMUEL 3:28–29

When you forget whom you serve, you quickly fall prey to the basest human instincts. Leaders are not exempt.

Joab, a nephew of King David and a successful army commander, showed great arrogance toward the king by chiding him for entering into a treaty with Abner, a former enemy. Joab basically called David a fool for allowing Abner to escape unharmed. Joab secretly plotted to kill Abner, not because he posed a threat to David's kingdom, but out of personal vengeance. He sent messengers to retrieve Abner so that he could murder him in cold blood. When David heard what Joab had done, he praised the dead man but pronounced a curse upon Joab and his family.

God tells us that vengeance belongs to Him. Leaders who cannot humble themselves to serve God and those He has raised up will eventually act out of selfish motives and hurt the kingdom.

The Maxwell Leadership Bible

MAKE COMMUNICATION CLEAR

His disciples said to Him, "See, now,
You are speaking plainly, and using no figure of speech!
Now we are sure that You know all things ...
By this we believe that you came forth from God."

JOHN 16:29–30

The success of your marriage, job, and personal relationships all depend greatly on communication. People will not follow you if they don't know what you want or where you are going. You can be more a more effective communicator if you follow four truths:

1. *Simplify your message:* The key to effective communication is simplicity. Forget about impressing people with big words or complex sentences. If you want to connect with people, keep it simple.

2. *See the person:* As you communicate with people—whether individuals or groups—ask yourself these questions: Who is my audience? What are their questions? What needs to be accomplished?

3. *Show the truth:* Credibility precedes great communication. Believe in what you say. Then, live what you say. There is no greater credibility than conviction in action.

4. *Seek a response:* As you communicate, never forget that the goal of all communication is action. Every time you speak to people, give them something to feel, something to remember, and something to do.

The 21 Indispensable Qualities of a Leader

PICKING YOUR TEAM

Therefore, brethren, seek out from among you seven
men of good reputation, full of the Holy Spirit and
wisdom, whom we may appoint over this business.

ACTS 6:3

Red Auerbach, long–time president of the Boston Celtics, said, "How you select people is more important than how you manage them once they're on the job. If you start with the right people, you won't have problems later on." You have to begin with the right raw materials in order to create a winning team.

I want the people close to me to . . .

Know my heart: This takes time for both of us and desire on their part.

Be loyal to me: They are an extension of me and my work.

Be trustworthy: They must not abuse authority, power, or confidences.

Be discerning: They make decisions for me.

Have a servant's heart: They carry a heavy load because of my high demands.

Be a good thinker: Our two heads are better than my one.

Be able to follow through: They take authority and carry out the vision.

Have a great heart for God: My heart for God is my driving force in life.

Developing the Leaders Around You

AVOID DESTRUCTIVE PARTNERSHIPS

Do not be unequally yoked together with unbelievers.
For what fellowship has righteousness with lawlessness?
And what communion has light with darkness?

2 CORINTHIANS 6:14

Healthy leaders often partner with others to reach their goals. In fact, we live in an age of partnerships, both in the corporate world and in the church. Paul reminds us that nothing is more dangerous to a leader than an unhealthy or destructive partnership. Note several signs of a bad partnership:

- The parties don't share the same values.
- The parties don't agree on the goal.
- One or both parties must compromise their convictions.
- One party selfishly demands that the other surrender.
- One party benefits and the other loses.

Good partnerships do not foster co–dependence or independence, but interdependence. Each party feels secure, is stretched, and enjoys synergy. The partnership multiplies the productivity of both parties.

The Maxwell Leadership Bible

HOPE SPRINGS ETERNAL

There is surely a future hope for you,
and your hope will not be cut off.

PROVERBS 23:18 (NIV)

One of the greatest gifts leaders can give to those around them is hope. Never underestimate its power. Winston Churchill was once asked by a reporter what his country's greatest weapon was against the Hitler's Nazi regime. Without pausing for a moment he said: "It was what England's greatest weapon has always been—hope."

People will continue working, struggling, and trying if they have hope. Hope lifts people's morale. It improves their self-image. It re-energizes them. It raises their expectations. It is the leader's job to hold hope high, to instill it in the people he leads. Our people will have hope only if we give it to them. And we will have hope to give if we maintain the right attitude. Battle of Verdun hero Marshall Foch observed, "There are no hopeless situations: there are only men who have grown hopeless about them." Maintaining hope comes from seeing the potential in every situation and staying positive despite circumstances.

Developing the Leaders Around You

ACCEPTING THE RESPONSIBILITY OF A LEADER'S TRUST

And Jehoshaphat feared, and set himself to seek the LORD, and proclaimed a fast throughout all Judah. So Judah gathered together to ask help from the LORD; and from all the cities of Judah they came to seek the LORD.

2 CHRONICLES 20:3–4

A leader can delegate anything except responsibility. Leaders simply cannot give it away. They can model it; they can teach it; they can share it. But in the words of Harry Truman, the buck stops with the leader.

When Jehoshaphat became king of Judah, he assumed a trust. He was to lead the people and manage the nation's resources. One of his greatest challenges came when an army from three countries laid plans to attack Judah. Jehoshaphat faced the same options we all face in a crisis: give up, back up, or stand up. At such time we find out the quality of our leadership:

1. *Dropouts*: leaders who give up and fail to take responsibility.

2. *Cop–outs*: leaders who make excuses for why they aren't responsible.

3. *Hold–outs*: leaders who waiver too long to take responsibility.

4. *All–outs*: leaders who own the responsibility and take action—like Jehoshaphat.

The Maxwell Leadership Bible

DON'T LET GO
OF YOUR DREAM

*But Joshua the son of Nun and Caleb the son
of Jephunneh, who were among those who had spied
out the land, tore their clothes; and they spoke to all the
congregation of the children of Israel, saying, "
The land we passed through to spy out is an exceedingly
good land. If the LORD delights in us, then He will
bring us into this land and give it to us" . . . And all
the congregation said to stone them with stones.*

NUMBERS 14:6–8, 10

During its early stages, a dream is an incredibly
fragile thing. As corporate leadership expert and
friend Bobb Biehl says, "Dreams are like soap bubbles
floating close to jagged rocks on a windy day."

New dreams are fragile because we haven't had time
yet to let them grow or develop. When a seedling oak is
only a year old, a child can tear it out by the roots, but
once it's had some time to become firmly established, even
a hurricane can't knock it down.

Young dreams are also more easily shot down because
if they are attacked, it is usually by close confidants,
because they're the only people who know about them.
Our hopes and desires may be able to weather the
criticism of a stranger, but they have a more difficult time
surviving when undermined by a friend.

Your Road Map for Success

LEADERSHIP TRANSITIONS

And the king took an oath and said, "As the LORD
lives, who has redeemed my life from every distress,
just as I swore to you by the LORD God of Israel, saying,
'Assuredly Solomon your son shall be king after me, and
he shall sit on my throne in my place,'
so I certainly will do this day."

1 KINGS 1:29–30

Two things greatly helped Solomon in his succession to the throne of Israel; both gave him the authority he required to rule. First, God chose him to be the next king. Second, David chose him as his successor.

Transitions in leadership often cause significant problems for groups and organizations. Notice what David did to smooth the transition process in his kingdom:

He made a public commitment.

He brought key influencers into the process.

He gave Solomon some of his own resources, easily recognizable to the people.

He set up a public commissioning for Solomon.

He publicly endorsed Solomon's leadership.

He initiated a celebration to transition the leadership to his successor.

The Maxwell Leadership Bible

LET GOD USE
YOUR STRENGTHS

But Saul increased all the more in strength,
and confounded the Jews . . . proving that
this Jesus is the Christ.

ACTS 9:22

Psychologist Sheldon Kopp says, "All of the significant battles are waged within the self." That's true. The greatest of the battles people wage is against their own flaws and failures. To have an opportunity to reach your potential, you must know who you are and face your flaws.

To do that:

1. See yourself clearly.
2. Admit your flaws honestly.
3. Discover your strengths joyfully.
4. Build on those strengths passionately.

You can reach your potential tomorrow if you dedicate yourself to growth today. Remember, to change your world, you must first change yourself.

Failing Forward

LEAVE MORE THAN
AN INHERITANCE

For when he dies he shall carry nothing away;
His glory shall not descend after him.

PSALM 49:17

God encourages us to fix our eyes on the things that endure. In light of eternity, leaders cannot become consumed with the temporary. Only a vision that outlives them, a vision connected to eternity, will fulfill a godly leader. In other words, we must build a legacy.

A huge difference exists between a legacy and an inheritance. Anyone can leave an inheritance. An inheritance is something you leave to your family or loved ones. (It also fades.) A legacy is something you leave *in* your family and loved ones. Consider these differences:

INHERITANCE	LEGACY
1. Something you give to others	1. Something you place in others
2. Temporarily brings them happiness	2. Permanently transforms them
3. Eventually fades as it is spent	3. Lives on long after you die
4. Your activity may or may not pay off	4. Your activity becomes achievement

The Maxwell Leadership Bible

MODEL THE WAY

It takes more than talk to keep workers in line;
mere words go in one ear and out the other.

PROVERBS 29:19 (THE MESSAGE)

People are first influenced by what they see. If you have children, then you've probably observed this. No matter what you tell your children to do, their natural inclination is to follow what they see you doing. For most people, if they perceive that you are positive and trustworthy and have admirable qualities, then they will seek you as an influencer in their lives.

When you meet people who don't know you, at first you have no influence with them at all. If someone they trust introduces you to them, then you can temporarily "borrow" some of their influence. But as soon as they have some time to observe you, you either build or bust that influence by your actions.

Becoming a Person of Influence

IN STEPS A LEADER

Then David said to Abigail: "Blessed is the LORD God of Israel, who sent you this day to meet me! And blessed is your advice and blessed are you, because you have kept me this day from coming to bloodshed and from avenging myself with my own hand."

1 SAMUEL 25:32–33

After Samuel's death, David moved to the Wilderness of Paran. There he encountered shepherds tending the flocks of the wealthy Nabal—an insolent, rude, and contentious man who happened to be married to a beautiful, intelligent, and intuitive woman named Abigail.

When Nabal offended David, Abigail very quickly took steps to defuse a volatile situation. She gathered a feast and went out to meet David. Abigail's decisive actions calmed David and diverted him from avenging himself on Nabal's whole household. Regardless of her husband's inappropriate behavior, Abigail responded forthrightly and respectfully, and God Himself soon avenged David by removing Nabal from the equation.

David knew a woman of God when he saw one, and after Nabal's death he married Abigail. David valued Abigail's strength and felt greatly attracted to this highly capable female leader.

The Maxwell Leadership Bible

CALL IN THE RESERVES

After this the Lord appointed seventy–two others
and sent them two by two ahead of Him to every town
and place where He was about to go.

LUKE 10:1 (NIV)

It's not difficult to see the importance of having well–trained, capable reserve players who sit on the bench in sports. In major league baseball, the teams who win championships do so because they have more than just a good pitching rotation and solid fielding. They possess a bench and a bullpen with strong players who can substitute or pinch–hit. In the NBA, players and fans have long recognized the impact of the bench by talking about the all–important sixth man, the person who makes a significant contribution to the team's success yet isn't one of the five starters on the basketball court. And football coaches express the need to have two skilled quarterbacks on their rosters. A great starter alone is simply not enough if a team wants to go to the highest level.

Any team that wants to excel must have good substitutes as well as starters. That's true in any field, not just sports. You may be able to do some wonderful things with a handful of top people, but if you want your team to do well over the long haul, you've got to build your bench. A great team with no bench eventually collapses.

The 17 Indisputable Laws of Teamwork

WHAT DO YOUR PEOPLE WANT?

Then I returned and considered all the oppression that is done under the sun: And look! The tears of the oppressed, but they have no comforter—on the side of their oppressors there is power, But they have no comforter . . . Again, I saw that for all toil and every skillful work a man is envied by his neighbor. This also is vanity and grasping for the wind. The fool folds his hands and consumes his own flesh. Better a handful with quietness than both hands full, together with toil and grasping for the wind. Then I returned, and I saw vanity under the sun: There is one alone, without companion: he has neither son nor brother. Yet there is no end to all his labors, nor is his eye satisfied with riches. But he never asks, "For whom do I toil and deprive myself of good?" This also is vanity and a grave misfortune.

ECCLESIASTES 4:1, 4–8

While Ecclesiastes 4 seems to continue the book's theme of futility, it actually attempts to address the issue of motivation. Solomon says that he observes people in a variety of contexts, and nothing seems to satisfy them. As leaders, we must understand people's motivational needs. What do they seek in life? Note Solomon's observations about what motivates most men and women:

Comfort and fulfillment (affiliation)
Competition and triumph (achievement)
Consumption and greed (influence)

The Maxwell Leadership Bible

September

*The sign of great leaders
is not what they accomplish on their own,
but what they accomplish through others.*

CONNECT WITH
YOUR LEADERSHIP HERITAGE

So all Israel was recorded by genealogies,
and indeed, they were inscribed in the book of the kings
of Israel. But Judah was carried away captive
to Babylon because of their unfaithfulness.

1 CHRONICLES 9:1

The first nine chapters of 1 Chronicles furnish a genealogy of Israel's leaders—almost a third of the book! The enormous space give to these ancestral lists illustrates the vast importance of heritage to a Hebrew leader. Our generation and culture seem to place a much lower value on tradition and family stock than did others in history. What do we learn from the lineages of Jewish leaders?

They remained connected to their heritage.

They saw their place in history and gained perspective from it.

They were able to honor and pay respect to their forefathers.

They saw their lineage as a family blessing and passed on this blessing.

They used their heritage to provide a sense of stability for their children.

They sensed tendencies of ancestral giftedness and calling.

They could retain their identity even when exiled to a foreign land.

The Maxwell Leadership Bible

WHEN YOU FAIL,
FAIL FORWARD

Then he began to curse and swear, saying, "I do not know the Man!" Immediately a rooster crowed. And Peter remembered the word of Jesus who had said to him, "Before the rooster crows, you will deny Me three times." So he went out and wept bitterly.

MATTHEW 26:74–75

Everybody fails, errs, and makes mistakes. You've heard the saying "To err is human, to forgive divine." Alexander Pope wrote that over 250 years ago. And he was only paraphrasing an ancient saying that was common during the time of the Romans. Recently I came across something called "Rules for Being Human." I think several of these describe well the state we're in:

Rule #1: You will learn lessons.

Rule #2: There are no mistakes—only lessons.

Rule #3: A lesson is repeated until it is learned.

Rule #4: If you don't learn the easy lessons, they get harder.

Rule #5: You'll know you've learned a lesson when your actions change.

You see, writer Norman Cousins was right when he said, "The essence of man is imperfection." Failure is simply a price we pay to achieve success. If we learn to embrace that new definition of failure, then we are free to start moving ahead—and failing forward.

Failing Forward

LEADERS TOUCH A HEART
BEFORE THEY ASK FOR A HAND

Now when all Israel saw that the king did not listen to them, the people answered the king, saying: "What share have we in David? We have no inheritance in the son of Jesse. To your tents, O Israel! Now, see to your own house, O David!" So Israel departed to their tents.

1 KINGS 12:16

A leader can't connect with people only when he is communicating among groups; he must connect with individuals. The stronger the relationship and connection between individuals, the more likely the follower will help the leader. Successful leaders always initiate; they take the first step and make the effort to continue building relationships.

Connecting with people isn't complicated, but it takes effort. Observe the truths about connection that Rehoboam, son of David, ignored:

Your people are more willing to take action when you first move them with emotion.

When you give first, your people will give in return.

When you connect with individuals, you gain the attention of crowds.

When you reach out to your people, they will reach back toward you.

Whether you have just taken over a leadership position or are well established, you must connect with your people if you are to succeed.

The Maxwell Leadership Bible

ARE YOU A WHOLE PERSON?

God hates cheating in the marketplace;
He loves it when business is aboveboard.

PROVERBS 11:1 (THE MESSAGE)

A person with integrity does not have divided loyalties (that's duplicity), nor is he or she merely pretending (that's hypocrisy). People with integrity are "whole" people; they can be identified by their single–mindedness. People with integrity have nothing to hide and nothing to fear. Their lives are open books. V. Gilbert Beers says, "A person of integrity is one who has established a system of values against which all of life is judged."

Integrity is not what we do, so much as who we are. And who we are, in turn, determines what we do.

We are all faced with conflicting desires. No one, no matter how "spiritual," can avoid this battle. Integrity is the factor that determines which desire will prevail. We struggle daily with situations that demand decisions between what we want to do and what we ought to do. Integrity establishes the ground rules for resolving these tensions. It allows us to predetermine what we will be regardless of circumstances, persons involved, or the places of our testing. It frees us to be whole persons no matter what comes our way.

Developing the Leader Within You

OUR COMFORT ALLOWS US TO COMFORT OTHERS

Blessed be the God and Father of our Lord Jesus Christ, the Father of mercies and God of all comfort, who comforts us in all our tribulation, that we may be able to comfort those who are in any trouble, with the comfort with which we ourselves are comforted by God.

2 CORINTHIANS 1:3–4

God promises to comfort us in our troubles, then asks us to share that comfort with others. We are to empower others with the power God gives us. Leaders who empower others offer these gifts:

Accountability—They help others keep their commitments to God.

Affirmation—They speak words of support and encouragement.

Assessment—They evaluate others' progress, offering an objective perspective.

Advice—They offer words of wise counsel and direction.

Admonishment—They lend words of caution, rebuke, or correction.

Assets—They give tangible resources to help their people reach their goals.

Acceptance—They provide unconditional love, regardless of the recipients' identity.

Application—They help others find places to apply and practice what they learn.

The Maxwell Leadership Bible

MAKING THE TOUGH CALL

But Paul insisted that they should not take with them the one who had departed from them in Pamphylia, and had not gone with them to the work.

ACTS 15:38

Some of the toughest decisions a leader faces concern poor performers. A leader who does not effectively handle them will hurt:

- The organization's ability to achieve its purpose
- The morale of top performers
- The leader's own credibility
- The low performer's self–image and potential effectiveness

To discover the proper course concerning a poor performer, a leader needs to ask, "Should this person be trained, transferred, or terminated?" The answer will determine the appropriate course of action. If low performance is due to skills that are poor or undeveloped, it calls for training. Sometimes an employee is a low performer because he is being expected to perform a job that does not match his gifts and abilities. If the employee has a good attitude and a desire to succeed, he can be transferred to a position matching his gifts. By far the most difficult of the tough decisions a leader faces concern terminating an employee, but terminating a poor performer benefits the organization and everyone in it.

Developing the Leaders Around You

SELF–PROMOTION . . . SELF–DESTRUCTION

Then Ambimelech the son of Jerubbaal went to Shechem, to his mother's brothers, and spoke with them and with all the family of the house of his mother's father, saying, "Please speak in the hearing of all the men of Shechem: Which is better for you, that all seventy of the sons of Jerubbaal reign over you, or that one reign over you?' Remember that I am your own flesh and bone."

JUDGES 9:1–2

At first glance, Abimelech might seem like an ideal candidate for leadership. A gifted communicator and skilled tactician, he set his heart on becoming the ruler of his people. He had a passion to lead. But passion does not mean fitness.

After the death of his father, Gideon, ambitious Abimelech kept his eye on the leadership of Israel, but he never sought God's view of his career choice. He employed "worthless and reckless men" to enforce his will. And as leader he murdered seventy potential competitors. In the end, the self–promoting power–seeker and his cronies all died under the terrifying frown of God.

Self–promotion may "work" in the short run, but over the long haul God makes sure that it fails. Godly leaders must remind themselves of the Lord's instruction: "Humble yourselves under the mighty hand of God, that He may exalt you in due time. (1 Peter 5:6).

The Maxwell Leadership Bible

A CREDIBLE LEADER

So Samuel grew, and the LORD was with him and let none of his words fall to the ground. And all of Israel from Dan to Beersheba knew that Samuel had been established as a prophet of the LORD.

1 SAMUEL 3:19–20

Have you ever wondered what gave Samuel such credibility with others? When he spoke, people listened.

Samuel's success began when he was just a boy under his mentor, Eli. God spoke to Samuel during the night, then the lad spoke for God to Eli. Despite the hardness of God's message to Eli, Samuel spoke the truth in love. This encounter began a long pattern for Samuel.

Soon, the Israelites sought out Samuel to speak words of direction for their future. They needed help to retrieve the Ark of the Covenant. They needed strategy against the Philistines. They eventually sought his permission to crown a king.

The influence of the prophet just kept growing. It grew so vast that when King Saul failed in his leadership, Samuel removed him. Imagine, having the sole authority fire the king! Samuel exhorted, he affirmed, he corrected, he prophesied, he reminded, and he taught the people. He spoke the truth, and he spoke it in love.

The Maxwell Leadership Bible

OVERCOMING POOR MORALE

The people came to Moses, and said, "We have sinned; .
..pray to the LORD that He take away the serpents from
us." So Moses prayed for the people ...
Moses made a bronze serpent, and put it on a pole;
and so it was, if a serpent had bitten anyone,
when he looked at the bronze serpent, he lived.

NUMBERS 21:7, 9

Nothing is more unpleasant than being on a team when nobody wants to be there. When that is the case, the team is usually negative, lethargic, or without hope. If you find yourself in that kind of situation, then do the following:

Investigate the situation—The place to start is by addressing what the team is doing wrong. Begin by fixing what's broken.

Initiate belief—The only way for a team to change is if people believe in themselves. As the leader, you must initiate that belief.

Create energy—The desire to change without the energy to change just frustrates people. To bring a greater level of energy to the team, you need to be energetic. Eventually, your energy will spread.

Communicate hope—The greatest need of players at this stage is hope. Help them to see the potential of the team.

When morale is low, the only way to get the ball rolling is to start pushing it yourself.

The 17 Indisputable Laws of Teamwork

THE IRONY OF SPIRITUAL LEADERSHIP

Trust in the LORD with all your heart, And lean not on your own understanding; In all your ways acknowledge Him, And He shall direct your paths.

PROVERBS 3:5–6

Proverbs chapters 2 and 3 pose an apparent paradox in spiritual leadership. We are to get wisdom and understanding, yet we are not to lean on it apart from the Lord. Even good wisdom divorced from God can become a snare. So how are godly leaders to think? They think:

Big—They realize God's vision is usually bigger than theirs.

Other people—They always include others in the mix.

Continually—They're not satisfied with today's answers.

Bottom line—They want to see results and fruit.

Continual growth—They want to keep improving.

Without lines—They let God outside of the box.

Victory—They want to see God's rule come to earth.

Intuitively—They have a sense of what will work.

Servanthood—They want to serve and add value to people.

Quickly—They evaluate quickly and see possible answers.

The Maxwell Leadership Bible

Coming Together as a Team

Apollos, a native of Alexandria, came to Ephesus...He
began to speak boldly in the synagogue.
When Priscilla and Aquila heard him, they invited
him to their home and explained to him the way
of God more adequately. When Apollos wanted to go
to Achaia, the brothers encouraged him...On arriving,
he was a great help to those who by grace had believed.
Acts 18:24, 26–27 (niv)

As people who care about each other grow together and work toward a common goal, they get to know each other better. They begin to recognize and appreciate each player's unique qualities. And that leads to the development of a team "fit."

A good team fit requires an attitude of partnership. Every team member must respect the other players. They must desire to contribute to the team, and they must come to expect a contribution from every other person. Above all, they must learn to trust each other. Trust makes it possible for people to rely on one another. It allows them to make up for each other's weaknesses instead of trying to exploit them. It enables one team member to say to the other, "You go ahead and do this task because you are better at it than I am," without shame or manipulation. Trust allows the people on the team to begin working as a single unit, to begin accomplishing the things that they together recognize as important.

Developing the Leaders Around You

Bloom Where
You are Planted

The LORD would speak to Moses face to face, as a man
speaks with his friend. Then Moses would return
to the camp, but his young aide Joshua son
of Nun did not leave the tent.

EXODUS 33:11 (NIV)

Rare are the people who begin their careers as stars. And those who do sometimes find that their success is like that of some child actors: After a brief flash in the pan, they are never able to recapture the attention they got early on.

Most successful people go through an apprenticeship or period of seasoning. Look at quarterback Joe Montana, who was inducted into the NFL Hall of Fame in 2000. He spent two years on the bench as a backup before being named the San Francisco 49ers starter. And as he was breaking records and leading his team to Super Bowls, the person who sat on the bench as a backup to him was Steve Young, another great quarterback.

Some talented team members are recognized early for their great potential and are groomed to succeed. Others labor in obscurity for years—learning, growing, and gaining experience. Then after a decade of hard work, they become "overnight successes."

Given the right encouragement, training, and opportunities, nearly anyone with desire has the potential to emerge as an impact player.

The 17 Indisputable Laws of Teamwork

PERSONAL QUALIFICATIONS FOR LEADERSHIP

*Surely the princes of Zoan are fools; Pharaoh's wise
counselors give foolish counsel . . . Let them know
what the LORD of hosts has purposed against Egypt.
The princes of Zoan have become fools; The princes
of Noph are deceived; They have also deluded Egypt,
Those who are the mainstay of its tribes.*

ISAIAH 19:11–13

What qualifies a person to be a leader? Most
natural leaders don't aspire to be great leaders; they
aspire to be great persons. Personal qualifications lead to
leadership qualifications. When leaders lead their own
lives well, others naturally want to follow.

Consider Mother Teresa of Calcutta, India. It's
doubtful she ever said, "I am going to set out to be a great
leader!" Yet that is what she became by determining to be
the person God created her to be.

If we want our leadership to last, we must pay
attention to four crucial elements:

Character—enables us to do what is right even when
it seems difficult.

Perspective—enables us to understand what must
happen to reach a goal.

Courage—enables us to initiate and take risks to step
out toward a worthy goal.

Favor—enables us to attract and empower others to
join us in the cause.

The Maxwell Leadership Bible

A LIVING SACRIFICE

For even the Son of Man did not come to be served, but to serve, and to give His life a ransom for many.

MARK 10:45

If a team doesn't reach its potential, ability is seldom the issue. It's rarely a matter of resources. It's almost always a payment issue. The team fails to reach its potential when it fails to pay the price. If you lead a team, then one of the difficult things you must do is convince your teammates to sacrifice for the good of the group. The more talented the team members, the more difficult it may be to convince them to put the team first.

Begin by modeling sacrifice. Show the team that you are willing to . . .

- Make financial sacrifices for the team.
- Keep growing for the sake of the team.
- Empower others for the sake of the team.
- Make difficult decisions for the sake of the team.

Once you have modeled a willingness to pay your own price for the potential of the team, you have the credibility to ask others to do the same. Then when you recognize sacrifices that teammates must make for the team, show them why and how to do it. Then praise their sacrifices greatly to their teammates.

The 21 Indisputable Laws of Teamwork

COPING WITH
DIFFICULT PEOPLE

Therefore David said to the Gibeonites, "What shall I do for you? And with what shall I make atonement, that you may bless the inheritance of the LORD?"

2 SAMUEL 21:3

Every leader faces difficult people and draining circumstances. The Gibeonites were difficult for David. The following difficult personality types commonly accost leaders today:

PERSONALITY TYPE	COPING STRATEGY
The Sherman Tank: rides over people	Consider the issue; stand up if important
The Space Cadet: lives in another world	Find and develop their unique gifts
The Volcano: explosive, unpredictable	Remove from crowd, listen, be direct
The Thumb Sucker: self–pity, pouts	Don't reward; expose them to real trouble
The Wet Blanket: always down	Be honest, don't cater; don't let them lead
The Garbage Collector: attracts the worst	Challenge their statements; force honesty
The User: demands lots of time, energy	Set boundaries; require accountability

The Maxwell Leadership Bible

MAKING THE MOST OF THE GIFT

If a man's gift is prophesying, let him use it
in proportion to his faith. If it is serving, let him serve;
if it is teaching, let him teach; if it is encouraging,
let him encourage; if it is contributing to the needs
of others, let him give generously; if it is leadership,
let him govern diligently; if it is showing mercy,
let him do it cheerfully.

ROMANS 12:6–8 (NIV)

Just about everyone has experienced being on a team where people had to take on roles that didn't suit them: an accountant forced to work with people all day, a basketball forward forced to play center, a guitarist filling in on keyboard, a teacher stuck doing paperwork, a spouse who hates the kitchen taking on the role of cook.

What happens to a team when members constantly play "out of position"? First, morale erodes because the team isn't playing up to its capability. Then people become resentful. The people working in an area of weakness resent that their best is untapped. And other people on the team who know that they could better fill a mismatched position on the team resent that their skills are being overlooked. Before long, people become unwilling to work as a team. When people aren't where they do things well, things don't turn out well.

The 17 Indisputable Laws of Teamwork

THE VELVET–COVERED BRICK

*Paul, called to be an apostle of Jesus Christ through
the will of God, and Sosthenes our brother,
To the church of God which is at Corinth, to those
who are sanctified in Christ Jesus, called to be saints,
with all who in every place call on the name of Jesus
Christ our Lord, both theirs and ours: Grace to you and
peace from God our Father and the Lord Jesus Christ.*

1 CORINTHIANS 1:1–3

As the human founder of the Corinthian church, Paul had a really big task before him. Paul loved his Corinthian brothers and sisters in Christ. But when he received reports that divisions, immorality, and pride had crept into the church, he knew he had to confront the sin.

Paul felt grieved—perhaps even angered—over the reports he received about his Corinthian colleagues. We can see in his letter the anguish he felt over what has been going on in the church, but we also read of an overriding sense of love and concern for these dear friends.

It was as if Paul were hitting the Corinthian church on the head with a velvet–covered brick—the brick being his condemnation of their sin, the velvet being his love for those whom God had set apart for good works.

It isn't always easy to speak correction to those we know are clearly in the wrong. But the Lord uses strong leaders to correct His people, courageous leaders who can speak the truth in love.

The Maxwell Leadership Bible

See the Heart
and the Potential

*Then Abram fell on his face, and God talked to him,
saying: "As for Me, behold, My covenant is with you,
and you shall be a father of many nations.
No longer shall your name be called Abram,
but your name shall be Abraham.*

GENESIS 17:3–5

I believe every person carries the seed of success. The ability to find another's seed of success takes commitment, diligence, and a genuine desire to focus on others. You have to look at their gifts, temperament, passions, successes, joys, and opportunities. And once you find that seed, you need to fertilize it with encouragement and water it with opportunity. If you do, the person will blossom before your eyes. Raising people to a higher level and helping them be successful is more than just giving them information or skills. The good news is that when you understand some basic concepts about people, it opens the door to your ability to develop others. Remember . . .

Everyone wants to feel worthwhile.

Everyone needs and responds to encouragement.

People are naturally motivated.

People buy into the person before buying into their leadership.

The more you understand people, the greater your chance of success in mentoring.

Your Road Map for Success

LEADERSHIP IN THE HOME

Wives, submit to your own husbands, as to the Lord.
Husbands, love your wives, just as Christ also loved
the church and gave Himself for her. Children,
obey your parents in the Lord, for this is right.

EPHESIANS 5:22 &25, 6:1

Contrary to what many teach, leadership in the home is not about power or control. Paul asks for mutual submission and calls husbands to be Christ–figures. And how did Christ lead the church? He provided, taught, wept, healed, and died on a cross. Spiritual leadership means giving up yourself for someone else. It means assuming responsibility for the health and development of your relationships. Evaluate your home leadership in each of the following categories:

Initiative—Do I give direction and take responsibility for my primary relationships?

Intimacy—Do I experience intimacy with God and others through open conversations?

Influence—Do I exercise biblical influence by encouraging and developing others?

Integrity—Do I lead an honest life, unashamed of who I am when no one is looking?

Identity—Am I secure in who I am in Christ? Or am I defensive?

Inner circle—Do I exhibit the fruit of the Sprit in my life, including self–discipline?

The Maxwell Leadership Bible

BEING BEFORE DOING

Live right, and you will eat from the life–giving tree.
And if you act wisely, others will follow.

PROVERBS 11:30 (CEV)

I believe people tend to think of leadership only in terms of action. But leadership is so much more than just that. Leadership is not just something you do; it's something you are. And that's one of the reasons good leaders have such strong magnetism. People are attracted to who they are.

All leaders desire results, but *being* must precede *doing*. To achieve higher goals, you must *be* a more effective leader. To attract better people, you must *be* a better person yourself. To achieve greater results, you must *be* a person of great character. A common problem occurs when a leader's real identity and the desired results don't match up. But when leaders display consistency of character, competence, and purpose, it makes a powerful statement to the people around them—and it draws those people to them.

If you desire to do great things with your life, then seek to become a better person and a better leader. Nothing great can be achieved alone. Any task worth doing requires the help of others. And if you want to attract good people, you've got to become a better person yourself. If you're willing to do that, then you can leave the results to God.

The 21 Most Powerful Minutes in a Leader's Day

LEADERSHIP IN GOD'S ECONOMY

*Now when Athaliah the mother of Ahaziah saw
that her son was dead, she arose and destroyed
all the royal heirs of the house of Judah.*

2 CHRONICLES 22:10

Some leaders step into positions of power out of love and a sense of mission. Others seek leadership merely to gain power over others and to revel in a smug feeling of superiority. Normally it doesn't take long to determine which sort of leader you've got. It took no time in the case of Athaliah. She would do anything to attain and hold her illegitimate title—including murder her own kin.

Leaders are not given authority to better themselves, to enlarge their income or social status, or to improve their standard of living. They are first and always servants of others. This idea appears throughout the Scripture. Consider what our Lord teaches us about servant leadership:

HUMAN ECONOMY	GOD'S ECONOMY
1. Pursuit of power and prestige.	1. Pursuit of love and service to others.
2. Improve wealth and status of the leader.	2. Improve the welfare of the people.
3. See others as enemies and competitors.	3. See others as brothers who complement.
4. Motive is to remove or kill opposition.	4. Motive is to meet needs and grow the cause.
5. The result: the leader is glorified.	5. The result: God is glorified.

The Maxwell Leadership Bible

HEART OF A CHAMPION

*Everyone who competes in the games goes into strict
training. They do it to get a crown that will not last;
but we do it to get a crown that will last forever.
Therefore, I do not run like a man running aimlessly;
I do not fight like a man beating the air.
No, I beat my body and make it my slave
so that after I have preached to others,
I myself will not be disqualified for the prize.*

1 CORINTHIANS 9:25–27 (NIV)

There is an old saying: Champions don't become champions in the ring—they are merely recognized there. Boxing is a good analogy for leadership development because it is all about daily preparation. Even if a person has natural talent, he has to prepare and train to become successful.

One of the most famous quotes of President Theodore Roosevelt uses a boxing analogy: "It is not the critic who counts, not the man who points out how the strong man stumbled, or where the doer of deeds could have done them better. The credit belongs to the man who is actually in the arena; whose face is marred by dust and sweat and blood; who strives valiantly; who errs and comes short again and again; who knows the great enthusiasms, the great devotions, and spends himself in a worthy cause."

The 21 Irrefutable Laws of Leadership

THREE QUESTIONS
FOR CHRISTIAN LEADERS

By the rivers of Babylon, There we sat down, yea,
we wept when we remembered Zion. We hung our
harps upon the willows in the midst of it. For there
those who carried us away captive asked of us a song.
And those who plundered us requested mirth. Saying,
"Sing us one of the songs of Zion!" How shall we sing
the LORD's song in a foreign land? If I forget you, O
Jerusalem, Let my right hand forget its skill! If I do not
remember you, Let my tongue cling to the roof of my
mouth—If I do not exalt Jerusalem above my chief joy.

PSALM 137:1–6

Three great issues erupt from the lyrics of this psalm: the writer dreams, the writer cries, and the writer sings. No wonder the people wept—the Jews had been exiled to Babylon. No wonder they sang—they could not forget Zion, the land of their birth. No wonder they dreamed—they hoped and prayed for the day of their return home.

These issues pose great questions for every leader:

What do you dream about? What would you do if you had no fear of failure?

What do you cry about? What burdens drive you to become passionate?

What do you sing about? What causes you to rejoice?

The Maxwell Leadership Bible

PRINCIPLE–CENTERED LEADERSHIP

*My son, give attention to my words; Incline your ear to
my sayings. Do not let them depart from your eyes;
Keep them in the midst of your heart; For they are life
to those who find them, And health to all their flesh.
Keep your heart with all diligence, For out of it spring
the issues of life. Put away from you a deceitful mouth,
And put perverse lips far from you. Let your eyes look
straight ahead, And your eyelids look right before you.
Ponder the path of your feet, And let all your ways
be established. Do not turn to the right
or the left; Remove your foot from evil.*

PROVERBS 4:20–27

Leaders who last do not merely react to their culture;
they base their leadership on timeless and universal
principles. They remain relevant because they marry
cultural context to timeless truth. Proverbs 4 encourages
leaders to become principle centered. Verses 20–27 teach us
that God's principles give us three crucial tools:

1. They are a guide; they help us stay on the right path.
2. They are a guard; they keep our hearts and bodies
   protected.
3. They are a gauge; they enable us to evaluate where we are.

Every leader ought to consume God's Word, then put
the truths he or she discovers in the form of principles that
can guide, guard, and gauge his or her life.

The Maxwell Leadership Bible

SAY NO TO THE STATUS QUO

Therefore, if anyone is in Christ,
he is a new creation; old things have passed away;
behold, all things have become new.

2 CORINTHIANS 5:17

Status quo is Latin for "the mess we're in." Leaders see what is, but they also have a vision for what could be. They are never content with things as they are. To be leading, by definition, is to be in front, breaking new ground, conquering new worlds, moving away from the status quo.

Dissatisfaction with the status quo does not mean having a negative attitude or grumbling. It has to do with a willingness to be different and to take risks. A person who refuses to risk change fails to grow. A leader who loves the status quo soon becomes a follower. Raymond Smith of the Bell Atlantic Corporation once remarked, "Taking the safe road, doing your job, and not making any waves may not get you fired (right away, at least), but it sure won't do much for your career or your company over the long haul. We're not dumb. We know that administrators are easy to find and cheap to keep. Leaders—risk takers—are in very short supply. And ones with vision are pure gold."

Risk seems dangerous to many people because they are more comfortable with the old problems versus what it takes to come up with new solutions. The difference is attitude. When you seek out potential leaders, seek people who seek solutions.

Developing the Leaders Around You

INGREDIENTS OF INFLUENCE

*So the children of Israel said to Samuel, "Do not cease
to cry out to the LORD our God for us, that He may
save us from the hand of the Philistines."*

1 SAMUEL 7:8

How did Samuel gain such influence? What made
everyone listen to him? At least three indispensable
qualities gained him the influence he won:

Competence—God blessed Samuel with many gifts.
He heard from the Lord, he could see the future unfold,
and he wisely knew what to do in crisis. His abilities
provided one reason that everyone listened to him.

Character—Unlike Eli, Samuel exuded integrity
and honestly faced each area of his life. People trusted
him and knew that he had Israel's best interests in mind.
They considered Samuel utterly trustworthy and
depended upon him to intercede for them with God.

Connection—Samuel knew how to connect with
people; he spoke their language. He expressed
compassion for their predicaments and brought courage
to their pursuits.

Fortunately for us, the formula for Samuel's success
still works today:

Competence + Character + Connection = Influence

The Maxwell Leadership Bible

SHARE THE DREAM

*Paul, an apostle of Jesus Christ by the will of God,
To the saints who are in Ephesus, and faithful
in Christ Jesus..."*

EPHESIANS 1:1

Any dream worth living is worth sharing with others. The person who shares his dream gets to watch it grow. The synergy of shared ideas often takes it to a whole new level. The dream becomes greater than the person launching it ever imagined it could be. And those who participate in it often adopt it as their own dream.

As you give others an opportunity to share your dream, paint a broad landscape for them so that they can catch your vision. Include . . .

A Horizon—to show the incredible possibilities ahead.

The Sun—to give them warmth and hope.

Mountains—to represent the challenges ahead.

Birds—to inspire them to soar like eagles.

Flowers—to remind them to enjoy the journey.

A Path—to offer direction and security.

Yourself—to demonstrate your commitment to the dream and to them.

Them—to show where they fit in and to communicate your belief in them.

When you are willing to share the dream by including others, there's almost no limit to what you can accomplish. The impossible comes within reach.

Your Road Map for Success

NEVER WORK ALONE

Paul chose Silas and departed, being commended by the brethren to the grace of God. And he went through Syria and Cilicia, strengthening the churches.

ACTS 15:40–41

I want to share a secret with you. It's the greatest principle I've ever learned in the area of developing others. Here it is: Never work alone. I know that sounds too simple, but it is truly the secret to developing others. Whenever you do anything that you want to pass along to others, take someone along with you.

This isn't necessarily a natural practice for many of us. The most common learning model in the United States is when a leader asks questions or lectures while the follower listens and tries to comprehend the instructor's ideas. But craftsmen use a different another model for developing others. They take apprentices who work along side them until they master their craft and are able to pass it along to others. Their model looks something like this:

I do it.

I do it—and you watch.

You do it—and I watch.

You do it.

In all the years I've been equipping and developing others, I've never found a better way to do it than this.

Your Road Map for Success

GIVE YOURSELF,
NOT JUST YOUR OPINION

"I have heard many such things;
Miserable comforters are you all!"

JOB 16:2

Eliphaz, Bidad, and Zophar accused Job of acting foolishly, of speaking wrongly, of leading wickedly. But they never got their message across for two reasons: First, they didn't have all the facts; and second, they didn't practice the Law of Connection.

Many leaders are tempted to make the same mistakes. We voice our opinions even though we remain ignorant of important information and lack any heart connection to our audience. Job called his friends, "miserable comforters." Every good communicator seeks first to understand before being understood. Note how they differ from public speakers:

PUBLIC SPEAKER	COMMUNICATOR
1. Seeks to be understood and liked	1. Seeks to understand and connect
2. Asks: What do I have?	2. Asks: What do they need?
3. Focuses on techniques	3. Focuses on atmosphere
4. Is self–conscious	4. Is audience–oriented
5. Wants to complete the speech	5. Wants to complete the people
6. Content–oriented	6. Change–oriented

The Maxwell Leadership Bible

BE ON PURPOSE

For we are His workmanship,
created in Christ Jesus for good works, which
God prepared beforehand that we should walk in them.

EPHESIANS 2:10

Nothing in life can take the place of knowing your purpose. If you don't try to discover your purpose, you're likely to spend your life doing the wrong things.

I believe that God created every person for a purpose. As psychologist Viktor Frankl said, "Everyone has his own specific vocation or mission in life. Everyone must carry out a concrete assignment that demands fulfillment. Therein he cannot be replaced, nor can his life be repeated. Thus everyone's task is as unique as his specific opportunity to implement it." Each of us has a purpose for which we were created. Our responsibility—and our joy—is to identify it.

Here are some questions to ask yourself to help you identify your purpose:

For what am I searching? All of us have a strong desire set in our hearts, something that speaks to our deepest thoughts and feelings, something that sets our souls on fire.

Why was I created? Think about the unique mix of abilities you have, the resources available to you, your own personal history, and the opportunities around you.

Do I believe in my potential? No one can consistently act in a manner inconsistent with the way he sees himself.

When do I start? The answer to that question is "NOW."

Your Road Map for Success

OCTOBER

Your thoughts determine your character...
The first person you lead is you.

THE FRUIT OF OBEDIENCE

You shall observe My judgments and keep My ordinances,
to walk in them: I am the LORD your God. You shall
therefore keep my statutes and My judgments, which
if a man does, he shall live by them. I am the LORD.

LEVITICUS 18:4–5

God calls His people to live at a standard higher than the unbelievers who surround them. In Leviticus chapters 18, 19 and 20, God reviews His higher standards regarding relationships, religion, and the rights and responsibilities of community members.

Why these higher standards? God intended Israel to be a light and a standard for the rest of the world, and Israel's leaders to be a light and a standard for the Jewish nation. God expects the same of leaders today. Why must we be faithful in keeping a higher standard than the rest of the world? To be like God. To make us qualified for ministry. To guarantee God's blessing on our life. And to receive God's reward for faithfulness.

And what characterizes those who choose to pursue life at God's higher standard?

They adopt godly values.

They care for the interests of others.

They live with integrity.

They keep their word.

They develop their gifts and potential.

They manage time and money well.

They pass on to others what they have received.

The Maxwell Leadership Bible

GROWING TO YOUR POTENTIAL

. . . in which you shine like stars in the universe . . .

PHILIPPIANS 2:15 (NIV)

It's been said that our potential is God's gift to us, and what we do with it is our gift to Him. But our potential is probably our greatest untapped resource. Why? We can do anything, but we can't do everything. Many people never really dedicate themselves to their purpose in life. They become a jack of all trades, master of none—rather than a jack of few trades, focused on one.

Here are four principles to put you on the road to growing toward your potential:

1. *Concentrate on one main goal.* Nobody ever reached their potential by scattering themselves in twenty directions. Reaching your potential requires focus.

2. *Concentrate on continual improvement.* Commitment to continual improvement is the key to reaching our potential. Each day you can become a little bit better than you were yesterday.

3. *Forget the past.* Jack Hayford, pastor of Church on the Way in Van Nuys, California, said, "We can't gain any momentum moving toward tomorrow if we are dragging the past behind us." Maybe you've made a lot of mistakes in your life, or you've had an especially difficult past. Work your way through it and move on.

4. *Focus on the future.* You can become better tomorrow than you are today. As the Spanish proverb says, "He who does not look ahead remains behind."

Your Road Map for Success

IMPORTANCE OF
CLEAR COMMUNICATION

Now Then Samuel said to the people,
"Come, let us go to Gilgal and renew the kingdom
there." So all the people went to Gilgal, and
there they made Saul king before the LORD.

I SAMUEL II:14–15

Leadership resources and studies tell us that having a message doesn't matter if leaders don't know how to communicate that message clearly and motive others. It's amazing how God wired us. We listen to leaders as they fling thoughts and ideas about the room, and then we want to get up and pursue those ideas. That's the power of communication.

Each time Samuel spoke, he followed the rules below:

Simplify the message—He spoke forthrightly, clearly, and simply. No one wondered what he meant.

See the person—He always empathized with others. He knew his audience.

Show the truth—He demonstrated credibility with his passion and his life. He lived what he said.

Seek the response—He always spoke with a purpose. When finished, he urged the people to obey God.

The Maxwell Leadership Bible

A STANDARD OF EXCELLENCE

Those who have served will gain an excellent standing ....
1 TIMOTHY 3:13 (NIV)

The word "competent" sometimes gets used to mean "barely adequate." When I talk about the quality of competence that is desirable in teammates, I mean it in the sense of its root word which means "complete." Competent team members have everything they need to do the job and do it well. People who are highly competent have some things in common:

1. *They are committed to excellence*—John Johnson in Christian Excellence writes, "Success bases our worth on a comparison with others. Excellence gauges our value by measuring us against our own potential."

2. *They never settle for average*—The word "mediocre" literally means "halfway up a stony mountain." Competent people never settle for average or mediocre.

3. *They pay attention to detail*—Dale Carnegie said, "If you do little jobs well, the big ones tend to take care of themselves."

4. *They perform with consistency*—Highly competent people give their best all the time. If 99.9 percent were good enough, then 811,000 faulty rolls of 35mm film would be loaded this year, 22,000 checks would be deducted from the wrong bank accounts in the next 60 minutes, and twelve babies would be given to the wrong parents today alone.

The 17 Essential Qualities of a Team Player

BE WILLING TO STAND UP

Hear me, O LORD, hear me, that
this people may know that You are the LORD God, and
that You have turned their hearts back to You again.

1 KINGS 18:37

The prophet Elijah knew about the idolatry of Israel and the wickedness of King Ahab. He knew the time for judgment had arrived. And he also knew that drought and famine were about to devastate Israel. He knew because he himself had announced God's judgment.

This all took place during a very sad time in the history of Israel, when the people had all but turned their backs on God and their king sinned openly and boldly. Elijah, consumed with holy indignation, prayed that it might not rain in Israel—and for more than three years, not a drop of rain fell. Streams dried up, crops failed, and people starved.

Later, all alone, the prophet stood on Mt. Carmel among 450 prophets of Baal, proving the impotence of their false god. In a spectacular demonstration of the power of the one true God, Elijah called fire down from heaven—and then directed the execution of Baal's priests.

Imagine the courage it took for one solitary man to pray for judgment on his own people, confront a wicked king, then stand before hundreds of false prophets and challenge their piety! Although the Lord took Elijah to heaven long ago, this courageous prophet still proclaims today that true leadership may mean standing alone and speaking difficult truth.

The Maxwell Leadership Bible

DO THE LITTLE THINGS
TO MAINTAIN MOMENTUM

These things I have spoken to you, that in Me you may
have peace. In the world you will have tribulation; but
be of good cheer, I have overcome the world.

JOHN 16:33

When your people are winning and morale is high,
you still have an important role as a leader. To help
the team maintain high morale and momentum . . .

Keep the team focused and on course—If team
members lose focus or get off course, then they'll
stop winning.

Communicate successes—Nothing boosts morale like
winning and then celebrating it.

Remove morale mashers—Once the team is rolling in
the right direction, keep it rolling. Leaders see
before others do, so they need to protect the team
from the things that will hurt the team.

Allow other leaders to lead—When a leader prepares
other team members to lead and then turns them
loose to do it, two things result. First, it uses the
existing momentum to create new leaders for the
team. It's easier to make new leaders successful if
they are part of a successful team. Second, it
increases the leadership of the team. And that
makes the team even more successful.

The process of building high morale is simple, but it
isn't easy. It takes strong leadership, and it takes time.

The 17 Indisputable Laws of Teamwork

IT'S NOT ABOUT POSITION

But the midwives feared God, and did not do as the king of Egypt commanded them, but saved the male children alive . . . Therefore God dealt well with the midwives, and the people multiplied and grew very mighty.

EXODUS 1:17, 20

Who changes the course of history? Kings? Potentates? Generals? The wealthy? Sure. But more often than not, men and women with little social standing most significantly reshape this world.

When the king of Egypt grew worried about the exploding numbers of Hebrew slaves, he summoned two midwives, Shiphrah and Puah, and instructed them to murder all Hebrew male newborns. But these midwives feared God and refused to obey such a wicked command. Despite the king's threats, they would not buckle under and continued to deliver healthy male Hebrews. Although they had no way of knowing it, their risky decision helped to spare the life of Moses, Israel's God–ordained deliverer.

In civil disobedience, Shiphrah and Puah risked their lives to protect the children God had placed in their care. Their bravery prompted God to show them kindness by blessing them with families of their own. No doubt their children and grandchildren took part in the great exodus from Egypt.

The Maxwell Leadership Bible

BE FIRST TO TAKE
YOUR GOOD ADVICE

My son, pay attention to my wisdom; Lend your ear to my understanding. That you may preserve discretion, And your lips may keep knowledge. For the lips of an immoral woman drip honey, And her mouth is smoother than oil; Remove your way far from her, And do not go near the door of her house, Lest you give your honor to others, And your years to the cruel one.

PROVERBS 5:1–3 & 8–9

It doesn't take a leader very long to realize that it's easier to give good advice than to follow it. Solomon proves the point. He tells us repeatedly and with great conviction that only fools fall into adultery. Solomon knew very well the spiritual issues at stake in marriage, for he declares, "The ways of man are before the eyes of the LORD, and He ponders all his paths" (Proverbs 5:21).

And yet, somehow, this same leader failed to heed God's explicit warning against kings taking many wives (Deuteronomy 17:17). Solomon blatantly disobeyed this command and married *seven hundred* women. The result? "His wives turned his heart after other gods; and his heart was not loyal to the LORD his God" (1 Kings 11:4).

Wise leaders not only give good advice; they heed it. How different the fortunes of Israel might have turned out had Solomon acted on the wisdom he so forcefully expressed to others!

The Maxwell Leadership Bible

GOD LEADS, WE FOLLOW

Now when they had gone through Phrygia and the region of Galatia, they were forbidden by the Holy Spirit to preach the word in Asia. After they had come to Mysia, they tried to go into Bithynia, but the Spirit did not permit them. So passing by Mysia, they came down to Troas. And a vision appeared to Paul in the night. A man of Macedonia stood and pleaded with him, saying, "Come over to Macedonia and help us." Now after he had seen the vision, immediately we sought to go to Macedonia, concluding that the Lord had called us to preach the gospel to them.

ACTS 16:6–10

All leaders need discernment. Paul had it and he used it to select new leaders, to size up what to say in a courtroom, and to know where to go next on his missionary trips. As Paul's team traveled through Asia, he must have been listening to the Holy Spirit in his quiet times. God prevented him from speaking any more in Asia and compelled him to move on. Next, the Spirit forbade Paul to minister in Mysia and Bithynia. In Troas, he had a vision in which a man begged him to visit Macedonia. Such was the dynamic leadership of God.

Discerning leaders usually share these common traits:

good listeners	flexible
intuitive	optimistic
well-networked	perceptive

The Maxwell Leadership Bible

A HOUSE DIVIDED

Ishbosheth, Saul's son, was forty years old when he
began to reign over Israel, and he reigned two years.
Only the house of Judah followed David.

2 SAMUEL 2:10

Saul's death led to all kinds of turmoil over who
would become the next king. Despite David's
anointing by Samuel, others saw a tempting opportunity
to seize power.

Transitions often bring difficult times. Leaders who
fail to plan for their departure invite trouble. Saul could
have been a hero had he cooperated with God in
preparing David to succeed him. He didn't have a more
submissive staff person in his entire palace than David.

Saul suffered from an "I" problem, and oversized ego
that blinded him. Saul could've helped himself had he
recognized these truths:

1. Because change makes people insecure, leaders must
   see ahead and prepare for them.

2. People can live without certainty, but not without
   clarity regarding future direction.

3. Wise choices today put "change in the pocket" of a
   leader regarding future choices.

4. Problem–solving skills and effective communication
   earn the leader trust and credibility.

The Maxwell Leadership Bible

ALARM BELLS FOR LEADERS

Do not be deceived, God is not mocked; for whatever a man sows, that he will also reap. For he who sows to his flesh will of the flesh reap corruption, but he who sows to the Spirit will of the Spirit reap everlasting life. And let us not grow weary while doing good, for in due season we shall reap if we do not lose heart. Therefore, as we have opportunity, let us do good to all, especially to those who are of the household of faith.

GALATIANS 6:7–10

We can't pull a fast one on God. He sees all and cannot be deceived. He notices our shortcuts and also our efforts when we do well. To ensure that we live by this truth, seek others to hold you accountable and act as your "alarm bells." Invite others to ask you tough questions, such as the following:

Is my personal walk with God up–to–date?

Am I keeping my priorities straight?

Am I asking myself the hard questions?

Am I accountable to someone in authority?

Am I sensitive to what God is saying to the whole body of Christ?

Am I over–concerned with building my image?

Do I put more stock in "events" rather than "process"?

Am I a loner in my leadership and personal life?

Am I aware and honest about my weaknesses?

Is my calling constantly before me?

The Maxwell Leadership Bible

LEADING ACROSS CULTURES

*Thus says Cyrus king of Persia: All the kingdoms of the
earth the LORD God of heaven has given me. And He
has commanded me to build Him a house at Jerusalem
which is in Judah. Who is among you of all His people?
May his God be with him, and let him go up to
Jerusalem which is in Judah, and build the house of the
LORD God of Israel (He is God), which is in Jerusalem.
And whoever is left in any place where he dwells, let
the men of his place help him with silver and gold,
with goods and livestock, besides the freewill offerings
for the house of God which is in Jerusalem.*

EZRA 1:2–4

Unlike King Rehoboam, the Persian king Cyrus
was able to connect with God's people. He first
displayed mercy and then identified with the values and
heart of his people. What enabled King Cyrus to connect
with the people? Ezra tells us he exhibited . . .

1. *Humility*—He realized his power came from God and
   should honor God.
2. *Responsibility*—He felt strongly he should build a
   place of worship for the Jews.
3. *Empowerment*—He allowed those who had a heart to
   build to fulfill their call.
4. *Resources*—He issued a decree to support the builders.
5. *Stewardship*—He managed people's gifts.
6. *Priorities*—He valued what the people valued.

The Maxwell Leadership Bible

CHARACTER BEFORE TALENT

For the ways of man are before the eyes of the LORD,
And He ponders all his paths. His own iniquities
entrap the wicked man, And he is caught in the cords
of his sin. He shall die for lack of instruction,
And in the greatness of his folly he shall go astray.

PROVERBS 5:21–23

How many leaders have ruined their lives and damaged the lives of others through immorality? Character has become a crucial issue today precisely because of the myriad leaders in the political, business, and religious worlds who have fallen morally. No doubt they fall partly because the enemy has targeted leaders for attack. Leaders need to remember that they influence many others beyond themselves; they never fall in a vacuum. They also need to realize that replacing fallen leaders is a slow and difficult process.

So how can we guard against falling? First, we must take care not to emphasize the gifts of a leader over his or her character. We have unhealthy tendency to see and reward the gift more than the character, but both are to be developed. We must strike the following balance if we are to finish well: Gift Deposited = Character Built.

WHAT I AM	WHAT I DO	THE RESULT
Humble	Rely on God	God's Power
Visionary	Set Goals	High Morale
Convictional	Do Right	Credibility

The Maxwell Leadership Bible

THE FIRST PRINCIPLE
OF WISDOM

The LORD appeared to Solomon in a dream by night;
and God said, "Ask! What shall I give you."
And Solomon said . . . "Give to Your servant an
understanding heart to judge Your people,
that I may discern between good and evil."

1 KINGS 3:5–6, 9

Near the beginning of Solomon's reign, God approached the young king with a proposal: Ask Me for anything you want. Much to God's delight, Solomon didn't ask for great riches, respect among world leaders, or an invincible nation. Solomon asked for wisdom, and God answered abundantly.

The Bible tells us that the Lord gave the king "wisdom and exceedingly great understanding, and largeness of heart like the sand on the seashore," and that his wisdom exceeded that of any other man. Solomon's expansive mind explored the disciplines of botany, zoology, and music, and pondered topics ranging from economics to communication to love. The wisdom of King Solomon helped Israel to prosper greatly. Solomon himself amassed wealth greater than all the kings of his time.

But by the end of his reign, this brilliant king somehow forgot the first principle of wisdom: "The fear of the LORD is the beginning of wisdom." (Psalm 111:10). Only wisdom energized by a vibrant walk with God makes godly leaders.

The Maxwell Leadership Bible

CONFRONTATION RESULTS IN PURITY AND SECURITY

For I indeed, as absent in body but present in spirit,
have already judged (as though I was present)
him who has so done this deed.

1 CORINTHIANS 5:3

Paul had to confront the problems the Corinthians faced, especially the issue of incest in the church. Unfortunately, the leaders failed to deal with this sin. Paul therefore instructs leaders in how to deal with a member who rebels against a life of obedience to the Lord.

Why is confrontation so difficult? We often misunderstand its purpose. Our goal among brothers should not be to punish or excommunicate, but to restore. Confrontation is a redemptive act of leadership. So what are the goals of healthy confrontation?

Clarification—I will get a better understanding of the person and what happened.

Change—I hope to get improvement from it. And it may be me!

Relationship—I will likely deepen my relationship with this person.

Purity—As word gets out, the organization will be purified and sobered.

Respect—The organization will likely raise the members' level of respect for the leadership.

Security—People feel safe knowing leaders are strong enough to take a stand.

The Maxwell Leadership Bible

DISCOUNT YOUR DISTRACTERS

Now it happened, when Sanballat, Tobiah, the Arabs,
the Ammonites, and the Ashdodites heard that the walls
of Jerusalem were being restored and the gaps were
beginning to be closed, that they became very angry,
and all of them conspired together to come and attack
Jerusalem and create confusion. Nevertheless we made
our prayer to our God, and because of them we set
a watch against them day and night.

NEHEMIAH 4:7–9

Nehemiah had to contend with the same kind of pest that plagues most true leaders today: distracters who torment and do everything possible to interfere with work. Sanballat first tried to stop the work by mocking and ridiculing the Jews. When that didn't work, he shifted his tactics to fear, entrapment, and political maneuvering. The contrast between Nehemiah and Sanballat could hardly be more pronounced. Nehemiah's leadership and character countered every assault of Sanballat and provided the impetus for his godly vision to be completed.

Contemporary leaders can learn several valuable lessons from studying Sanballat's assaults, threats, and schemes:

Expect distracters.

Don't give them the time of day.

Trust God to protect you and your reputation.

Keep your hands to the plow and don't look back.

The Maxwell Leadership Bible

SECURITY IS FOUND IN THE LORD, NOT IN FOLLOWERS

Unless the LORD builds the house, They labor in vain who build it; Unless the LORD guards the city, The watchman stays awake in vain.

PSALM 127:1

Unless God remains at the center of your efforts, you labor in vain. Whether we lead in the military, in construction, or sit behind a desk, we cannot fight, build, or plan well enough to gain anything permanent. Smart leaders not only include God in their strategy, they place Him at its center. He alone can provide leaders with security; we cannot get it from followers. Consider the following list of rules regarding security and people:

People cannot provide permanent security for a leader.

Leaders should never put their emotional health in the hands of someone else.

Spiritual and emotional health requires the truth.

Leaders must remember that hurting people naturally hurt people.

Trouble arises when leaders depend on people to do what only God can do. *The Maxwell Leadership Bible*

GUARD YOUR THINKING

*For as he thinks in his heart, so is he . . . Do not speak
in the hearing of a fool, For he will despise the wisdom
of your words . . . Apply your heart to instruction,
And your ears to words of knowledge . . . Do not let
your heart envy sinners, But be zealous for the fear
of the LORD all the day; For surely there is a hereafter,
And your hope will not be cut off. Hear, my son,
and be wise; And guide your heart in the way.*

PROVERBS 23:7, 9, 12, 17–19

Leaders understand the importance of their minds
to the future of their organizations. Consider some
of these timeless principles offered in Proverbs 23 about
our minds and a godly vision for tomorrow.

Your thoughts determine your character.

Be careful of your thoughts; they may break into
words at any time.

Don't waste your thoughts on those who don't
hunger for them.

The first person you lead is you, and the first organ
you master is your mind.

Don't let your mind drift away from God's truth and
into vain envy.

Stay confident that your vision will come to pass.

Discipline your thoughts to remain steadfast in what
you know is right.

The Maxwell Leadership Bible

WHAT IS YOUR ROLE?

*Then he turned his face toward the wall, and prayed
to the LORD, saying, "Remember now, O LORD, I pray,
how I have walked before You in truth and with
a loyal heart, and have done what was good in Your
sight." And Hezekiah wept bitterly.*

2 KINGS 20:2–3

Hezekiah was only one of two kings in Judah who completely followed the Lord. In the days of Esarhaddon king of Assria, Hezekiah lay on his deathbed. Isaiah the prophet had predicted the king's imminent death and told him to get his house in order. But Hezekiah poured out his heart to the Lord and reminded God of His covenant, and how the king had faithfully led Judah. As Isaiah left the royal court, God heard Hezekiah's prayer and determined to heal him. God kept the king alive for another fifteen years.

God did for the king what Hezekiah could not do for himself. Both God and Hezekiah knew their roles:

HEZEKIAH'S ROLE	GOD'S ROLE
1. Maintain a humble heart.	1. Demonstrate grace and power.
2. Submit to God's values.	2. Control the destiny of the land.
3. Ask God to meet needs.	3. Respond to needs of people.
4. Stay faithful to the covenant.	4. Stay faithful to the covenant.

The Maxwell Leadership Bible

A Leader Passes the Baton

*So he died in a good old age, full of days and riches
and honor; and Solomon his son reigned in his place.*

1 CHRONICLES 29:28

As his life was ebbing away, David prepared his son
Solomon to give oversight to the construction of
the temple. The old king was determined to ensure his
legacy by setting up the next leader and committing him
to the care of God Almighty. Look closely at what he did:

1. He rallied all the people together.
2. He affirmed God's choice of his successor.
3. He identified the great need for help.
4. He reminded the people of his own commitment.
5. He declared that the people were well on their way to
   the goal.
6. He asked for commitment.

The people loved this old king, and they knew he was
not asking them to do anything that he had not already
demonstrated an eagerness to complete himself. Because
people do what people see, David was able to motivate the
Israelites to do three things:

Sacrificially give toward the temple project.

Support Solomon and his leadership.

Rejoice in what God was doing among them.

The Maxwell Leadership Bible

GAINING AUTHORITY IN CHRIST

But God, who is rich in mercy, because of His great love with which He loved us, even when we were dead in trespasses, made us alive together with Christ, and raised us up together, and made us sit together in the heavenly places in Christ Jesus.

EPHESIANS 2:4–6

Paul took time to reflect on past human failures and God's present redemption. He insisted that God not only raised Jesus up and sat Him in heavenly places above all authority, but He did the same for all of us. We must identify with Christ in His life, death, resurrection, and ascension. We have been raised with Christ. No wonder Paul could lead with such boldness! He lived and led based on this paramount truth. What must we do to experience the same kind of authority in Christ?

Renew your perspective—We must see ourselves as He does and fix our minds on Him. We must base our life on this position rather than our experience.

Release your past—We must let go of old patterns. We will never lead in an empowering way if we hold on to our old self, our old baggage, our old citizenship. We must die to the past.

Remember your purpose—We drift when we lose sight of why God left us on earth. Our goal is to participate in God's redemptive plan for the world. If we embrace purpose, we gain power.

The Maxwell Leadership Bible

LEADERS CANNOT SHOW THE WAY UNTIL THEY KNOW THE WAY

Blessed are the undefiled in the way, Who walk in the law of the LORD! Blessed are those who keep His testimonies, Who seek Him with the whole heart! They also do no iniquity; They walk in His ways.

PSALM 119:1-3

The longest chapter in the Bible is a song about the priority of the Word of God. For 176 verses, Psalm 119 holds high the words and wisdom of God and convinces us to treasure it more than anything else in life.

Why is this so crucial for us? Leaders in our world face two realities:

1. Change happens faster than ever, so leaders must remain adaptable.

2. We need timeless values more than ever, so leaders must remain principle-driven.

Consider what Psalm 119 teaches about God's Word as our source for leadership principles. Our leadership will...

be blessed	remain pure and ethical
be strengthened and revitalized	insightfully answer criticism
enjoy liberty	gain wise counsel when needed
remain steady even when afflicted	display more insight than our teachers
be enlightened, intuitive	have a reliable guide

The Maxwell Leadership Bible

READ THE NEED, THEN LEAD

If your enemy is hungry, give him bread to eat;
And if he is thirsty, give him water to drink;
For so you will heap coals of fire on his head,
And the LORD will reward you.

PROVERBS 25:21–22

Leaders need to respond to individuals based on their needs rather than their faults. The Lord encourages us to see what others need—even our enemies—and respond accordingly.

Good leaders do this well. They don't lead out of a predetermined package of behaviors, but size up every situation and discern what must happen to reach the desired goal. Like a quarterback who reads the defense, then calls an audible from the line of scrimmage, good leaders remain flexible and may change their response, based not on what a person deserves, but on what they need to succeed. Good leaders follow this path in difficult situations:

They *need*—They aren't afraid to admit they need to listen and get understanding.

They *read*—They evaluate what has happened and what steps are best to take.

They *feed*—They communicate what they've observed to key players.

They *heed*—They act on the basis of their discovery, even if it means change.

They *lead*—They provide direction to those involved.

The Maxwell Leadership Bible

WHEN YOUR PRIORITIES
ARE RIGHT . . .

Then God said to Solomon: "Because this was in your heart, and you have not asked riches or wealth or honor or the life of your enemies, nor have you asked long life—but have asked wisdom and knowledge for yourself, that you may judge My people over whom I have made you king—wisdom and knowledge are granted to you; and I will give you riches and wealth and honor, such as none of the kings have had who were before you, nor shall any after you have the like."

2 CHRONICLES 1:11–12

Every leader must establish a list of priorities, then learn to put first things first. When Solomon became king of Israel, he was given the opportunity to ask God for anything. No doubt, King Solomon faced the same options we have today:

1. Easy things first—He could've chosen to focus on the easy tasks ahead of him.

2. Fun things first—He could've chosen to focus on riches or fame.

3. Urgent things first—He could've asked for help in building the temple.

4. Hard things first—He could've sought favor with those who didn't like him.

5. First things first—Instead, he chose to seek wisdom so he could glorify God.

The Maxwell Leadership Bible

REFORM BEGINS WITHIN

Now it happened, when the king heard the words
of the Book of the Law, that he tore his clothes.

2 KINGS 22:11

Throughout his thirty–one years of godly leadership, King Josiah wholeheartedly followed the Lord and devoted himself to leading the people well. His own spiritual passion soon began to influence Judah and eventually brought about public reform.

Even today Josiah remains a vivid example of a key biblical principle: Outward reform begins with inward renewal. The leader must experience personal change before he or she can implement public change. Leaders make an impact the same way an atomic bomb does: They implode before they explode.

How did the young king "implode" before he "exploded"? After ten years on the throne, while he was still a teenager, Josiah sent several men to the high priest to re–energize the process of repairing the temple. While cleaning up the rubble, the high priest found "the Book of the Law." Shaphan the scribe read it, then reported its contents to the young king. And how did Josiah respond? He imploded. He ripped his clothes. His tender heart and humility prompted him to embark on a national program of spiritual reform. The cycle worked this way for King Josiah:

Personal Renewal >>> Personal Change >>> Public Change Implemented >>> Public Reform

The Maxwell Leadership Bible

SUBMIT TO
GOD–GIVEN AUTHORITY

Let every soul be subject to the governing authorities.
For there is no authority except from God, and
the authorities that exist are appointed by God.
Therefore whoever resists the authority resists
the ordinance of God, and those who resist
will bring judgement on themselves.

ROMANS 13:1–2

Paul gets practical in how to apply our beliefs to our lives by challenging us to submit to God–given authorities. For children, this means parents; for adults, this means leaders in government, the workplace, and the church.

Why should we so submit? Is it because these leaders are the smartest, most reliable individuals on earth? No. God simply provides us with an authority test. Before we will ever become leaders of integrity, we must learn to follow other leaders, regardless of differences. In fact, the acid test of character comes when we disagree with legitimate authorities. When we refuse to demand our own way and instead submit to others, our hearts are right. This is when God can trust us to lead others.

The Maxwell Leadership Bible

LEADERSHIP LESSONS
FROM AN ANT

*Go to the ant, you sluggard! Consider her ways
and be wise, which, having no captain, overseer
or ruler, provides her supplies in the summer,
and gathers her food in the harvest.*

PROVERBS 6:6–8

Do you want to make a difference? Then pay
attention to the metaphor of the ant. It's amazing
that one of the smallest of God's creatures can become one
of His greatest teachers. The lessons the ant teaches us can
be summarized this way:

A—Attitude of Initiative

Ants don't need a commander to tell them to get
started.

N—Nature of Integrity

Ants work faithfully and need no outside
accountability to keep them doing right.

T—Thirst for Industry

Ants work hard and will replace their anthill when it
gets ruined.

S—Source of Insight

Ants store provisions in summer.

If we consider and learn from the ways of the ant, we
can grow wise.

The Maxwell Leadership Bible

ABUSE OF POWER

*And he wrote in the letter, saying, "Set Uriah in the
forefront of the hottest battle, and retreat from him,
that he may be struck down and die."*

2 SAMUEL 11:15

Pittacus wrote, "The measure of a man is what he
does with power. Second Samuel 11 tells the story
of a king who forgot that leaders wield power for one
reason only—to serve. Consider the "Path to Abusive
Power" in leaders:

Stage One: Surprise—"I get this?"

Stage Two: Self–Esteem—"I need this."

Stage Three: Satisfaction—"I deserve this."

Stage Four: Selfishness—"I demand this."

By watching King David weave a tangled web
following his sin with Bathsheba, we notice five common
abuses of power that still trip up leaders today. Calvin
Miller describes them this way:

1. Drifting away from those disciplines we still demand
   of our people.
2. Believing that others owe us whatever use we can
   make of them.
3. Attempting to fix things up rather than make things
   right.
4. Refusing to accept that we could be blindly out of
   God's will.
5. Believing that people in our way are expendable.

The Maxwell Leadership Bible

DECEPTION, MORE OFTEN THAN MISTAKES, DISQUALIFIES LEADERS

For I acknowledge my transgressions,
and my sin is always before me. Against You,
You only, have I sinned, and done this evil in Your
sight—that You may be found just when You speak,
and blameless when You judge.

PSALM 51:3-4

David wrote Psalm 51 shortly after he committed adultery with Bathsheba and had Uriah killed. When Nathan confronted him about his sin, the king fell to the floor and wept in bitter repentance. He publicly sought restoration as a king and as a spiritual man, as the psalm demonstrates. Because of his repentant heart, God allowed him to remain in office until he died.

Why then, are some leaders removed from office when they fail morally? The answer may lie in the way David maintained his trust in God. Those who do not repent after some failure—or who do so only for public show—often lose their positions. Some sins no doubt disqualify leaders from continuing in leadership, but more fail in leadership from their deceptions than from their mistakes. History teaches that the public usually forgives a leader who owns up to his mistakes, but refuses to forgive those who remain unrepentant.

When a leader deceives the people, they will no longer follow him or her.

The Maxwell Leadership Bible

WHEN PEOPLE ARE ESTEEMED, RELATIONSHIPS ARE REDEEMED

Do not boast about tomorrow, For you do not know what a day may bring forth...Wrath is cruel and anger a torrent, But who is able to stand before jealousy? Open rebuke is better Than love carefully concealed. Faithful are the wounds of a friend, But the kisses of an enemy are deceitful...Like a bird that wanders from its nest is a man who wanders from his place....Do not forsake your own friend or your father's friend... As iron sharpens iron, So a man sharpens the countenance of his friend...The refining pot is for silver and the furnace for gold, And a man is valued by what others say of him.

PROVERBS 27:1, 4–6, 8, 17, 21

Leaders know that people are an organization's most appreciable asset; therefore, people skills are a leader's most important attribute. Proverbs 27 presents some fundamentals on relationships. It teaches that if people are esteemed, relationships are redeemed.

1. *Don't brag.*
2. *Don't envy.*
3. *Be forthright.*
4. *Don't forsake your roots.*
5. *Stay close.*
6. *Add value.*
7. *Don't be moved by flattery.*

The Maxwell Leadership Bible

THE DANGER OF
TOO MANY PURSUITS

Whatever my eyes desired I did not keep from them.
I did not withhold my heart from any pleasure,
For my heart rejoiced in all my labor;
And this was my reward from all my labor.
Then I looked on all the works that my hands had done
and on the labor in which I had toiled;
And indeed all was vanity and grasping
for the wind. There was no profit under the sun.

ECCLESIASTES 2:10–11

We can learn from Solomon's costly mistakes. The king of Israel fervently pursued several unrelated goals in a vain attempt to satisfy himself. And by the time Solomon wrote these words, he had reached a high level of success—but still felt empty. The axiom remains true: If you chase two rabbits, both will escape.

How about you? Do you have a way of determining your focus, based on what really matters or what really counts? Consider the following checklist as you make decisions about where to invest your time and energy. When faced with a decision, ask yourself:

Is this consistent with my priorities?

Is this within my area of competence?

Can someone else do it better?

What do my trusted friends say?

Do I have the time?

The Maxwell Leadership Bible

November

People don't care how
much you know until they know
how much you care.

LEARN FROM
A MASTER COMMUNICATOR

Then Paul stood in the midst of the Areopagus and said, "Men of Athens, I perceive that in all things you are very religious; for as I was passing through and considering the objects of your worship, I even found an altar with this inscription: TO THE UNKNOWN GOD Therefore, the One whom you worship without knowing, Him I proclaim to you.

ACTS 17:22–23

In the four sermons that Luke records in the book of Acts, Peter, Stephen, and Paul all practiced the Law of Connection, which says that leaders touch a heart before they ask for a hand. Paul's sermon recorded in Acts 17 is a masterpiece. He connected brilliantly with people from a different culture, showing he understood both Greek society and human needs. Notice how a master communicator connected with his audience:

He began with affirmation.

He bridged his subjects with the familiar.

He enlarged their vision of God.

He used inclusive language.

He gave them encouragement and hope.

He identified with some of their own poets.

He gave them specific action steps.

Only when Paul had built relational bridges with the people, did he issue a clear call to repent.

The Maxwell Leadership Bible

See the Leader, Know the Followers

*When the righteous are in authority, the people rejoice;
But when a wicked man rules, the people groan . . .
The king establishes the land by justice, but he who
receives bribes overthrows it . . . The righteous considers
the cause of the poor, but the wicked does not
understand such knowledge . . . If a ruler pays
attention to lies, all his servants become wicked . . .
Where there is no revelation, the people cast off
restraint; but happy is he who keeps the law.*

PROVERBS 29:2, 4, 7, 12, 18

People reflect their leader. We cannot expect followers to grow beyond their leader. We cannot expect followers to turn out fundamentally different from their leader. Consider what Proverbs tells us about the influence of good and bad leaders:

Attitudes—When good leaders rule, people rejoice; when the wicked reign, people groan.

Stability—When moral leaders rule, they establish justice; compromising leaders tear things down.

Compassion—Good leaders express concern for the poor; bad leaders reflect no compassion for anyone.

Honesty—When leaders pay attention to lies, their staff begins to esteem the same deceptions.

Vision—Solid vision keeps everyone on track; chaos reigns wherever the vision lapses.

The Maxwell Leadership Bible

THE TWO GO TOGETHER

Be kindly affectionate to one another with brotherly love, in honor giving preference to one another; not lagging in diligence, fervent in spirit, serving the Lord.
ROMANS 12:10–11

Many leaders commit the error of separating leadership from relationships. This happens when people step into leadership positions and assume that everyone will follow them because of their position. Some leaders wrongly believe that their knowledge alone qualifies them to lead others. People don't care how much you know until they know how much you care. We cannot separate leadership from relationships. Leaders help themselves by developing good relational skills.

Paul instructs us how to lead through relationships:
Avoid hypocrisy.
Be loyal to colleagues.
Give preference to others.
Be hospitable.
Return good for evil.
Identify with others.
Be open–minded toward others.
Treat everyone with respect.
Do everything possible to keep peace.
Remove revenge from your life.

The Maxwell Leadership Bible

BROKER TALENT
FOR TEAM–BUILDING

There are diversities of gifts, but the same Spirit.
There are differences of ministries, but the same Lord.
And there are diversities of activities, but it is
the same God who works all in all.

1 CORINTHIANS 12:4–6

Leaders aren't supposed to do all the work of the church, but are to effectively broker the talent on their team. Good teams use every gift and enjoy both unity and diversity. Consider Paul's philosophy of team building:

The team possesses a variety of gifts or positions, but pursues the same goal and God.

Everyone has a contribution to make.

God is the source of each gift, so He deserves the glory.

God chooses who has what gifts, so we must not compete or compare.

Team members are to function like the organs and muscles in a body.

No team member is less important than another.

God's goal is team harmony and mutual care.

Although members are equally important, they are meant to be diverse.

We should not compete with each other, but complete each other.

The Maxwell Leadership Bible

GIVE YOUR ALL

Thus Jehu destroyed Baal from Israel. However Jehu did not turn away from the sins of Jeroboam the son of Nebat, who had made Israel sin, that is, from the golden calves that were at Bethel and Dan.

2 KINGS 10:28–29

Call him a man with a mission. Jehu not only accepted a charge from God to lead Israel as king, he also embraced divine instructions to destroy the house of Ahab and the worship of Baal. God told him not to spare anyone from Ahab's family and to eliminate all traces of Baal worship in Israel. Jehu led brilliantly in fulfilling God's commands, and God commended Jehu for carrying out his mission, even promising him great blessing because of his obedience.

But a problem eventually arose. While Jehu obeyed God to the last detail concerning the destruction of Ahab and the worship of Baal, he compromised his devotion to God by leaving intact some idols from Israel's past. Even after such great success, "Jehu took no heed to walk in the law of the Lord God of Israel with all his heart."

Jehu accomplished great things for the Lord and the kingdom of Israel, but his compromise led to another vile form of idolatry. In the end, his disobedience overshadowed his accomplishments as a leader.

The Maxwell Leadership Bible

LEADING FROM
THE INSIDE OUT

A good woman is hard to find,
and worth far more than diamonds.
PROVERBS 31:10 (THE MESSAGE)

Proverbs 31 no doubt gets more air–time on Mother's Day than any other passage of Scripture. The majority of the proverb describes a virtuous woman who leads her home with integrity, discipline, and giftedness. Like all leaders, this wife and mother is a leader not because she tries to be one, but because of *who she is.*

HER ASSETS

1. She is trustworthy.
2. She is a positive influence.
3. She is a hard worker.
4. She is a planner.
5. She is protective.

HER ACHIEVEMENTS

1. She meets the needs of her home.
2. She invests for her household.
3. She keeps herself in shape.
4. She helps her husband become successful.

HER ATTITUDES

1. Delightful
2. Healthy
3. Compassionate
4. Unselfish
5. Public

HER APPLAUSE

1. From her family
2. From her husband
3. From God's Word
4. From her works

The Maxwell Leadership Bible

LEADERSHIP AND
THE FRUIT OF THE SPIRIT

But the fruit of the Spirit is love, joy, peace,
longsuffering, kindness, goodness, faithfulness,
gentleness, self–control. Against such there is no law.
GALATIANS 5:22–23

Probably the most memorable verses in Galatians are those that list the "fruit of the Spirit." Fruit grows from planted seeds. Every leader should embrace this marvelous list of inward qualities. Evaluate yourself against them:

Love—Is my leadership motivated by love for people?

Joy—Do I exhibit an unshakable joy, regardless of life's circumstances?

Peace—Do people see my peace and take courage?

Longsuffering—Do I wait patiently for results as I develop people or goals?

Kindness—Am I caring and understanding toward everyone I meet?

Goodness—Do I want the best for others and the organization?

Faithfulness—Have I kept my commitments?

Gentleness—Is my strength under control? Can I be both tough and tender?

Self–Control—Am I disciplined to make progress toward my goals?

The Maxwell Leadership Bible

LIFTING THE LID

"Also, in time past, when Saul was king over us, you
were the one who led Israel out and brought them in;
and the LORD said to you, 'You shall shepherd
My people Israel, and be ruler over Israel'."

2 SAMUEL 5:2

Why did Saul fail as Israel's king, while David succeeded? The answer can be found in the Law of the Lid. Leadership ability is the lid that determines a person's level of effectiveness. And to reach the highest level of effectiveness, you have to raise the lid on your leadership ability.

David had many lids on his life, but they did not stop him:

1. His family
2. His leader
3. His background
4. His youthfulness and inexperience

Ultimately David became a great leader—yet not because he lacked limitations in life. He achieved much because he became a lid lifter.

Every leader has lids on his life; nobody is born without them. And they don't disappear when a person receives a title, achieves a position, or gets invested with power. The issue is not whether you have lids, but what you are going to do about them.

The Maxwell Leadership Bible

THE PRICE OF COMMITMENT

Thus Hezekiah did throughout all Judah,
and he did what was good and right and true before
the Lord his God. And in every work that he began
in the service of the house of God, in the law
and in the commandment, to seek his God,
he did it with all his heart. So he prospered.

2 CHRONICLES 31:20–21

The Bible describes King Hezekiah as a leader who "did what was good and right and true before the Lord his God. And in every work that he began . . . he did it with all his heart." Hezekiah paid the price to get the job done. But what is the price of commitment?

1. *Change of lifestyle*—Hezekiah couldn't live the way his father lived.

2. *Loneliness*—Hezekiah stepped out in obedience, alone at first.

3. *Faith in God*—Hezekiah believed that God would bless his efforts.

4. *Criticism*—Hezekiah weathered the harsh questions of an older generation.

5. *Hard work and money*—The king gave up time, energy, and budget to reach his goal.

6. *Daily discipline*—Hezekiah had to instill a daily regimen to bring about reform.

7. *Constant pressure*—The king endured the pressure of potential failure and misunderstanding.

The Maxwell Leadership Bible

IF THEY RESPECT YOU,
THEY FOLLOW

*Then Jesus said to them, "Follow Me, and I will make
you become fishers of men." They immediately
left their nets and followed Him.*

MARK 1:17–18

People don't follow others by accident. They
follow individuals whose leadership they respect.
And the more leadership ability a person has, the more
quickly he or she recognizes leadership—or its lack—in
others. When people get together for the first time as a
group, take a look at what happens. As they start
interacting, the leaders in the group immediately take
charge. They think in terms of the direction they desire
to go and who they want to take with them. At first,
people may make tentative moves in several different
directions, but after the people get to know one another,
it doesn't take long for them to recognize the strongest
leaders and to follow them.

In time, people in the group get on board and follow
the strongest leaders. Either that or they leave the group
and pursue their own agendas.

The 21 Irrefutable Laws of Leadership

Choosing a
Leadership Model

You know how we lived among you for your sake.
You became imitators of us and of the Lord; in spite of
severe suffering, you welcomed the message with the joy
given by the Holy Spirit. And so you became a model
to all the believers in Macedonia and Achaia.

1 Thessalonians 1:5–7 (niv)

As leaders, you and I are responsible for finding good models to emulate. Give great thought to which leaders you follow because they determine your course as a leader. I have developed six questions to ask before picking a model to follow:

1. Does my model's life deserve a following?
2. Does my model's life have a following?
3. What is the main strength that influences others to follow my model?
4. Does my model reproduce other leaders?
5. Is my model's strength reproducible in my life?
6. If my model's strength is reproducible in my life, what steps must I take to develop and demonstrate that strength?

The models we choose may or may not be accessible to us in a personal way. Studying national or historical figures can certainly benefit you, but not the way a personal mentor can.

Developing the Leaders Around You

Spend Minutes Wisely

LORD, make me to know my end, And what is the measure of my days, That I may know how frail I am. Indeed, You have made my days as handbreadths, And my age is nothing before You; Certainly every man at his best state is but vapor.

PSALM 39:4–5

In Psalm 90, David shows his mindfulness of his brief time on earth. He asks God to help him number his days, which ought to be the prayer of every leader. Wise leaders work to redeem the time they have.

A leader needs to wonder if the task is worth the time investment. What would happen if the leader wasn't the one doing it? Is there someone else who could do it just as well, and for whom the task would be time better spent? A good leader knows that time is like gold, and good "spending habits" are essential. It's just that in this case the units are minutes, not dollars.

If you don't know where your time goes—that's a danger signal. If you can save small bits of time and consolidate them into a chunk of time that can be spent on something worthwhile—that's like "found money." If leaders can number their minutes and hours, "numbering their days" will be easier.

The Maxwell Leadership Bible

EVALUATE, THEN EMPOWER

If anyone wants to provide leadership in the church, good! But there are preconditions.

1 TIMOTHY 3:1 (THE MESSAGE)

The place to start empowering people is by evaluating them. With inexperienced people, if you give them too much authority too soon, you can be setting them up to fail. With people who have lots of experience, if you move too slowly you can frustrate and demoralize them.

Sometimes when leaders misjudge the capabilities of others the results can be comical. For example, in 1898, Albert Einstein applied for admittance to the Munich Technical Institute and was rejected because he would "never amount to much." As a result, instead of going to school, he worked as an inspector at the Swiss Patent Office and with his extra time he refined his theory of relativity.

Remember that everyone has the potential to succeed. Your job is to see the potential, find out what he lacks, and equip him with what he needs. As you evaluate the people you intend to empower, look first at three areas:

1. *Knowledge*—Think about what people need to know in order to do anything you intend to give them.
2. *Skill*—Nothing is more frustrating than being asked to do things for which you have no ability.
3. *Desire*—No amount of skill, knowledge, or potential can help a person succeed if he doesn't have the desire to be successful.

Becoming a Person of Influence

THE FAST WAY
TO GAIN LEADERSHIP

The fear of the LORD is the beginning of knowledge,
But fools despise wisdom and instruction.

PROVERBS 1:7

Wisdom can be a leader's best friend, especially in times of decision. Suppose you find yourself in a large committee meeting in which a crucial decision must be made. The committee reaches an impasse and everything stops. Who will become the most influential person in that room? Answer: the one with the wisdom to draw a conclusion that not only works, but which receives the blessing of that committee.

Proverbs 1 describes wisdom as a woman crying out in the streets. What a beautiful picture! Wisdom does not hide herself, but shouts publicly! We must go out and find her and build a friendship with her: What can we learn about decision making from Proverbs?

1. The foundation for every decision is to honor and revere God.

2. We must build off our heritage and conscience: what values are we to embrace?

3. We must avoid the counsel of the ungodly.

4. We must pursue wisdom. What are the facts? What are the options?

5. We must move toward inward peace.

The Maxwell Leadership Bible

FINDING YOUR PLACE

*. . . being confident of this very thing,
that He who has begun a good work in you will
complete it until the day of Jesus Christ.*

PHILIPPIANS 1:6

Right now you may not be in a position to place others on your team. In fact, you may be thinking to yourself, How do I find my own niche? If that's the case, then follow these guidelines:

Be secure—If you allow your insecurities to get the better of you, you'll be inflexible and reluctant to change. And you cannot grow without change.

Get to know yourself—Spend time reflecting and exploring your gifts. Ask for feedback. Do what it takes to remove personal blind spots.

Trust your leader—A good leader will help you to start moving in the right direction. Or get on another team.

See the big picture—Your place on the team only makes sense in the context of the big picture. If your only motivation for finding your niche is personal gain, your poor motives may prevent you from discovering what you desire.

Rely on your experience—The only way to know that you've discovered your niche is to try what seems right and learn from your failures and successes. When you discover what you were made for, your heart sings.

The 17 Indisputable Laws of Teamwork

LEADERS AND FOLLOWERS HAVE SPECIFIC ROLES

Where the word of a king is, there is power; And who may say to him, "What are you doing?" He who keeps his command will experience nothing harmful; And a wise man's heart discerns both time and judgment ... All this I have seen, and applied my heart to every work that is done under the sun: There is a time in which one man rules over another to his own hurt.

ECCLESIASTES 8:4–5, 9

Solomon makes points about our relationship to the people who lead us. We are to submit to them, not because the person deserves it, but because the office deserves it and God decrees it. And what about leaders in authority? Solomon also issues a warning. When leaders try to exercise authority without a servant's heart, they eventually hurt themselves. Consider what he says:

ROLE OF THE FOLLOWER

1. Submit to God–given authority.

2. Trust God to accomplish His purpose.

3. Don't quit or become divisive.

ROLE OF THE LEADER

1. Exercise authority with wisdom and caution.

2. Recognize that no human controls all of life.

3. Lead others by serving, not bossing them.

The Maxwell Leadership Bible

YOU'RE A 10!

And when Jesus came to the place He looked up and saw him, and said to him, "Zacchaeus, make haste at your house." So he made haste and came down, and received Him joyfully. But when they saw it, they all complained, saying, "He has gone to be a guest with a man who is a sinner." Then Zacchaeus stood and said to the Lord, "Look, Lord, I give half of my goods to the poor; and if I have taken anything from anyone by false accusation, I restore fourfold." And Jesus said to him, "Today salvation has come to this house."

LUKE 19:5–9

I've never known a positive person yet who didn't love people and try to see the best in them. And one of the most effective ways to help you see the best in others is to do what I call putting a "10" on people's heads. Here's what I mean: We all have expectations of others, but we can choose whether those expectations are positive or negative. We can think that others are worthless or wonderful. When we make the decision to expect the best and actually look for the good instead of the bad, we're seeing them as a "10."

The ability to do this is important for a couple of reasons. First, we usually see in others what we expect to see. Second, people generally rise to meet our level of expectations.

Your Road Map for Success

FIND CLARITY,
NOT CERTAINTY

*Then the LORD answered Job out of the whirlwind, and
said: "Who is this who darkens counsel by words
without knowledge? Now prepare yourself like a man;
I will question you and you shall answer Me."*

JOB 38:2–3

In the Book of Job, God brings justice and
perspective with Him. He rebukes Eliphaz, Bildad,
and Zophar for projecting their opinions as though they
represented the mind of God (a danger every spiritual
leader faces). Before God is finished, He poses His own
question: Where were you when I created the world?

Many leaders feel a great temptation to pretend they
know everything that's coming down the pike. They feel
an unreasonable need to project self–confidence, not
realizing that people soon recognize their pretension.
Leaders often fail to understand that people do not need
a leader to have every answer.

Consider this: Individuals can live without certainty
from a leader, but not without clarity. Leaders must be
genuine with their people. Unless a word has come to us
directly from the mouth of the Lord, we cannot know what
is coming in the future. Don't speak with certainty on an
issue of which you are unsure! Yet when you do speak, speak
with clarity, even if your words paint only a small part of the
whole picture. Your people do not need certainty on every
issue, but they do need clarity on every issue.

The Maxwell Leadership Bible

Watch Them Blossom

I remind you to stir up the gift of God which is in you through the laying on of my hands. For God has not given us a spirit of fear, but of power and of love and of a sound mind.

2 TIMOTHY 1:6-7

People rise or fall to meet our level of expectations for them. If you express skepticism and doubt in others, they'll return your lack of confidence with mediocrity. But if you believe in them and expect them to do well, they'll wear themselves out trying to do their best. And in the process, both of you benefit.

If you've never been one to trust people and put your faith in them, change your way of thinking and begin believing in others. Your life will quickly begin to improve. When you have faith in another person, you give him or her an incredible gift, maybe the best gift you can give another person. Give others money, and it's soon spent. Give resources, and they may not be used to the greatest advantage. Give help, and they'll often find themselves back where they started in a short period of time. But give them your faith, and they become confident, energized, and self-reliant. They become motivated to acquire what they need to succeed on their own. And then later if you do share money, resources and help, they're better able to use them to build a better future.

Become a believer in people, and even the most tentative and inexperienced people can bloom.

Becoming a Person of Influence

AS THE LEADER GOES, SO GOES THE NATION

He did evil in the sight of the LORD, and walked in the way of Jeroboam, and in his sin by which he had made Israel sin.

1 KINGS 15:34

Leadership ability is the lid on the success of a nation or organization. When Israel or Judah lived under good kings, things went well. Under bad kings, things went sour. The heart and skill of a leader will always tremendously affect the life of the people under his direction. This is a law, both timeless and universal. See how this law played out under the Hebrew kings of the Old Testament:

GOOD KINGS

1. Drew loyalty from their people
2. Enjoyed victory over sin
3. Enjoyed peace within within the kingdom
4. Were affirmed by God's God's prophets
5. Enjoyed prosperity

6. Opposed evil kings

BAD KINGS

1. Drew rebellion from their people
2. Saw bondage to sin
3. Suffered turmoil the kingdom
4. Were rebuked by prophets
5. Often endured natural disasters and war
6. Opposed good kings

The Maxwell Leadership Bible

COMPETENCE DOESN'T COMPENSATE FOR INSECURITY

And from that time on
Saul kept a jealous eye on David.

1 SAMUEL 18:9

Insecure leaders are dangerous—to themselves, their followers, and the organizations they lead. That's because a leadership position becomes an amplifier of personal flaws. Whatever negative baggage you have in life only gets heavier when you're trying to lead others.

Unsure leaders have several common traits:

1. *They don't provide security for others*—To become an effective leader, you need to make your followers feel good about themselves.

2. *They take more from people than they give*—Insecure people are on a continual quest for validation, acknowledgment, and love. Because of that, their focus is on finding security, not instilling it in others.

3. *They continually limit their best people*—Show me an insecure leader, and I'll show you someone who cannot genuinely celebrate victories. The leader might even take credit personally for the best work of the team.

4. *They continually limit their organization*—When followers are undermined and receive no recognition, they become discouraged and eventually stop performing at their potential. And when that happens, the entire organization suffers.

The 21 Indispensable Qualities of a Leader

WHERE DOES GOD FIT IN?

*"Woe to the rebellious children," says the LORD, "Who
take counsel, but not of Me, and who devise plans, but
not of My Spirit, that they may add sin to sin; who
walk to go down to Egypt, and have not asked My
advice, to strengthen themselves in the strength of
Pharaoh, and to trust in the shadow of Egypt! Therefore
the strength of Pharaoh shall be your shame, and trust
in the shadow of Egypt shall be your humiliation. For
his princes were at Zoan, and his ambassadors came to
Hanes. They were all ashamed of a people who could
not benefit them, or be help or benefit, but a shame
and also a reproach."*

ISAIAH 30:1–5

Leaders and organizations constantly make plans.
Yet Isaiah issues a warning to every leader who
develops plans without consulting God's design. Leaders
must remember just how tentative strategic plans need to
be. No one knows the future except God. Keep in mind
the following equation as you plan:

Our Preparation + God's Providence = Success

Leaders must constantly ask if their plans fit God's
revealed will for them and their organization. Then they
must ask if their plans remain relevant to the needs of their
mission, their values, their vision, and their long–range
objectives. Finally, they need to ask if their plans fit the
needs of their culture and time.

The Maxwell Leadership Bible

Make Your Home a Haven

Better a dry crust with peace and quiet than a house full of feasting, with strife.

Proverbs 17:1 (NIV)

I once heard someone joke that home is the place where family members go when they are tired of being nice to other people. Unfortunately some homes actually seem to work that way. A salesman spends his day treating his clients with kindness in order to build his business, but he's rude to his wife when he comes home. Or a doctor spends the day being caring and compassionate with her patients, but comes home exhausted and blows up at her children.

To build a strong family, you have to make your home a supportive environment. Psychologist William James said, "In every person from the cradle to the grave, there is a deep craving to be appreciated." Feeling appreciated brings out the best in people. And when that appreciation comes in the home and is coupled with acceptance, love, and encouragement, the bonds between family members grow, and the home becomes a safe haven for everyone.

Your Road Map for Success

LEADERS LOSE
THE RIGHT TO BE SELFISH

*We then who are strong ought to bear with the scruples
of the weak, and not to please ourselves. Let each of us
please his neighbor for his good, leading to edification.
For even Christ did not please Himself; but as it is
written, "The reproaches of those who reproached You
fell on Me." For whatever things were written before
were written for our learning, that we through the
patience and comfort of the Scriptures might have hope.
Now may the God of patience and comfort grant you to
be like–minded toward one another, according to Christ
Jesus, that you may with one mind and one mouth
glorify the God and Father of our Lord Jesus Christ.*

ROMANS 15:1–6

How can leaders increasingly gain a servant's heart?
This passage reminds us that leadership is about
serving others, not wielding power. A servant…

1. *Denies self*—we are to please others, not ourselves.
2. *Develops others*—we are to add value to others.
3. *Accepts mistreatment*—we are to forgive wrongs.
4. *Imitates Christ*—we are to look to Jesus as our model.
5. *Is a student*—we are to remain teachable.
6. *Pursues the harmony of relationships*—we are to pursue
   unity and peace.

The Maxwell Leadership Bible

BELIEVE IN YOURSELF

"Let no man's heart fail because of him;
your servant will go and fight with this Philistine."
1 SAMUEL 17:32

People will not follow a leader who does not have confidence in himself. In fact, people are naturally attracted to people who convey confidence. An excellent example of this can be seen in an incident that occurred in Russia during an attempted coup. Army tanks surrounded the government building that housed President Boris Yeltsin and his pro–democracy supporters. High–level military leaders had ordered the tank commander to open fire and kill Yeltsin. As the army rolled into position, Yeltsin strode from the building, climbed up on a tank, looked the commander in the eye, and thanked him for coming over to the side of democracy. Later the commander admitted that although they had not intended to go over to his side, Yeltsin had appeared so confident and commanding that the soldiers decided to join him.

Confidence is a characteristic of a positive attitude. The greatest achievers and leaders remain confident regardless of circumstances. Strong, confident leaders recognize and appreciate confidence in others. Confidence is not simply for show. Confidence empowers. Good leaders have the ability to instill within their people confidence in themselves. Great leaders have the ability to instill within their people confidence in *them*selves.

Developing the Leaders Around You

OFFER VULNERABLE OBEDIENCE

Let me be weighed on honest scales,
that God may know my integrity.

JOB 31:6

One of the beautiful facets of the Book of Job is that it displays how a man can be very human, and yet very heavenly at the same time.

Job feels all the emotions of a man who has endured great loss. He becomes angry, depressed, and anxious, and he declares his feelings openly. At the same time, he never drifts from his strong character; he remains consistent through everything. The moment it appears he will curse God and give up on Him, he affirms his promise to be faithful even when he doesn't understand what is happening. Job pledges to maintain his integrity despite his circumstances.

Such a commitment is a crucial key to leadership. Here's why:

1. Leaders must be visionary, yet they cannot see everything in the future.
2. Instead of pretending to be in control, leaders must model being under control.
3. Leaders must model humanity and identify with the limitations of followers.
4. Leaders must model an anchored life, acting from character, not emotions.
5. While leaders don't know what tomorrow holds, they do know Who holds tomorrow.

The Maxwell Leadership Bible

FEEL BAD? THEN GIVE!

*And there is one who withholds more than is right,
but it leads to poverty. The generous soul
will be made rich, and he who waters
will also be watered himself.*

PROVERBS 11:24–25

One of the greatest causes of negative thinking and poor mental health is self–absorption. Selfishness inclines people toward failure because it keeps them in a negative mental rut. That is the reason that Dr. Karl Menninger responded the way he did when someone asked, "What would you advise a person to do, if he felt a nervous breakdown coming on?" Most people expected him to reply, "Consult a psychiatrist," because that was his profession. To their astonishment Menninger replied, "Lock up your house, go across the railway tracks, find someone in need, and do something to help that person."

My friend Kevin Myers says, "Most people are too insecure to give anything away." I believe that's true. Most people who focus all their attention on themselves do so because they feel that they're missing something in their lives, so they're trying to get it back.

Developing a giving spirit, as Menninger implies, helps a person to overcome some of those feelings of deficiency in a positive and healthy way. That's why Menninger says, "Generous people are rarely mentally ill people." A person is less likely to focus on himself if he trying to help someone else.

Failing Forward

OH, IT'S NOTHING

*Then news of these things came to the ears of the
church in Jerusalem, and they sent out Barnabas to go
as far as Antioch. When he came and had seen the
grace of God, he was glad, and encouraged them all
that with purpose of heart they should continue with
the Lord. For he was a good man, full of the
Holy Spirit and of faith. And a great many
people were added to the Lord.*

ACTS 11:22–24

If any early church leader could be called a servant,
it is Barnabas. He initiated and did whatever it
took to raise morale, men, or money. He led with clarity
and by example by becoming a servant. He considered no
task too small. What allowed Barnabas to demonstrate
such a lifestyle? He had . . .

Nothing to prove—Barnabas didn't have to play
games. He never sought the limelight. When he
mentored Paul, he happily let the emerging
apostle rise above him.

Nothing to lose—Barnabas didn't have to guard his
reputation or fear that he would lose popularity.
He came to serve, not to be served. This enabled
him to focus on giving, not getting.

Nothing to hide—Barnabas didn't maintain a facade or
image. He remained authentic, vulnerable, and
transparent. He could rejoice with other's victories.

The Maxwell Leadership Bible

BOOSTING LOW MORALE

Then Jonathan said to the young man who bore his armor, "Come, let us go over to the garrison of these uncircumcised; it may be that the LORD will work for us."

1 SAMUEL 14:6

When morale is low, the leader must do productive things to give the team a boost. In the beginning, any movement is a great victory. But to create positive morale, you need to pick up some speed. You need to be productive. After all, you can't steer a parked car! To get the team moving:

Model behavior that has a high return—People do what people see. The best way for them to learn what you expect of them is to model it yourself.

Develop relationships with people of potential—To get any team going in the right direction, you need players who can produce. Find the people who have the potential to be productive and start with them. Don't ask too much of them too soon. Leaders touch a heart before they ask for a hand.

Set up small victories and talk teammates through them—Nothing helps people grow in skill and confidence like having some wins under their belts. Begin with the people who have the greatest potential.

Communicate vision—Keep the vision before your team continually because vision gives team members direction and confidence.

The 17 Indisputable Laws of Teamwork

LEADERS BROKER
HUMAN RESOURCES

*So David reigned over all Israel, and administered
judgment and justice to all his people. Joab the son of
Zeruiah was over the army; Jehoshaphat the son of
Ahilud was recorder; Zadok the son of Ahitub and
Abimelech the sone of Abiathar were the priests;
Shavsha was the scribe; Benaiah the son of Jehoiada
was over the Cherethites and the Pelethites; and
David's sons were chief ministers at the king's side.*

1 CHRONICLES 18:14–17

David understood that he was to broker human
gifts and talents. As Scripture says, he
"administered judgment and justice to all his people."
The next verses report how the king placed individuals
in appropriate tasks according to their gifts.

Effective leaders know their primary job isn't to amass
personal accomplishments, but to accomplish as much as
possible through the gifts of others. How do leaders
inspire their associates to such great heights?

1. *Know the keys to their heart*—What do they sing
   about, cry about, dream about?

2. *Know the gifts in their possession*—What do they do
   well that gets results?

3. *Know the opportunities in their path*—What next step
   fits their maturity?

The Maxwell Leadership Bible

December

*Commitment is the one quality
above all others that enables a potential leader
to become a successful leader.*

GO TO THE VERY END

For I am already being poured out
as a drink offering, and the time of my departure
is at hand. I have fought the good fight,
I have finished the race, I have kept the faith.

2 TIMOTHY 4:6–7

Even people who lack talent and fail to cultivate other vital qualities can contribute if they possess a tenacious spirit. Being tenacious means:

1. *Giving all that you have, not more than you have*—Some people mistakenly believe that being tenacious demands from them more than they have to offer. As a result, they don't push themselves. However, being tenacious requires that you give 100 percent—not more, but certainly not less.

2. *Working with determination, not waiting on destiny*—Tenacious people don't rely on luck, fate, or destiny for their success. They know that trying times are no time to quit trying.

3. *Quitting when the job is done, not when you're tired*—Robert Strauss said, "Success is a little like wrestling a gorilla. You don't quit when you're tired—you quit when the gorilla is tired." If you want your team to succeed, you have to keep pushing beyond what you think you can do. It's not the first but the last step in the relay race, the last shot in the basketball game, the last yard with the football into the end zone that makes the difference, for that is where the game is won.

The 17 Essential Qualities of a Team Player

GO THE DISTANCE

"Leave your country, your people and your father's
household and go to the land I will show you.
I will make you a great nation and I will bless you;
I will make your name great and you will be a
blessing. I will bless those who bless you and
whoever curses you I will curse; and all peoples
on earth will be blessed through you."

GENESIS 12:1–3 (NIV)

Genesis 11:31 tells us that Abraham's father, Terah, set out for Canaan from Ur of the Chaldeans long before Abraham made a similar trip. But for some reason, Terah stopped in Harah and never continued his journey. Did Terah receive an original call from God…but neglect to follow through? We don't know.

We do know that Abraham never made such a mistake. Although he made other leadership errors, Abraham always seemed to follow through on his commitments. When God called him to depart to an unknown land, he went the distance. When enemies abducted Lot and his goods, Abraham pursued the kidnapers and subdued them (Genesis 14:14–16). When commanded to circumcise the males of his household, Abraham did it that very day (Genesis 17:23). And when God asked Abraham to sacrifice his beloved son, Isaac, only a last–second angelic intervention spared the young man's life (Genesis 22:1–9). No wonder that God, the Ultimate Leader, called Abraham, "My friend" (Isaiah 41:8)!

The Maxwell Leadership Bible

TOUCH A HEART FIRST

*I am the good shepherd; and I know My sheep,
and am known by My own . . . My sheep hear
My voice, and I know them, and they follow Me.*

JOHN 10:14, 27

One of the most common mistakes people make is trying to lead others before developing relationships with them. It happens all the time. A new manager starts with a company and expects the people working there to respond to her authority without question. A coach asks his players to trust him when they don't even know each other. A divorced father who hasn't seen his children in years reinitiates contact and expects them to respond to him automatically. In each of these instances, the leader expects to make an impact on his people before building the relationship. It's possible that the followers will comply with what the leader's position requires, but they'll never go beyond that.

As you prepare to develop other people, take time to get to know each another. Ask them to share their stories with you—their journeys so far. Find out what makes them tick, their strengths and weaknesses, their temperaments, and so forth. And spend some time with them outside of the environment where you normally see them. It will develop your relationship in a way it hasn't before, and it will help you grow.

Your Road Map for Success

LIFE CYCLE

When all that generation had been gathered to their
fathers, another generation arose after them who did
not know the LORD nor the work which He had done
for Israel. Then the children of Israel did evil in the
sight of the LORD, and served the Baals.

JUDGES 2:10–11

The Book of Judges provides a vivid biography of
leaders, followers, and human nature, and describes
a cycle repeated even today:

Rebellion—When things go well, people drop their
guard. Peacetime brings a greater chance of
rebellion than wartime.

Repression—Repression follows rebellion. Whether
God sends an enemy or the people cause their
own misery, they endure hardship, calamity,
invasion, or natural disaster. Poor life choices
result in retribution.

Repentance—Extreme hardships often trigger
community–wide repentance. Individuals begin to
refocus on what is really important and purify their
motives and behavior. Organizations cut budgets,
downsize, and check egos.

Restoration—Purification leads to restoration. When
people begin to obey God, peace returns to the
land once more. And the cycle of fallen human
behavior has run its full course.

The Maxwell Leadership Bible

DECISION TO DELEGATE

For this reason I left you in Crete, that you should set in order the things that are lacking, and appoint elders in every city as I commanded you.

TITUS 1:5

One of the most common mistakes a coach can make is to misjudge the level of a player. If the leader doesn't work with each player according to where he is in his development, the player won't produce, succeed, and develop. According to management consultant Ken Blanchard, all team members fit into one of four categories with regard to the type of leadership they need:

Players who need direction. These players don't really know what to do or how to do it. You need to instruct them every step of the way.

Players who need coaching. Players who are able to do more of the job on their own will become more independent, but they still rely on you for direction and feedback.

Players who need support. Players able to work without your direction still may require resources and encouragement.

Players to whom you delegate. At this stage, players can be given a task, and you can be confident that it will be done. They only need you to lead. Provide them with vision on the front end and accountability on the back end, and they will multiply your efforts toward success.

Developing the Leaders Around You

THE LEADER'S REFUGE

He who dwells in the secret place of the Most High
shall abide under the shadow of the Almighty.
I will say of the LORD, "He is my refuge and
my fortress; My God, in Him will I trust."

PSALM 91:1-2

We discover one of the most comforting chapters in the Bible in Psalm 91. It describes the security believers can enjoy through faith in God. Leaders especially can benefit from this set of promises. Study them and enjoy them:

PROMISE	LEADER'S BENEFIT
1. God's presence	1. It doesn't have to be lonely at the top.
2. God's protection	2. As you take initiative and risks, God keeps you safe.
3. God's peace	3. You don't have to feel insecure in unknown territory.
4. God's perspective	4. God gives an eternal view of life that keeps you steady.
5. God's provision	5. Regardless of your needs, God meets them.
6. God's power	6. In adversity, God delivers and helps you reach your goal.

The Maxwell Leadership Bible

IT TAKES ONE TO MAKE ONE

When the Philistines were at war again with Israel,
David and his servants with him went down and
fought against the Philistines; and David grew faint.
Then Ishbi–Benob, who was one of the sons
of the giant . . . thought he could kill David.
But Abishai the son of Zeruiah came to his aid,
and struck the Philistine and killed him.

2 SAMUEL 21:15–17

According to Albert Schweitzer, "Example is not the main thing in influencing others . . . it is the only thing." Part of creating an appealing climate is modeling leadership. People emulate what they see modeled. Positive model, positive response. Negative model, negative response. What leaders do, the potential leaders around them do. What they value, their people value. Leaders set the tone. Leaders cannot demand of others what they do not demand of themselves.

As you and I as leaders grow and improve, so will those we lead. We need to remember that when people follow behind us, they can only go as far as we go. If our growth stops today, our ability to lead will stop along with it. Neither personality nor methodology can substitute for personal growth. We cannot model what we do not possess. Begin learning and growing today, and watch those around you begin to grow.

Developing the Leaders Around You

WHAT KIND OF
LEADER ARE YOU?

But whoever desires to become great among you,
let him be your servant. And whoever desires
to be first among you, let him be your slave.

MATTHEW 20:26–27

The Old Testament uses several Hebrew terms that we translate as "servant," each one presenting a slightly different picture of the heart of a servant:

Ebed—A love–slave or servant. This term describes someone who is at the complete disposal of another (Deuteronomy 15:12–18). Likewise, leaders must be at the disposal of the Lord and their people.

Abad—One who gives up personal rights in order to work in the fields or tabernacle (Numbers 18:7, 23). In a similar way, leaders must sacrifice their rights and stay surrendered to the cause.

Sakyir—A hired servant who works for pay, by day or by year (Leviticus 25:39–42). A leader must avoid the perspective of a "paid professional" and flee when times get hard.

Sharath—Someone who will perform menial tasks to accomplish an overall goal (Exodus 28:35–43). Leaders must serve the mission.

Leaders must never forget that God calls them to serve. If our Lord could wash His disciples' feet as a *sharath*, then how could we frown at becoming an *ebed*?

The Maxwell Leadership Bible

MEASURING INFLUENCE

Epaphras, my fellow prisoner in Christ Jesus, greets you,
as do Mark, Aristarchus, Demas, Luke, my fellow
laborers. The grace of our Lord Jesus Christ
be with your spirit. Amen.

PHILEMON 23–25

A person's ability to make things happen in and through others depends entirely on their ability to lead them. Without leadership, there is no teamwork, and people go their own way. If your dream is big and will require the teamwork of a lot of people, then any potential leaders you select to go with you on the journey will need to be people of influence. After all, that's what leadership is—influence. And when you think about it, all leaders have two things in common: They're going somewhere, and they're able to persuade others to go with them.

As you look at the people around you, consider the following:

Who influences them?

Whom do they influence?

Is their influence increasing or decreasing?

To be a good judge of potential leaders, don't just see the person—see all the people who that person influences. The greater the influence, the greater the leadership potential and the ability to get others to work with you to accomplish your dream.

Your Road Map for Success

ANOINTED TO LEAD

*Now it was so, when Moses came down from Mount
Sinai (and the two tablets of the Testimony were in
Moses' hand when he came down form the mountain),
that Moses did not know that the skin of his face shone
while he talked with Him . . . Afterward all the
children of Israel came near, and he gave them
as commandments all that the LORD
had spoken with him on Mount Sinai.*

EXODUS 34:29, 32

When Moses brought down the commandments,
his face shone with the glory of God. The nature
and character of God had begun to rub off on Moses, and
the glory took such tangible form that he had to wear a
veil over his face. The Israelites sensed both God's presence
in Moses' leadership and a divine anointing to lead.

Do others describe your leadership as "anointed"?
What does it mean to be anointed? Here's one way to break
it down. Anointed leadership is characterized by:

1. *Charisma*—The anointed enjoy a sense of giftedness
   that comes from God. It seems magnetic.

2. *Character*—People see God's nature in your
   leadership. They trust you.

3. *Competence*—You have the ability to get the job done.
   Your leadership produces results.

4. *Conviction*—Your leadership has backbone. You
   always stand for what is right.

The Maxwell Leadership Bible

YOUR FRIENDS' BEST FRIEND

*God loves the pure–hearted and well–spoken;
good leaders also delight in their friendship.*
PROVERBS 22:11 (THE MESSAGE)

Your integrity is one of the best friends that your friends will ever have. When the people around you know that you're a person of integrity, they know that you want to influence them because of the opportunity to add value to their lives. They don't have to worry about your motives. Recently we saw a cartoon in the *New Yorker* that showed how difficult it can be to sort out another person's motives: A group of hogs was assembled for a feeding, and a farmer was filling their trough to the brim. One of the pigs turned to the others and said, "Have you ever wondered why he's being so good to us?" A person of integrity influences others because he wants to bring something to the table that will benefit them—not put them on the table to benefit himself.

If you're a basketball fan, you probably remember Red Auerbach, president and general manager of the Boston Celtics from 1967 to 1987. He truly understood how integrity adds value to others, especially when people are working together on a team, and his method of recruiting was different from that of most NBA team leaders. When reviewing a prospective player for the Celtics, his primary concern was the young man's character. He figured that the way to win was to find players who would give their best and work for the benefit of the team.

Becoming a Person of Influence

REPENTANCE BRINGS REWARD

*Then Job answered the LORD and said: "Behold, I am
vile; What shall I answer You? I lay my hand over my
mouth. Once I have spoken, but I will not answer;
Yes, twice, but I will proceed no further."*

JOB 40:3–5

When God confronted Job with His power and
majesty, Job responded with absolute humility.
The chastened man didn't try to defend himself or
rationalize his feelings. He confessed his humanity, then
shut his mouth. Even after Job acknowledged his
insignificance and presumption, God delivered a second
speech, graphically describing His power to control
everything. God said He glories in the might of behemoth
and the ferocity of leviathan, and asked Job if he dare go
near either one. This time Job responded with deep
repentance, clearly marking the difference between his
friends and him.

Good leaders feel secure enough to repent when
wrong. They don't have to project their self-worth, defend
their every move, or make excuses for their failures. In the
end, God rebuked Job's friends and rewarded Job—but
not until the end.

The Maxwell Leadership Bible

Color My World

*Thus Saul saw and knew that the LORD was with
David, and that Michal, Saul's daughter, loved him;
and Saul was still more afraid of David.
So Saul became David's enemy continually.*

1 SAMUEL 18:28−29

Nearly everyone has emotional filters that prevent them from hearing certain things that other people say. Your experiences, both positive and negative, color the way you look at life and shape your expectations. And particularly strong experiences, such as traumas or incidents from childhood, can make you tend to react strongly whenever you perceive you are in a similar situation.

If you've never worked through all your strong emotional experiences, you might be filtering what others say through those experiences. If you're preoccupied with certain topics, if a particular subject makes you defensive, or if you frequently project your own point of view onto others, you may need to spend some time working through some of your issues before you can become an effective listener.

Sigmond Freud said, "A man with a toothache cannot be in love," meaning that the toothache doesn't allow him to notice anything other than his pain. Similarly, any time a person has an axe to grind, the words of others are drowned out by the sound of the grindstone.

Becoming a Person of Influence

THE IMPORTANCE
OF STARTING WELL

It shall be a statute forever throughout your generations,
that you may distinguish between holy and unholy, and
between unclean and clean, and that you may teach the
children of Israel all the statutes which the LORD has
spoken to them by the hand of Moses.

LEVITICUS 10:9–11

God does not take it lightly when the leaders He calls disregard His commandments. When Nadab and Abihu broke God's laws (Leviticus 10:1–7), He executed them on the spot.

Sounds harsh, you say? Consider this. Any movement in its infant stages must set a standard or pattern of operations. If God allowed compromise at the beginning, things would surely grow worse. The same principle came into play in the new church when God took the lives of Ananias and Sapphira (Acts 5:1–11).

Nadab and Abihu broke the Law of Solid Ground, which states that trust is the foundation of leadership. As holy priests and trusted leaders, they were supposed to model obedience for the people. God could not permit them even the slightest renegade move, the smallest maverick act, for that would give permission for others to compromise as well.

The Maxwell Leadership Bible

MOVING YOUR TEAM IN THE RIGHT DIRECTION

*Then all the tribes of Israel came to David at Hebron
and spoke, saying "The LORD said to you,
'You shall shepherd My people Israel, and be ruler
of Israel.'" Therefore all the elders of Israel came
to the king at Hebron, and King David made
a covenant with them at Hebron before the LORD.
And they anointed David king over Israel.*

2 SAMUEL 5:1–3

Do you remember what it was like when you first
got your driver's license? Just going for a drive was
probably a thrill. It didn't really matter where you went.
But as you got older, having a destination became more
important. The same is true with a team. Getting the team
together and moving it are accomplishments. But *where*
you're going matters. You've got to begin doing the difficult
things that help the team to improve and develop high
morale. Among other things, you must:

Make changes that make the team better.

Receive the buy–in of team members.

Communicate commitment.

Develop and equip members for success.

The two toughest stages in the life of a team are when
you are trying to create movement in a team that's going
nowhere, and when you must become a change agent.
Those are the times when leadership is most needed.

The 17 Indisputable Laws of Leadership

GOOD LEADERS
OWN UP TO THEIR MISTAKES

And David said to God, "Was it not I who commanded
the people to be numbered? I am the one who has
sinned and done evil indeed; but these sheep, what have
they done? Let Your hand, I pray, O LORD my God, be
against me and my father's house, but not against Your
people that they should be plagued."

1 CHRONICLES 21:17

Times of failure not only reveal a leader's true character, but also present opportunities for significant leadership lessons.

Following a major victory over the Philistines, King David made a major mistake. The king chose to listen to Satan, stopped trusting God for the defense of his nation, and undertook a census.

David's willingness to take responsibility for his foolish action demonstrated his depth of character. He repented and accepted punishment from the hand of God, trusting in the grace of God. Even so, David's error snuffed out the lives of seventy thousand Israelites. When leaders mess up, many people suffer.

Many leaders attempt to hide failures, blame others, or run from God. But David admitted his failure and repented. Although he faced many difficulties, David worked to restore his relationship with God and did whatever he could to minimize the consequences of his failure in the lives of others.

The Maxwell Leadership Bible

THE KEY TO CONTINUED SUCCESS

And the things that you have heard from me among many witnesses, commit these to faithful men who will be able to teach others also.

2 TIMOTHY 2:2

Leadership is like a running head start for the team. Leaders see farther than their teammates. They see things more quickly than their teammates. They know what's going to happen and can anticipate it. As a result, they get the team moving in the right direction ahead of time and for that reason, the team is in a position to win.

The greater the challenge, the greater the need for the many advantages that leadership provides. And the more leaders a team develops, the greater the edge that leadership provides becomes. If you want to win—and keep winning for a long time, train players on the team to become better leaders.

The power of leadership carries over into every field. The business run by a good leaders often finds its market niche first and outperforms its rivals, even if the rivals possess greater talent. The non–profit organization headed by strong leaders recruits more people, equips them to lead, and serves a greater number of people as a result.

Look behind the scenes of any great undertaking, and you will always find a strong leader. That's why I say that the difference between two equally talented teams is leadership.

The 17 Indisputable Laws of Teamwork

KNOW YOUR PEOPLE
BEFORE PLACING THEM

*Also the sons of Hassenaah built the Fist Gate; they laid
its beams and hung its doors with its bolts and bars.
And next to them Meremoth the son of Urijah, the son
of Koz, made repairs. Next to them Meshullam the son
of Berechiah, the son of Meshezabel, made repairs.
Next to them Zadok the son of Baana made repairs.*

NEHEMIAH 3:3–4

Thomas Jefferson once said, "No duty the
executive has to perform is so trying as to put the
right man in the right place." Shortly after his arrival in
Jerusalem, we see Nehemiah busily at work putting the
right people in the right places. The text lists specific men
as the builders of specific gates. Why? Nehemiah placed
them in stations according to their natural gifts and
interests and had them build the portion of the wall right
in front of their homes. Talk about motivation!

Nehemiah recognized the principles that make
organizations progress:

Motivation without organization equals frustration.

The strongest organizations are the simplest.

Leaders love everybody, but move with the movers.

Good organizations establish clear lines of authority.

People do what you inspect, not what you expect.

Leaders provide a supportive climate.

Successful organizations recognize and reward effort.

The Maxwell Leadership Bible

ASK FOR COMMITMENT

After these things He went out and saw a tax collector named Levi, sitting at the tax office. And He said to him, "Follow Me." So he left all, rose up, and followed Him.

LUKE 5:27–28

In his book *The One Minute Manager®*, Ken Blanchard says, "There's a difference between interest and commitment. When you are interested in doing something, you do it only when it is convenient. When you are committed to something, you accept no excuses." Don't equip people who are merely interested. Equip the ones who are committed.

Commitment is the one quality above all others that enables a potential leader to become a successful leader. Without commitment, there can be no success. Football coach Lou Holtz pointed out, "The Kamikaze pilot who was able to fly fifty missions was involved—but never committed." To determine whether your people are committed, first you must make sure they know what it will cost them to become a leader. That means that you must be sure not to undersell the job. Let them know what it's going to take to do it. Only then will they know what they are committing to. If they won't commit, don't go any further in the equipping process. Don't waste your time.

Developing the Leaders Around You

FIRST ACHIEVE
VICTORY OVER SELF

*Then the king stood in his place and made a covenant
before the LORD, to follow the LORD, and to keep His
commandments and His testimonies and His statues
with all his heart and all his soul, to perform the words
of the covenant that were written in this book.*

2 CHRONICLES 34:31

How does a leader seek victory over self? Consider
how Josiah conquered himself.

1. *He remained open and teachable*—Instead of trying to
   convince everyone that he knew it all, Josiah humbled
   himself. He departed from the ways of his arrogant
   father and sought God.
2. *He removed obstacles carried forward from the past*—
   A leader has to win battles involving past problems.
   Josiah swept the country clean of idols.
3. *He realized what he needed to give and gave it*—Victory
   always carries a personal cost. For Josiah, that meant
   repairing the temple and reinstating the Passover.
4. *He recognized the key to victory*—For Josiah, the key to
   victory was repentance.
5. *He retained a personal commitment to succeed*—People
   never become more committed than their leader.
   Josiah's personal commitment inspired the people to
   be faithful despite their evil desires and history.

The Maxwell Leadership Bible

Whole-Hearted Devotion

Whatever you do, work at it with all your heart, as working for the Lord, not for men.

Colossians 3:23 (niv)

Experts spend a lot of time trying to figure out what makes people successful. They often look at people's credentials, intelligence, education, and other factors. But more than anything else, passion is what makes the difference.

Take a look at four truths about passion and what it can do for you as a leader:

1. *Passion is the first step to achievement*—Your desire determines your destiny. The stronger your fire, the greater the desire—and the greater the potential.

2. *Passion increases your willpower*—There is no substitute for passion. It is fuel for the will. If you want anything badly enough, you can find the willpower to achieve it.

3. *Passion changes you*—If you follow your passion—instead of others' perceptions—you can't help but become a more dedicated, productive person. In the end, your passion will have more influence than your personality.

4. *Passion makes the impossible possible*—Human beings are so made that whenever anything fires their soul, impossibilities vanish. A fire in the heart lifts everything in your life A leader with great passion and few skills always outperforms a leader with great skills and no passion.

The 21 Indispensable Qualities of a Leader

FOLLOW MY LEAD

Israel served the LORD all the days of Joshua,
and all the days of the elders who outlived Joshua,
who had known all the works of the LORD
which He had done for Israel.

JOSHUA 24:31

Look at every phase of Joshua's life, and you see a man who gave himself wholeheartedly to completing whatever task was assigned to him. From the first, he immediately obeyed the instruction of Moses (Exodus 17:9–10). Thereafter Joshua took on the role of Moses' assistant. Joshua again displayed his obedience when he agreed to spy out the Promised Land. Upon his return from the reconnaissance mission, he and Caleb, alone among the spies, were ready to obey God and enter Canaan. Forty years later when Moses handed the reins of power to his protégé, Joshua again obeyed the call (Joshua 1:5–11).

In the end, the people of Israel followed Joshua's example and did what God asked of them—and as a result inherited the land God had promised.

By the time of his death, Joshua was known simply as "the servant of the LORD" (Judges 2:7–8). That is high praise! While today we consider Joshua an exceptional leader, nowhere does Scripture describe him as a man of extraordinary might, intellect, or talent. Obedience made him extraordinary. And when you're a servant of the Lord, that is all you really need.

The Maxwell Leadership Bible

OFFER OTHERS
A SENSE OF BELONGING

I will walk among you and be your God,
and you shall be My people.

LEVITICUS 26:12

Belonging is one of the most basic needs that every person has. Positive influencers understand this need for a sense of belonging and do things that make people feel included. Parents make sure their children feel like important members of the family. Spouses make the person to whom they are married feel like a cherished equal partner. And bosses let their employees know that they are valued members of the team.

Great leaders are particularly talented at making their followers feel like they belong. Napoleon Bonaparte, for example, was a master at making people feel important and included. He was known for wandering through his camp and greeting every officer by name. As he talked to each man, he would ask about his hometown, wife, and family. And the general would talk about a battle or maneuver in which he knew the man had taken part. The interest and time he took with his followers made them feel a great sense of camaraderie and belonging. It's no wonder that his men were devoted to him.

If you desire to become a better leader, develop an other–person mindset. Begin looking for ways to include others.

Becoming a Person of Influence

A LEADER OF DISCERNMENT

> *So David said to Nathan,*
> *"I have sinned against the LORD."*
>
> 2 SAMUEL 12:13

Like Samuel before him, the prophet Nathan served as a leader to leaders. God used Nathan to correct his erring leader. Nathan could act as he did because of his keen, God–given discernment.

Discernment goes deeper than knowledge, resembling intuition. At times, discernment is a gift; at other times, it results from much experience. Discernment brings a profound perception of what is occurring, either on the outside or the inside of a person.

To improve your discernment as a leader:

1. *Learn to hear God's voice*—Get quiet and read Scripture. Reflect on the mind of God.
2. *Build problem–solving skills*—If you can see root issues of problems, you can solve those difficulties.
3. *Analyze your successes*—What worked? Can you identify the heart of the matter?
4. *Evaluate your options*—Discernment involves both your gut and your head.
5. *Expand your opportunities*—Get more experience to help you deepen your wisdom.
6. *Explore what others think*—Choose leaders you admire and study how they think.
7. *Listen to your gut*—Most people are afraid to listen to their God–given intuition.

The Maxwell Leadership Bible

KEEP TRAINING, KEEP RUNNING

Let us lay aside every weight, and the sin which so easily ensnares us, and let us run with endurance the race that is set before us, looking unto Jesus, the author and finisher of our faith, who for the joy that was set before Him endured the cross, despising the same, and has sat down at the right hand of the throne of God.

HEBREWS 12:1–2

We cannot lead anyone else farther than we have been ourselves. Too many times we are so concerned about the product we try to shortcut the process. There are no shortcuts when integrity is involved. Eventually truth will always be exposed.

Recently I heard a consultant interviewed about quality control. The consultant said, "In quality control, we are not concerned about the product. We are concerned about the process. If the process is right, the product is guaranteed." The same holds true for integrity; it guarantees credibility.

My basketball coach, Don Neff, emphasized to our team, "You play like you practice; you play like you practice." When we fail to follow this principle, we fail to reach our personal potential. When leaders fail to follow this principle, eventually they lose their credibility.

Developing the Leader Within You

HEADS YOU WIN, TAILS YOU WIN

So he shepherded them according to the integrity of his heart, And guided them by the skillfulness of his hands.

PSALM 78:72

David's leadership succeeded through a two-sided coin: his hands and his heart, or outward skill and inward integrity. Every great spiritual leader must have this combination. David's excellent leadership combined both heart and art. To have one without the other leads to failure. Consider the following list of eleven keys to excellence, aimed at helping us to develop our leadership skills today. Leaders must . . .

1. Value excellence
2. Not settle for average
3. Pay attention to detail
4. Remain committed to what really matters
5. Display integrity and sound ethics
6. Show genuine respect for others
7. Go the second mile
8. Demonstrate consistency
9. Never stop improving
10. Always give 100%
11. Make excellence a lifestyle

The Maxwell Leadership Bible

CLOSER THAN A BROTHER

But He answered and said to the one who told Him,
"Who is My mother and who are My brothers?"
And He stretched out His hand toward His disciples
and said, "Here are My mother and My brothers!"
MATTHEW 12:48–49

When you're looking for potential leaders, if someone you're considering lacks loyalty, he's disqualified. Don't even consider taking him on the journey with you because in the end, he'll hurt you more than help you. So what does it mean for others to be loyal to you?

They love you unconditionally—They accept you with your strengths and weaknesses intact. They care for you, but don't put you on a pedestal.

They represent you well to others—Loyal people may take you to task privately or hold you accountable, but they never criticize you to others.

They are able to laugh and cry with you as you travel together—This makes the trip less lonely.

They make your dream, their dream—Some people will share the journey with you only briefly. But a few—a special few—will want to come alongside you and help you for the rest of the way.

When people combine loyalty with other talents and abilities, they can be some of your greatest assets. If you find people like that, take good care of them.

Your Road Map for Success

THE RIGHT TO LEAD

So the LORD said, "I will destroy man whom
I have created from the face of the earth,
both man and beast, creeping thing and birds of the
air, for I am sorry that I have made them."
But Noah found grace in the eyes of the LORD.

GENESIS 6:7–8

There's something about righteousness—the kind of morally virtuous lifestyle powered from above—that qualifies a person to lead God's people. Noah, the man God chose to rescue the human race from extinction, demonstrated just this kind of righteousness.

God didn't choose Noah randomly. He knows whom He can count on to get things done—and it's not necessarily the one with the most skill, talent, or social standing. Rather, it's the one who daily walks with Him, the one who hears His voice and follows His lead.

No doubt Noah had his own weaknesses and frailties. But he walked with God, and it was that close walk that made him righteous before the Lord (Genesis 6:9). Noah's righteousness qualified him to be used by God to help save the human race from annihilation, and in the bargain kept him and his loved ones from certain death.

Noah still stands as an example of the kind of person God wants to use. God hasn't changed, and even now He looks for righteous leaders who can help Him change the world.

The Maxwell Leadership Bible

CLOSE TO THE HEART OF GOD

Draw near to God and
He will draw near to you.

JAMES 4:8

When Samuel first heard God's voice, he was "in the tabernacle of the LORD where the ark of God was" (1 Samuel 3:3). That was a good place to be, because that location was as close to the presence of God as a person could be in those days—unless, of course, he were the high priest who entered the Holy of Holies once a year.

Close to God is where every leader belongs. That doesn't mean you have to be in a place of formal worship; it just means you need to have an attitude of worship wherever you are. It's a posture of the heart.

That's a lesson I learned while in college and then took into the ministry. When I was attending Circleville Bible College, I used to go out to a deserted house after my classes and spend time with God every afternoon. It became my special place to connect with Him. Since then, I've always had a special place I visit to listen to God.

If you want to become the kind of person that others listen to, then get better acquainted with God. Connect with Him on a consistent basis, and you will greatly increase the likelihood that you will connect with others.

The 21 Most Powerful Minutes in a Leader's Day

ARE YOU A NAVIGATOR?

The preparations of the heart belong to man,
But the answer of the tongue is from the LORD.
All the ways of a man are pure in his own eyes,
But the LORD weighs the spirits. Commit your
works to the LORD, And your thoughts
will be established.

PROVERBS 16:1–3

Effective leaders practice the Law of Navigation, which says that anyone can steer the ship, but it takes a leader to chart the course. The verses in Proverbs 16 remind leaders to:

• Check the source of their wisdom
• Check their motives
• Check the outcome they are pursuing

Consider five key words to understanding how God helps leaders to navigate their way through life:

Process—God's plan usually unfolds over time. What is He revealing progressively?

Purpose—God wants to accomplish His purposes. Why were you created?

Potential—God will use your gifts and passion. Does this goal fit who you are?

Prioritize—God will ask you to adjust your time and energy. What steps must you take?

Proceed—God will eventually require you to act. When should you start?

The Maxwell Leadership Bible

TAKE ME TO YOUR LEADER

Now I saw heaven opened, and behold, a white horse.
And He who sat on him was called Faithful and True,
and in righteousness He judges and makes war . . . And
the armies in heaven, clothed in fine linen, white and
clean, followed Him on white horses . . . And He
Himself will rule them with a rod of iron. He Himself
treads the winepress of the fierceness and wrath of
Almighty God. And He has on His robe and on His
thigh a name written: King of Kings and Lord of Lords.

REVELATION 19:11, 14–16

In this passage from the last book of the Bible, John, the writer of Revelation, is of course describing Jesus Christ, the one who will ultimately rule the world at the end of time. In most of the Bible, Jesus is described as a humble and lowly servant. He healed the sick. He forgave the sinful. He washed the feet of fishermen, tax collectors, and the man who would betray him. And he meekly submitted to torture and gruesome death on the cross.

But make no mistake. Jesus is no weakling! In the book of Revelation, we see another side of His character and leadership. He is a captain of war who can rally huge heavenly armies to defeat a strong and bitter enemy. And He not only wins the day, but all eternity. That is a mark of great leaders. They have the strength to conquer, yet they stoop to help the weak and raise them up to join in the victory.

I believe in leadership. I've dedicated more than thirty years of my life teaching it. But as Jesus Himself said, "What profit is it to a man if he gains the whole world, and loses his own soul?" (Matthew 16:26). If you do not have a relationship with the King of kings, Jesus Christ, then I want to invite you to enter into one. If you acknowledge that Jesus is the Son of God, repent of your sins, ask for forgiveness, and invite Jesus into your heart, you will be saved, and he will become *your* Lord of lords. And you will join Him, the ultimate leader, in eternity.

ACKNOWLEDGMENTS

Grateful acknowledgment is made to the following publishers for permission to reprint this copyrighted material. All copyrights are held by the author, John. C. Maxwell.

The Maxwell Leadership Bible (Nashville: Thomas Nelson, Inc, 1982).

Developing the Leader Within You (Nashville: Thomas Nelson, Inc., 2001).

Developing the Leaders Around You (Nashville: Thomas Nelson, Inc., 1995).

The 21 Irrefutable Laws of Leadership (Nashville: Thomas Nelson, Inc., 2002).

The 21 Indispensable Qualities of a Leader (Nashville: Thomas Nelson, Inc., 1999).

Becoming a Person of Influence (Nashville: Thomas Nelson, Inc., 1997).

The 21 Most Powerful Minutes in a Leader's Day (Nashville: Thomas Nelson, Inc., 2000).

Failing Forward (Nashville: Thomas Nelson, Inc., 2000).

The 17 Indisputable Laws of Teamwork (Nashville: Thomas Nelson, Inc., 2001).

The 17 Essential Qualities of a Team Player (Nashville: Thomas Nelson, Inc., 2002).

Your Road Map for Success (Nashville: Thomas Nelson, Inc., 2002).

NOTES

Notes

Notes

NOTES